Twelve Weeks In Spring

Twelve Weeks In Spring

June Callwood

LESTER
&ORPEN
DENNYS
PUBLISHERS

FIRST EDITION

Canadian Cataloguing in Publication Data
Callwood, June
Twelve weeks in spring

ISBN 0-88619-162-9 (bound) ISBN 0-88619-115-7 (pbk.)

1. Frazer, Margaret. 2. Cancer – Patients – Ontario – Biography. 3.
Cancer – Patients – Home care. I. Title.

RC265.6.F73C35 1986 362.1'96994'00924

C86-094162-0

Half the royalties from *Twelve Weeks in Spring* are being donated to
Casey House a hospice for people with AIDS
(Acquired Immune Deficiency Syndrome).

Design by Gordon Robertson
Cover art by Rosalind Goss
Typeset in 11 pt. Goudy Old Style by Projet Marketing Inc.
Printed and bound in Canada by Imprimerie Gagné Ltée
for
Lester & Orpen Dennys Limited
78 Sullivan Street, Toronto, Canada M5T 1C1

Introduction

After Margaret Frazer died, a newspaper account described how some sixty friends formed a team to stay with her around the clock for three months so that she could die at home. A few days later, I encountered a philanthropist of great renown. He said he was sorry to read of Margaret's death, but she did have almost an ideal end. It made him wistful, he said. He wouldn't mind dying like that, but he didn't have sixty friends.

"Yes you do," I said at once. "You have hundreds, maybe thousands."

Almost everyone knows enough people to cushion their dying. One of the wonders of human nature is that most people are capable of fine behaviour in an emergency. Like the unknown hero when an airliner hit a bridge over the Potomac river – "the man in the water" who helped five people into a sling lowered by a helicopter, only to perish himself – people respond in a time of peril with a strength they never knew before and are grateful to find that splendid self within.

A genuine crisis – and death is the final and perhaps greatest testing time – releases that better being. For the individual who experiences it, it has the distinct feeling of growth; for the human tribe, it is a redemptive experience.

One of the lessons of Margaret's death is a redefinition of friendship. When Margaret's terminal cancer was diagnosed, the crisis she faced in her aloneness was something that needed no explanation or interpretation. She needed help and people came together suddenly to give it, but most of them were little more than acquaintances of hers. Very few were friends in the way the word is usually meant: that is, one half of a serious, intimate relationship with someone whose loyalty and support have been tested, someone who has become as close as kin.

It slowly dawned on the sixty of us involved in her care that

1

many of the people who might have been regarded as Margaret's *real* friends were distinctly absent.

One explanation might have been that they felt superfluous. There were so many of us on the Margaret team, and we were organized and efficient. Certainly, at least one of Margaret's neighbours who wanted to help felt too intimidated by our bustle to offer. Perhaps, though, long-time friends are less able to bear watching the deterioration of the body and the personality than people whose relationship has been casual. A woman dear to Margaret did a few shifts and then stopped; she couldn't bear it. A woman even dearer refused to join the team at all. A woman dearest of all came for only an hour, the visit stiff and uneasy, and was not at the funeral.

Though many of the team knew Margaret only slightly, affection and regard for her certainly had a part in the phenomenal response. She was an easy person to care about: an interesting, honest, quirky, funny woman. Few of us doubted, however, that what also drew us to Margaret's side was our own need to become reconciled to death. One of the team, Fran Sowton, put it best when she said, with a grin, "We're all boning up for our own finals."

It was notable, too, that almost everyone who volunteered to be with Margaret through the three months of her dying had experienced the death of someone close, very often their mothers, and needed to feel that grief again to bear it better.

Moreover, all of us, I think, had the hope that in experiencing Margaret's death at such close hand, we might be better prepared to face our own. When people explore what they dread, sometimes they become less afraid.

Hospitals were never intended to be places where people go to die. The primary function of hospital care is to heal. In such an environment a person whose death cannot be prevented will nevertheless be subjected to the same zeal and heroic measures as a young accident victim whose life can be saved. The consequence for the terminally ill is a medical miracle: the invention of living death, a state in which patients may linger for weeks or even years. Their hearts and lungs can be maintained indefinitely, but all else has died. What relatives and friends visit is a corpse that breathes.

When our friend Margaret Frazer learned in February 1985 that she had developed cancer tumours in several parts of her body, she dealt with the horror of that news much as most people do: she knew intellectually that she was dying, but she couldn't believe it. Her compromise was a determination not to die precipitately, not to go before she was ready.

In lingering death this organ or that stops functioning or causes pain, but substantial amounts of the person are untouched until nearly the end. Margaret could accept that something lethal existed within her and would kill her eventually, but her senses were keen, she was mentally alert, she enjoyed good conversation and laughter, and she longed to see her garden awaken in the spring. The best parts of Margaret Frazer were still in working order, and she thought them infinitely worth cultivation. So did we.

The surgery that confirmed the brutal diagnosis of irreversible cancer took place in March, but the next step wasn't clear. She wasn't sick enough to remain in an active-treatment hospital, but she wasn't well enough to care for herself. It would have been a catastrophic defeat for her to remain in hospital where the focus would be on her illness rather than her wellness. So long as she was tended by nurses and doctors, she would feel full of death.

She craved normalcy: her own bed with a view of the garden, Mozart in the afternoons, herbal tea in a blue-and-white cup, a rocking chair in a room walled by books. If she could go home, she felt, her situation would not be hopeless. And even if death could not be avoided, she wanted to face it with all the treasures of her lifetime around her.

Her only surviving close relative, a sister, was more than a thousand miles away. Margaret, a retired school teacher with a modest pension, lived alone with her cat in a paid-up house on a pretty street in the north part of Toronto. She had never married; the several relationships she had formed over her lifetime had ended long before her illness. Like millions of people in North America in this generation, she had no family in the traditional sense. In its place she had what everyone has, hundreds of people who knew her, scores of people who liked her, a handful whose lives had been really touched by hers.

Most people live within many human villages. Their families and close friends form the most obvious of these communities, but they belong as well to a village of people at their workplace, another village of people with whom they attend church or fitness classes, another inhabited by school friends, another composed of people they see regularly at meetings of community organizations or unions, the friends of friends they run into repeatedly at parties, and neighbours whose names they may scarcely know.

Most of these villages tend to be small, and the attachments within them appear tenuous and impermanent. What Margaret's death demonstrated, however, is that the tribe works. In an emergency, all the villages spill forth people who will help if a way to do it presents itself.

Since human relationships rarely are life-long, it appears likely that most North Americans will face serious illness without the ties that insure them against dying among strangers.

Margaret Frazer, sixty-eight when she died, had been a pioneer all her life, stimulated by change, open to new ideas, eager to experiment. She would be amused and pleased to know that the circumstances of her dying were rich in innovation and implications in a way consistent with the creative work that dominated the last ten years of her life.

Margaret said to me, twice, "I hope someone is going to write about this." She was clear about that, and she explained why. She thought we had put together something that would help others.

So this book has that ideal in mind. The team hoped that the Margaret experience would provide a workable blueprint for others to follow so that non-related people could provide palliative care to a family member, a friend, or a stranger.

Since then we have all known periods of doubt. We realized

that some of the factors in Margaret's situation are hard to replicate. Her home, for instance, was close to transportation and had ample space for privacy and overnight shifts. Certainly Margaret Frazer herself was extraordinary: "excellent" as the child next door put it. Margaret was able to allow sixty people to give her intimate care without resisting or resenting them. Her acceptance required considerable sacrifice for an independent woman who valued her privacy and had always been made uncomfortable by kindness or praise. She found the fortitude to receive a gift she could never repay, and in so doing she gave us a gift we'll treasure all our lives.

There were concerns that the team had unusual qualities: many people had time and flexibility for a long commitment, for one; many possessed caring skills, for another. The first doubt that the experience could be duplicated was expressed by a woman at Margaret's wake who noted that most of the people on the team were women whose natures had taken them into such professions as nursing and social work. She observed that most were feminists with a commitment to help a woman in trouble and to work collaboratively with other women. Also, many were practising Christians – not only within their church, but outside it as well.

She speculated that if Margaret had been a man, or if Margaret's friends had worked in business offices, the team would not have happened.

The team's success had much to do with a third element, a warm, skilled, and generous doctor, Linda Rapson, who threw away the book that instructs the medical profession to be detached. She saw Margaret through three months of her terrible disease with the attention and devotion of a loving daughter. She sustained Margaret and made it possible for the untrained people to feel confident that expert medical supervision and prompt response were available when needed. Without Linda Rapson, Margaret would have been back in hospital in short order.

Now it's more than a year since Margaret died, and the doubts are gone. What happened at 47 Deloraine in the spring of 1985

5

is the model we wished it to be when we began. We have realized that the mechanics will differ in every palliative-care situation, just as patients differ; but the hearts behind the schedules and lists of chores beat the same. We see that although all palliative-care teams are unique – home-made and individualized – they still belong to the same tribe. We know that not many doctors make house calls in tennis shoes and brush the patient's hair, but plenty of doctors and other health professionals are coming to understand how to ease pain and control symptoms, work with volunteers, and "not bug the patient".

The lesson of Margaret's dying is better than a list of the ingredients. We see now that we were demonstrating something deeper and more lasting: we showed that people can help one another when disaster strikes, and maybe even sooner. We simply rushed to give aid, sorted out how best to do that, and examined ourselves frequently to evaluate whether we were helping or hurting. Also, we kept the faith.

That's a workable model. No human crisis will ever be exactly like Margaret Frazer's, and therefore no solution can be identical. It will be enough, it will be more than enough, if Margaret Frazer's legacy is that people realize they *can* help a dying person.

Sheila File and others of Margaret's team from the Church of the Holy Trinity learned in the winter of 1985 that another of the church's parishioners was dying of cancer. They organized themselves to give support to this man and to his wife, who was giving him bedside care. The patient, very different from Margaret Frazer, was uncommunicative and withdrawn. The wife asked for suggestions.

"Why don't you rub his feet?" Sheila said. "He might love a foot massage. And it's a way of touching him."

He did. And it was.

As Linda Rapson observed, everyone has practical skills. All it takes is a flower, lemon squares, stroking, a hug. Easy stuff.

The Beginning

Margaret Frazer and I had arranged to meet on the evening of February 14, 1985, Valentine's Day, at a restaurant across the street from Toronto's Roy Thomson Hall. We hadn't seen one another for months, not since November 29 when she turned up, thinner than I had ever seen her, at the opening of a residence for teenaged mothers on Madison Avenue, a new venture of Jessie's Centre for Teenagers that we both supported. I had commented then that she seemed to have lost some weight – was she feeling all right? – and she had answered, with a negligent shrug, that she had maybe picked up a bug during her recent trip to China that summer. She was seeing a doctor about it.

She'd looked thin, I remembered, a month before that, in October, when we went together to a performance of *Tosca* by the Canadian Opera Company. I had mentioned her weight at the time, but she had said she hadn't really noticed it herself because she'd been so busy. The "China bug" theory seemed far-fetched so I was pleased to hear that she was seeing a doctor.

Following that brief conversation, we kept in touch by telephone through the Christmas upheaval and beyond. The subject of her health was never mentioned. We had mutual interests in fund raising, I for Jessie's, which had been launched only three years earlier to help teenaged parents and was still unsteady financially, and she for Nellie's, an emergency shelter for women. We were each absorbed by events in the women's movement – both of us born-again feminists – and in the activities of the Supportive Housing Coalition, which a year earlier had succeeded in persuading the provincial government to fund houses for homeless ex-psychiatric patients. One of these houses was named the Margaret Frazer House in her honour. We talked about literature, since she was a retired high-school teacher of English with perfect pitch for good writing and I am a journalist who appreciated a commendation from her almost more than anyone's, and about politics, especially at the municipal level, which was closest to the social-justice, direct-service issues that absorbed us both.

Our special relationship, however, was based on music. To my great pleasure, Margaret had taken on responsibility for what we referred to as my musical education. Early in our friendship, when I first became aware of her consuming passion for music, I told her apologetically that I too loved symphonies but never found time to go or anyone to go with. She found the explanations for such pitiful impoverishment unacceptable. Accordingly, every few weeks, she would call with a choice of several concert dates. We would agree on one, sometimes two, arrange to meet an hour or so ahead of time for a chat over a light dinner or a glass of wine, and part with a hug when the program ended.

Our friendship seemed so comfortable and such an integral part of the small circle of people on whom I depend that it had the feel to me of a lifelong relationship. In fact we had known one another for only a little more than ten years. My first contact with her came early in the fall of 1974, when she wrote to introduce herself as an English teacher at Bloor Collegiate in Toronto who was using my columns in the *Globe and Mail* as part of her Grade 11 course. Her comments about the writing were startling, interesting, uncluttered, and encouraging, reminding me of a brilliant and acerbic history teacher I had adored at Brantford Collegiate.

"That was the only fan letter I've ever written in my life," she once assured me. She was making me the gift of a compliment at the expense of truth. In her effects I found a letter from Earle Birney expressing his gratitude for a letter about his epic poem, *David*. He called her letter "heart-warming" and added, "I feel sure, from the way you have written me, that a good deal of its [*David's*] success with your class can be credited to its teacher." There was also a letter from Walter Susskind, dated 1957 when he was conductor of the Toronto Symphony Orchestra, thanking Margaret for her praise of a Mozart concert but taking gentle exception that "your comments about the new players are a little too scathing, though I am...prepared to cede you quite a few points."

I felt the same glow after reading her letter to me. I replied with a note of gratitude, and she wrote a second letter in a sprightly and humorous tone I found irresistible. We arranged to meet over lunch on November 11, 1974, Remembrance Day, when schools would be closed. It was the first and only time in my life that I have responded that way to a letter from a stranger.

The woman who waited for me at the restaurant in 1974 was small, grey-haired, close to sixty, primly dressed, and somewhat flustered. After some initial shyness on both sides, I fell under the spell of her gusto and lively intelligence. We talked about politics and found we both supported the New Democratic Party, but with the same reservations. We talked about changes in education and agreed that the spirit of the sixties reformers had been lost. We talked about journalism, on which subject she was informed and astute, and about the emerging feminist movement that delighted us both.

Engrossed, I failed to check the time until almost three hours had passed and I was late for an appointment.

My theory about friendships is that they last, as a good marriage does, when there is a fair trade between the participants. For ten years what I gained from Margaret Frazer was exposure to her questing heart, the steadiness of her loyalty and integrity, her sunny optimism, her capacity to see the point and stick to it, and her alert, thirsty, and enterprising curiosity that ranged beyond my own interests and enriched me.

"I'm really enjoying my yoga classes," Margaret remarked one day. I was amazed. I'd often toyed with the idea of taking yoga in the way that people think idly they'd like to learn to fly or do cross-country skiing, but it was Margaret, eight years older than I am, who actually did it.

When we separated after that first meeting with assurances that we would see one another again soon, I mentioned off-hand-edly that she might be interested in helping Nellie's, a newly opened emergency hostel for women in crisis that was having a

11

full-blown crisis of its own. Caught in the downward spiral of lack of funds, Nellie's was facing oblivion. The staff was over-worked, under-paid, and burning out, and the board of directors was demoralized.

Margaret promised to consider the possibility of volunteering at Nellie's, and she certainly followed through. Two summers later, in 1977, she played a significant role in keeping the hostel open. That was a year after she took an early retirement from teaching at the age of fifty-eight. "I didn't wait one minute longer than was needed to get my full pension," she explained one evening when we were headed to a choral recital at Massey Hall. She was skipping like an excited child, snuggling my arm in hers as we threaded the traffic-choked streets. "I love teaching, but it takes up too much time, and there are so many things I want to do."

"Such as?"

"Well, I want to learn to play the flute. And I want to read all of Virginia Woolf."

She never did find time for Virginia Woolf. Instead, she did something quite remarkable for a retired schoolteacher with no funds but her pension, no influence anywhere, and a modest circle of friends who didn't really know much about her. She plunged into two circles of activity, one focused on Nellie's that led her into a maze of committees dealing with housing and feminist issues, and the other centred on Holy Trinity, the Ang-lican church whose singular congregation was then battling for its life against two Goliaths, Eaton's of Canada, which wanted to usurp its space for the proposed Eaton Centre, and the Anglican Church of Canada, which looked askance at Holy Trinity's uncon-ventional approach to Christianity. Both activities were on the leading edges of social change, where she proved to be a spunky, resourceful, determined, and confident David.

Her life came in two parts. One half encompassed her childhood and thirty years as a high-school teacher; the other half spanned the last ten years of her life, when she turned her retirement into a monument of good works. The Margaret Frazer who taught school had a wardrobe of sensible shoes, tweed skirts, and blue blouses. The Margaret Frazer who helped Amnesty International, the peace movement, and the Rape Crisis Centre, and who could be found serving soup at Holy Trinity's lunch counter for lonely downtown workers was dressed in moccasins, slacks, and a Mexican shirt. At the age of fifty-eight, an uncommon time of life to put forward a thousand glorious blossoms, she opened herself to adventure and service and set free a stubborn rebel who had been inside all along.

On the day, ten years after our first meeting, when we were making our Valentine's Day plans to attend the concert, there was a significant change in the routine we had followed dozens of times before. The first sign that something was wrong was when Margaret complained about feeling tired. I had never heard her make such an admission. She went on to say that she was cutting back on her activities because she didn't have the strength to keep up. "I've resigned from the Supportive Housing Coalition."

I was speechless. The coalition had been a favourite activity of hers. "I haven't been able to eat," she was saying. "I've got a new doctor, though, and she's doing lots of tests." Her tone was matter-of-fact, but I sensed a note of fear. Belatedly, I remembered how wasted she had looked in November.

Keeping my voice as casual as hers had been, I offered to get the symphony tickets, something she usually did, and she agreed to let me. We lived far from one another, so we had always arrived and departed independently, but I said, "I can't pick you up, Margaret, because I've got a meeting at five o'clock that night, but if you can make your way downtown on public transit I'll drive you home."

When she accepted, I felt real alarm.

She didn't see me when I arrived at the restaurant. She was slumped in a chair in the lobby, looking older than her sixty-eight years, her cheeks sunken hollows. People were laughing at a nearby table; in view of her frightful appearance, it had a callous sound. I made some arm-flapping gestures to catch her attention, and we greeted one another with radiant smiles.

Over a hurried meal, which she ordered reluctantly, saying, "Maybe I can eat a bit of fish," she explained that something was wrong with her pancreas. "The message that I'm hungry isn't getting to my brain," she told me, assuming an amused inflection. "I think I'm getting better, though, because I do have some appetite in the morning. So I've started eating a good breakfast."

I wanted to believe her. I estimated that she had lost about twenty pounds. On a woman of small stature with very little excess weight, the effect was pronounced.

She pushed the fish around her plate with her fork. She had taken one small bite, maybe two. "I look dreadful," she went on in the same blithe way. "I hate to see myself in the mirror when I get out of the shower. I look like those people who survived the concentration camps. My doctor wants me to keep weighing myself, so I got some scales. I'm down to ninety-three pounds."

I had underestimated the weight loss by close to twenty pounds. I didn't know what to say.

"At least we know it isn't cancer," she said, still using her cheery voice. "All the tests but the last one, a CT scan, have eliminated cancer. I haven't heard about it yet because my doctor is on vacation, but I get the results Monday."

I called Monday, and she sounded startled that I had remembered. Her appointment, she explained, was later in the day. When I called Tuesday afternoon, February 19, she answered the telephone with her usual lilt, a rising inflection like a child's expectation of a happy surprise.

"What happened?"

"Well, they found something in the pancreas," she replied in the same buoyant tone. "The doctor says there is a 99 per cent chance that it's cancer."

I said, "Oh, shit."

"Yes," she went on brightly. "They won't be operating. The doctor says it's no use, but there'll be chemotherapy and all sorts of things!"

"I'll buy you a lovely wig," I promised. Floundering in my own shock, I found myself imitating her brittle airiness. I assumed that we would drop the pose at some point and weep together, but I was wrong. Except for two occasions, we were to maintain an almost euphoric lightness during the four months and one day left in her life. Our banter was a shield against breaking down, but it was also a kind of prison. It obliged us, for the most part, to communicate our love and despair without words.

She chuckled. "There was no mention of hair loss, so maybe that won't be necessary."

My first impulse after the call was to gather Margaret's friends in a circle around her. The decision of where to begin was simple. I dialled Jessie's and asked for Elizabeth Greaves. Elizabeth is a small woman who walks with a glide. At forty-one the single parent of a teenaged daughter known fondly as Plum, she's a legend in Toronto. She spent almost five years on the staff of Nellie's hostel, the longest anyone to that time had been able to endure the stress of meeting the needs of thirty women a night, all of them in crisis. From that experience she developed into a gentle-spoken but ferociously tenacious catalyst on half a dozen housing committees all over the city, wherever front-line workers had joined battle with the bureaucracy in order to obtain improvements in the wretchedly inadequate services for homeless women. In 1983 the City of Toronto recognized her contribution by presenting her with the Constance B. Hamilton award, which is given annually for outstanding service on behalf of women.

What was foremost in my mind, however, was Elizabeth's formidable capacity for friendship. She is rarely without a house guest, for instance: either someone who needs nursing for hurts of the body or spirit, or someone who is broke, or someone just drifting through town.

In a storm, you can tie your boat to Elizabeth; she'll hold. Once she befriended a teenager who came to Nellie's between jail sentences, a strong young woman with a volatile temper. I asked about this person one day, and Elizabeth told me, regretfully, that she had been expelled from Nellie's for the inexcusable act of threatening another resident – who admittedly was baiting her – with a knife.

15

"Where is she now?" I asked, concerned.

Elizabeth said serenely, "Don't worry, she's fine. She's living with me and baby sitting Plum."

When I told Elizabeth that Margaret Frazer had inoperable cancer, she made a sound of pain. After a moment, her voice low and broken, she said she would notify people at Jessie's, where she was working as a counsellor of teenaged mothers, and her former colleagues at Nellie's. At the end she said, "What can we do?" I answered helplessly, "I don't know. We'll think of something."

Later that day Joyce Brown, a staff member at Nellie's, called to give me the date of a rescheduled housing-committee meeting. A serene woman of thirty-four, Joyce wears her long, light-brown hair fastened at the nape of her neck. Her voice is high and musical but so soft it is almost inaudible. She has a graduate degree in social work and exhibits the attentiveness to detail that is the hallmark of all great organizers. When Nellie's obtained funds to open the Margaret Frazer House, an eight-bedroom former mansion adjacent to Nellie's that now houses ten women with histories of psychiatric breakdown, Joyce was the unanimous choice to co-ordinate the final renovations, the purchase of furnishings, equipment, and supplies, and the efforts of committees working on staffing, program, fund raising, and policy.

Joyce finished explaining to me about the rescheduled meeting, and I asked, "Has Liz told you yet about Margaret?"

"No, what's up?"

When I informed her of the cancer, Joyce was stunned. "I was talking to Margaret not half an hour ago," she told me. "She sounded just the same, and she didn't say anything about it."

I was disconcerted. "I don't think she minds people knowing," I said doubtfully. "When she told me about it earlier today, she didn't ask me to keep it secret."

Joyce called Margaret immediately. She said she had just learned that Margaret was "really quite sick". Margaret's attitude was almost brusque. It was true she was ill, she acknowledged very matter-of-factly, but there was a lot that could be done in

16

her situation and she would just have to learn what was needed in order to start getting well. Time would tell.

Thus distanced, as I had been, Joyce murmured assurances and left Margaret her privacy.

That Sunday at Holy Trinity church, anxious friends barraged Margaret with advice. Elaine Hall, who works in an alternative health clinic, asked her, "Are you medically oriented?" Sheila Mackenzie volunteered to consult a herbal healer about Margaret's case. Anne Grasham, a nurse, suggested a naturopath.

Over the next week or so, Margaret and I talked frequently on the telephone. Her attitude remained bright and shining. She was having a battery of tests, she said, and the doctors no longer thought chemotherapy was a possibility. In fact, though she didn't tell me, more tumours had been located. Her doctors had informed her that cancer had invaded her ovaries and lymph glands and that they were concerned as well that part of her bowel was being destroyed. She insisted to me that she was feeling fine. "I'm even eating better," she assured me, "and that's the important part."

Immediately after learning that her cancer was spreading, she made a brave note in a journal she kept intermittently. "The news is worrying," she wrote, "but I felt clear in my mind. Played the flute, just scales, and the tone was clear and strong, better than most of my last lesson where the clarity came only at the end."

Margaret was a founding member of an ambitious amateur chorus, the Concord Singers, who were talented and fiercely rehearsed to the level of professionals. Margaret was by far the oldest of the Concord Singers and approached the seasonal auditions in trepidation that she would be dropped. She was troubled that her voice had slipped from soprano into the alto range, but none the less had always managed to survive the leader's exacting standards. This year she was the group's second alto.

A few times a year the Concord Singers could be heard in concerts presented in various churches for a modest admission fee, and it was my habit to attend at least one of these a season. Months earlier, I had purchased tickets for one that was scheduled for March 1. I assumed that Margaret would have to cancel her participation. To my astonishment, she told me with asperity that she had every intention of singing that night, though the program was a demanding one that concluded with a sustained forty minutes of Virgil Thomson.

"Why wouldn't I be there?" she asked me in a withering tone.

I thought, Because you're dying. Because you're a skeleton. Because you haven't the strength. I said, "I can't think of a single reason." At that, she had the grace to laugh.

That night seemed the coldest of the winter, and the church was full of bone-aching chill. My husband and I sat huddled in our overcoats, hands stuffed in the pockets. The music, however, was beautiful. The voices of the Concord Singers soared like fluted prayers into the church's Gothic vault, and the stringed accompaniment was delicate and sweet. Margaret's face, a ghastly white, was easy to locate in the second row of the chorus. The hard light of the church filled her eye-sockets with shadow. She looked from the distant pew where we sat like a singing skull.

At the conclusion of the first half of the program, the chorus went quickly, almost at a run, along a side aisle and bolted down a stairway. As Margaret fled past, close to me but unseeing, she looked ready to collapse. I had the sensation of not having enough air to breathe, and we left.

I told her the next day that the concert had been the finest I had ever heard the Concord Singers give, which was true, but that we had been obliged to leave at intermission because my husband had work to do, which wasn't true. She said she had noted our absence and worried. Then she blurted a confession, that she had been so tired after the concert that she had sat alone for fifteen or twenty minutes in the deserted changing room, waiting for the strength to stand and join the others at a reception.

That day her doctor recommended that she go to Wellesley Hospital for surgery to correct the possible blockage in her bowel. There was nothing that could be done about the other tumours, she was told, but possibly the bowel could be repaired.

She went on with her life as if nothing was changed. She had her hair done that day and then selected material for the dining-room chairs she wanted reupholstered. She told her tenant that she would be going into hospital, and he promised to look after her cat, Cleo, and water her plants.

"We went over them all," she wrote in her journal. "I gave him an aloe vera and he kissed me. It is so exhilarating to be with him.

"It took some time to send a telegram to Phyllis [her sister]. Frustrating trying to find the number in the book. Then energy ran out. I got into bed, turned on the radio. It is CBC-FM Bach celebration – Menuhin. Just to hear him talk about Bach's music was deeply moving – near tears. He played too.

"I must get things in order for the singing at the H.T. [Holy Trinity] weekend and for publicity for Concord.

"June phoned. She and Trent were at the Concord concert to the intermission. T's first concert – in many years? Ever? He was impressed. She wants to take me to the hospital on Wednesday.

"This day makes me think of the effect of one's emotional state on cancer troubles."

I called again on Tuesday, March 5, to confirm the arrangements we had made for me to drive Margaret to the hospital the next day. She told me that her doctors had decided to operate on her bowel and revealed that additional cancerous tumours had been located in her uterus and lymph glands. She described this in the manner of someone reciting household nuisances. I couldn't speak for a moment, and then I said, "You're a mess." Her voice lifted. "A walking mess," she agreed with a chuckle.

Wednesday was an intensely cold day, and I feared for Margaret's frailty in the elderly, uncomfortable, and drafty sports car I drive. I brought pillows to cushion her protruding bones and a blanket to tuck around her. At the last minute I dashed into a florist shop and purchased some spring flowers. As I drove across the city with those inadequacies beside me, I was struck full force by a wave of grief.

I arrived promptly at the designated time, and Margaret was so ready that she opened the door as I was knocking. We've

19

discussed our compulsive punctuality many times and have concluded that it has something to do with our generation. I saw her small old-fashioned suitcase standing bravely in the hall. Her coat was laid out on a chair and, as I helped her into it, we chatted in hearty voices about Cleo, her eight-year-old cat, and her plants, all of which, as she explained when I asked feverishly, would be in the care of her tenant, Vincent Levesque, a young chiropractic student from Quebec. He lived in a self-contained and exceedingly dismal apartment in Margaret's basement.

I found myself commenting on the weather. Pulling on her knitted gloves, Margaret agreed with no trace of irony that the winter had been dreadful.

She looked around distractedly to see if she had forgotten anything. I followed her eyes and marked the possessions she held dear: her piano with a music stand beside it, a Frances Loring plaster cast of a boy with a flute, a small cherrywood rocking chair upholstered in brocade, her mother's plates in a glass-walled china cabinet, the copper kettle she had brought back from England. We didn't speak as she closed her front door behind us, checked that it was locked, and walked slowly to the car.

Margaret lived alone, except for her cat and an occasional tenant in the basement. Both her parents, stern Baptists, were dead. She had never married. She told me once that they had imbued her with such a terror of sex that she avoided the company of men until she was past her youth, "and by the time I woke up, it was too late."

She had not been without serious relationships. One time a boozy young man of my acquaintance joined us in a restaurant and brashly asked her if she'd ever had an affair. Before I could crown him with my briefcase, she replied calmly, "I've had four. Two with men and two with women."

I was never sure whether she had responded factually or had simply wanted to startle her assailant into silence. Once I reminded her of the exchange and she gave a chuckle. "Is that what I said?" she asked, bemused. Well, yes. She continued to smile like Mona Lisa reflecting on a delicious secret until I realized the subject was closed.

Her four-bedroom house, purchased twenty years earlier when a school teacher's careful savings could stretch to cover what were then modest down payments and mortgage requirements, was of brick with a spacious porch and latticed casement windows across the front. Situated in the northern part of Toronto, close to the city limits, it was a block from Yonge Street's cornucopia of shops and handy to a subway station.

Her street, Deloraine Avenue, was lined on both sides by houses like hers: solid, unpretentious, and well-maintained, their garages tucked behind in the style of fifty years ago, and all of them fronted in summer by well-groomed lawns and bright flower beds under an arch of mature maples twice as tall as the roofs.

Margaret was the oldest of three sisters but had no family in Toronto. Her next sister, Phyllis Frazer Cockram, born in 1920, lived in Florida with her husband, Ted, who was suffering from the early stages of Alzheimer's disease and could not travel easily. The youngest, Lynn Frazer Caldwell, born in 1926, had disappeared mysteriously fifteen years before. Without explanation or warning, she had simply stopped writing. One Christmas Margaret's gift went unacknowledged. She had mailed it to the address in Dominica, in the West Indies, where Lynn was living with her husband, Tom, an engineer engaged in a construction project there. The absence of a thank-you letter was curious, but Margaret didn't wonder about it until months had passed and her letters also went unanswered. All efforts to trace her sister in Dominica failed; she was gone without leaving a forwarding address.

Margaret told me this while we sat in the depressing basement cafeteria of Wellesley Hospital, sipping lukewarm machine-made drinks from Styrofoam cups, cocoa for her, black coffee for me. The hospital admitting department had directed us to a wing of the ninth floor, where we were advised that her room wasn't ready for occupancy. It had to be disinfected, a nurse told us crisply. She suggested we come back in about an hour.

The hour was passing slowly, and we somehow had wandered to the subject of Margaret's sisters, a territory new to me. "I'm sure Lynn must be dead," Margaret said, quite indifferently. "Otherwise I know I'd hear from her. We were quite close."

21

I couldn't imagine not knowing for fifteen years what had happened to my sister. Stunned, I saw for the first time the reality of Margaret's aloneness, so different from my situation in a close-knit family whose members keep in constant touch. Unwittingly, in the haphazard discussion she had revealed a truth that should have been evident to me all along. Margaret's optimistic bounce and the myriad activities into which she plunged enthusiastically, all flags flying, were such a diverting show I hadn't seen that her breathless existence was as precarious as a juggler's act. Now, the flurry of those balls-in-the-air stilled by her devastating illness, she stood revealed as a solitaire. My eyes stung to contemplate this other Margaret, the one inside all the others, the dying woman with no intimates.

She caught my expression and read it. Her back straightened, and she stopped her moody contemplation of her cocoa, launching vigorously into a discussion of the failings of the Concord Singers. Attendance at their concerts was poor because the organization was unprofessional, she declared. The problem, she thought, was that the leader refused to delegate authority in any area. He was a gifted musician, she went on, her voice growing stronger and her chin lifting higher, and she was proud of him when instrumentalists, a breed not given to holding choir conductors in much esteem, accorded him respect.

"But he needs help in promotion and selling tickets," she snapped, cracking her hand on the Formica table. Her indignation felt good to us both and carried us along blindly. Erect and fiery, she explained that she had brought mailing lists with her to the hospital, and in the days ahead she planned to work on an organizational chart that the Concord Singers had just better adopt.

I was cheering this when she stopped and slumped in her chair, suddenly too exhausted to continue. I realized that the colour I had noted approvingly in her face was really jaundice, and I saw as she leaned back that her body was so wasted she had rolled her pants at the waist to keep them from dragging on the ground.

Slowly, an apprehensive silence between us, we returned to the ninth floor to ask if the room was ready. Margaret leaned

22

weakly against the corridor wall while a nurse explained that the cleaners still had not scrubbed the room. Would we please wait? I said we would not. My friend was very ill, and it was necessary for her to lie down at once. The nurse measured me and looked at Margaret. It developed that a spacious corner room was being held for a doctor who had not yet arrived. If Margaret didn't mind lying on top of the bed rather than in it, she could stretch out there.

Margaret slipped off her shoes and curled up on the bed in a fetal position. I found a blanket to put around her and slipped a pillow cover over another blanket to make a pillow for her head. All the while, horrified by her enfeeblement, I chattered insanely about the attitude I said she should maintain while in hospital. She wasn't to make a run for the Undemanding Patient of the Week Award, I lectured her. She was also not to be the best friend and confidante that the staff ever had. Instead she was to state her needs clearly, without apologies, and keep all exchanges impersonal.

"You are not to be adorable," I instructed her severely, hanging up her coat in the doctor-to-come's closet. "Being adorable is tiring. It takes energy, and you've got to conserve your strength."

She was vastly amused. She closed her eyes, grinning, and I kissed her and left.

Elizabeth Greaves, an old hand at hospital survival, also had given Margaret a briefing. Elizabeth was born with kidney defects that several times have required bouts of alarming surgery, from which traumas she has emerged with some sensible strategies for coping. One of them is that people facing a serious situation need the comfort and quiet of a private room, despite the extra expense. Another is that someone should stay with the patient through the first day after surgery to take care of small but vital needs. Still another, somewhat grim, is that people who undergo surgery should first put their affairs in order.

"You never know, Margaret," Liz told her with a melting smile. "There's always a risk when you have an anaesthetic. Last time

I went to hospital, I made out a new will. You want to make sure that people you care about get the money, and you don't want the government to be able to grab it."

Margaret agreed to the private room, though such a self-indulgence was rare in her parsimonious existence, and gave in to Liz's insistence that someone from Nellie's be with her throughout the day after the operation. However, she balked at updating her will. Margaret admitted that the existing document was worthless, the main beneficiary long dead, but she seemed loath to do anything about it. Liz dropped the subject.

I visited Room 908 the next day and found that Margaret had nested. Books were stacked on her bedside table, and flowers covered every available surface. Her jaundice had deepened; she looked fresh from a Florida beach. She was lying on a natural fleece to protect her bony bottom, and her bed was covered with a cheerful patchwork quilt. The quilt and fleece came from Jay MacGillivray, twenty-nine, another of the Nellie's collective. Jay's thoughtful contributions to Margaret's comfort and cosiness were evidence both of her kindness and her moxie about making hospitals habitable. Jay has spent an arduous lifetime acquiring such expertise, hospitalized sometimes for months with life-threatening afflictions. In addition to uncertain health caused by her circulatory difficulties, Jay has a serious hearing impairment.

Margaret told me, very pleased, that a piece of festively embroidered felt mounted on the room's dun-coloured bulletin board was a gift from Eileen Swinton, a cricket-thin woman who had abandoned her Ph.D. program in 1977 to head a triumphant fund-raising campaign for Nellie's. Margaret was Eileen's admiring assistant and apprentice in the Nellie's campaign office. When Eileen, a Buddhist, left volunteer work at Nellie's to devote herself full time to a boutique selling crafts from Nepal, Margaret stepped into her shoes in a seamless transition.

Margaret's room had seen a torrent of visitors. Margaret counted them off at my request, and most of them were strangers to me. Included were members of the Concord Singers and also a group known as CAMMAC, the Canadian Amateur Musicians, Musi-

24

ciens Amateurs du Canada, with whom Margaret spent two weeks every summer at a music camp in Quebec, improvising, performing, and taking lessons. She always described those summer sessions, closing her eyes in bliss, as "gorgeous". Also, people from her congregation at Holy Trinity had been dropping in. I'd never met any of them, either.

I didn't stay long. After nursing our oldest child, Jill, through frightful injuries she suffered when she was partially crushed under the wheels of a cement-mixer truck, I am sensitive to the deep fatigue that accompanies pain and illness. Margaret lay curled up under Jay's patchwork quilt, looking small, withdrawn, and sweet. Her surgery would take place the next day. She wasn't interested in talking about it.

The next afternoon, March 8, a Friday, I called from Phoenix, Arizona, where I had gone with my husband, Trent Frayne, *Globe and Mail* sports columnist, so we could have some time together while he covered baseball spring training. Joyce Brown answered the telephone in Margaret's room.

Joyce said Margaret was not yet back from the recovery room, but the news was bad. The surgeon had found no bowel obstruction, but there was no point in touching the tumours he saw. "He just opened her abdomen, had a look, and sewed her up," Joyce said.

Through the window of our motel room I could see children splashing gleefully in a bright blue pool while scrubby palm trees lashed a clear blue sky.

"I feel strange being the one to be with her when she gets back to her room," Joyce went on slowly. "I'm not really as close to Margaret as the rest of you."

I said she was representing us all. In fact, she was the best possible representative, being a self-possessed woman who radiates a sense of peacefulness and order that would serve Margaret well.

Joyce had expected that Margaret would be in surgery and the recovery room for many hours and had made arrangements accordingly to do some errands. Learning that Margaret would be back in her room at any minute, she called for a Nellie's reinforcement.

Alison Guyton dropped what she was doing and came at once.

Alison is a key player in one of the great moments of Margaret's life, the naming of the home for ex-psychiatric patients in her honour. That was Alison's idea. Alison, thirty-one and the mother of two daughters, is a British-born woman with natural elegance. Trained as a counsellor of people with addiction problems, she came to the Nellie's staff just as Elizabeth Greaves was leaving. Liz had spent frustrating months in the Supportive Housing Coalition, on which she and Margaret were the Nellie's representatives, and Alison would be replacing her.

Liz told Alison that she thought the coalition was being ignored by government because of a lack of documentation. No proof existed of the numbers of homeless women discharged from psychiatric facilities who were caught in the revolving door of hostel-hopping or else lived in sordid and dangerous rooming houses. She urged Alison to compile research data to back up the arguments about the need for supportive housing that the Nellie's staff was trying in vain to make with three levels of government. Alison had no experience with research, but she was game. With the help of Dale Martin, later a Toronto alderman and skilled in that field, she plunged in.

The Supportive Housing Coalition divided off a regional subcommittee, the East Area Mental Health Coalition, to focus on the more manageable problem of a single district. Margaret Frazer and Alison moved into this new group as well, along with others from Nellie's. Alison recalls vividly a meeting of the east end group when a prominent Nellie's board member expressed skepticism that the problem was really as serious as the staff was saying.

"Don't you think you're getting a bit hysterical?" this woman asked Alison.

Alison, a soft, vulnerable person, was crushed. That night she and Margaret Frazer happened to leave the meeting together and boarded the same subway. Riding home, Alison confided her distress at the criticism. Margaret came to the rescue promptly with praise and bandages. "Don't worry what anyone says," she told Alison warmly, giving her arm a reassuring squeeze. "You're right, all of you, and you know it. You're the ones in the situation and you know firsthand what you're talking about. You stick to your guns and it will work out fine."

I could picture that exchange: Alison gentle, wounded, and uncertain, and Margaret with her blue eyes glittering, brimming with enough confidence and conviction for them both.

Alison pursued her research with such credible results that the paper she prepared, "The Role of Nellie's in Providing Post-Psychiatric Care", became a valued document. It caught the attention of Larry Grossman, then Minister of Health. Grossman met with Alison, and her arguments influenced his subsequent decision to provide funds for a cluster of houses in Toronto to shelter homeless ex-psychiatric patients.

Nellie's was assured of funding for one of these residences in an ideal site, a huge abandoned house only a few steps away from Nellie's itself. Joyce Brown was relieved of her staff duties to prepare the house for operation. At one of the early planning meetings, deciding the name was on the agenda. Alison said, "We should call it Margaret's, after Margaret Frazer. She's the one who has always been *there* for Nellie's. The committee met for years when it didn't look as if anything would happen, but Margaret kept plugging along. She has stuck with us through the whole long process."

Leslie MacDonald, another member of the Nellie's collective, objected. "People might think we've named it for Margaret Trudeau," she said. "We'll have to use Margaret's full name."

The response was unanimous, and it fell to Alison, since it was her idea, to approach Margaret.

"She was such a private person that I had no idea what the reaction would be" Alison recalled. "She might have refused, she might have said, 'Don't be silly!' – I just couldn't imagine how she would take it. But when I told her what we wanted to do, she said nothing. But she didn't say no."

The opening day in February 1984 went like a Viennese waltz, with Margaret fluttering in an unaccustomed state of embarrassment in the background while Joyce and members of the new staff proudly conducted tours of the sparkling premises.

"Isn't this nifty?" Margaret said with a beatific smile when I tracked her down in the kitchen where she was stirring spices into the hot cider. "Nifty" was a favourite word, unexpected in an English teacher with a lifelong aversion to sloppy language.

I said, "I'm going to write a *Globe* column about this to say how wonderful you are."

She made a face. "That will be one of your shorter efforts, I presume."

When Alison arrived at the hospital, Margaret was back from the recovery room, sleeping off the anaesthetic. In a while she opened her eyes and, expecting Joyce, seemed surprised to see Alison bending over her. Her first blurred request was for her dentures, which had been removed in preparation for surgery, and Alison helped put her teeth back in her mouth. A while later Margaret roused again and said she was cold, though the room was warm. Alison wrapped Jay's patchwork quilt around her and stroked Margaret's hair, telling her soothingly to rest.

A doctor came in and addressed Margaret loudly as "Mrs. Frazer", demonstrating a lack of knowledge of his patient that outraged Alison. He told Margaret that the surgery had changed nothing. He had taken some tissue for a biopsy, he added, but he wouldn't have the results until the next day. Margaret nodded uninterestedly, and he left.

Eileen Swinton came for a moment and was desolated by the news. Ruth McKeown stopped by and burst into tears. Ruth, a social worker who runs a mental health agency, had known Margaret through the Supportive Housing Coalition and was visiting her every day.

Later that afternoon, Joyce relieved Alison, by which time Margaret seemed more aware of her surroundings. Joyce braced herself for the questions Margaret might ask about her prospects, but none came. People arrived singly and in pairs through the day and evening as Joyce sat attentively by the bedside. Along with the Nellie's women she knew, there were Margaret's music friends and others from the Holy Trinity congregation. Notable in the latter group was Elaine Hall, a stately, composed woman with steady eyes, a shy way of speaking, and iron-grey hair smoothed back in a bun from a high brow. Joyce liked her on sight.

Margaret, floating in a haze of sedation and pain, acknowledged them all with a dim smile and slept a lot.

Early the next morning Margaret asked a nurse what the brevity of the surgery signified. The nurse answered straightforwardly, saying the cancer was too advanced for anything to be done about it. Margaret was quiet. The nurse took her hand and stayed with her most of the morning. Occasionally Margaret wept, and the nurse wiped the tears with a tissue.

Dr. William Whitla found Margaret asleep soon after the nurse had left. Bill Whitla is a most accomplished man. He is chairman of humanities at York University, where he teaches nineteenth-century British literature, and he's also ordained in the Anglican Church, an honorary assistant priest at Holy Trinity. Margaret often had mentioned him to me, always with admiration. I could see that she was enormously proud of the friendship.

He was quietly writing her a note when she woke up.

"Are you sore?" he asked.

"The stitches pull a bit," she admitted, "but I'm all right." Then she said bitterly, "As an operation, though, they haven't done much."

After a pause she burst out, "Bill, I'm ready to die, but I want to play the flute!" Her eyes filled with tears, and so did his.

After a bit her mood changed. She became indignant, affronted that her body had the temerity to interfere with her plans. "I don't know why I should die," she declared vehemently. "I've got so many things I want to do!"

Bill saw her attitude, he told me later, as not so much a denial of the existence of the cancer but of its power over her. Margaret's outrage was that disease should have such a victory.

By the afternoon, when people came with smiling faces and stricken eyes, Margaret was her old chipper self.

I returned from Phoenix and, on March 16, a Saturday, went to see Margaret. Her room was a bazaar of posters, fruit, plants, flowers, magazines, books, and one fat silver balloon, the charming gift of Sheila Mackenzie, on which was inscribed "P.S.: I LOVE YOU". Someone had provided a tape deck with earphones, beside which teetered a stack of tapes, mostly Bach and Mozart. We greeted one another joyfully, and Margaret assured me she was fine, just fine. She looked haggard.

I asked questions about visitors and learned that they were coming non-stop. Sometimes there were as many as four and five people in the room at a time, and some of them seemed to feel that Margaret would appreciate long, long chats. I suggested that I could put a sign on the door asking visitors to stay for no more than ten minutes, and Margaret agreed with a sigh of relief.

I marched to the nurses' station, announced I had the patient's approval, and borrowed some tape to stick the notice on Margaret's door.

A few minutes later a man arrived, a poised person with a grey chin-whisker and a genial kindly expression. Margaret introduced us. He was Bill Whitla. I learned he had been bringing Holy Communion to Margaret in hospital.

Liz Greaves and I agreed that we would visit Margaret on alternate days, rather than each of us every day as we had been doing. Liz had been pursuing a rehabilitation program with Margaret, each visit encouraging her to walk the length of the hospital corridor and, on one occasion, taking Margaret wrapped in a cocoon of blankets for a wheelchair stroll around the block. I promised Elizabeth I would maintain the routine.

Most of us believed that Margaret would be transferred to Princess Margaret Hospital, the cancer-treatment facility next door. As the days passed, however, there were clear indications that this would not happen. A decision about Margaret's post-hospital care was becoming urgent because her stitches were to be removed that week. I knew how dear her home was to her and felt she would be happiest there, but clearly she would not be able to care for herself in that big empty house.

One night Liz called me with a plan: Margaret could live with her and Plum. Liz had even worked out the logistics of where Margaret would sleep and how nursing her would be managed. I was doubtful. Margaret probably would rather be in her own home, I thought, and it was up to us to figure out a way to do that. Liz promptly agreed.

Margaret, however, informed me that she would be going to St. John's Hospital, a convalescent home of high repute run by an order of Anglican nuns, St. John the Divine. Margaret had been to St. John's some years earlier when she was recovering from gall-bladder surgery, and she was looking forward with pleasure to returning. I thought the arrangement had a peculiar ring, since St. John's is for patients who are recovering their health, a category in which it was unlikely that Margaret belonged.

A few days went by. Margaret willingly walked every day in the corridor, leaning on my arm and taking the small shuffling steps of the pain bound. She was beautifully dressed for these excursions in a lovely blue velour dressing-gown loaned to her by Eileen Swinton just before Eileen left for India on a buying trip. Though Margaret had obvious difficulty struggling into her slippers and the gown, she was determined to accept all invitations to try. "I must exercise," she would declare. "I've got to get my strength back so I can go home and work on getting well."

One day, exhausted but glowing, she clung tightly to Liz's arm and practised on the hospital stairs. Margaret explained, "I've got to get used to stairs so I can go home."

I accepted her declarations that she was getting well without argument, though it seemed to me and to Liz that Margaret was becoming weaker every day. Still, there were some hopeful signs: for one, the jaundice had disappeared.

"I'm going to beat this cancer," Margaret said one afternoon, watching me sharply for my reaction.

"Looks like it," I grinned. "You're some fighter." She rewarded me with a squeeze.

I discovered that Margaret was keeping a record of everything people did for her, listed by the day. "March 23: Sheila Mackenzie phoned twice from Aurora; June Callwood, three red roses; Dorothy Rogers, cushion to match quilt; Nancy Endicott, juices, talk about Jessie's, Nellie's; Joan Andrews with a tape from the CAMMAC evening; Kathleen Smith, three tapes; Glenys McMullen;" and so on.

Margaret's networks were converging on Room 908. Every day I met more people from Holy Trinity and found them a quiet-spoken, distinguished, and capable-looking group. Margaret presided from her bed like an IODE regent at high tea, grandly making the introductions. Her stack of tapes and books was growing at an alarming rate, and so was the horticulture show. Her room began to resemble a thriving greenhouse. On one visit, as I busied myself watering the plants and culling dead flowers from the bouquets, Margaret's tranquil voice floated from her bed into the bathroom where I was dumping odorous water out of a vase. "You're the third person today to do that," she informed me sweetly. "The last one was my flute teacher."

Helen Gough, a Holy Trinity woman, made the gift of her walkman and some tapes she thought Margaret would like. On the night she left the machine with a grateful Margaret, Helen went home and had a dream about Margaret in which she and Margaret were climbing a mountain path. The path was steep, and they were having difficulty finding their way. Margaret took charge, asking a guide sharply if he was sure this was the way. The guide left them in a clearing. They followed in the direction he had gone, but Helen was enveloped in a mist and couldn't see where to put her feet. Margaret came to her side and pointed to a path through the rocks. Helen began to pick her way toward it, and the haze cleared up. Then Helen woke up.

Helen wrote down what she could remember of the dream in a letter to Margaret. It ended: "I don't know how to interpret dreams. What seems clear in this one, however, is that your presence helps me to surface that aspect of my unconscious that knows the way, and encourages me to take it." Because Margaret did not come with her along the rocky path, Helen assumed that

32

the dream was also about Margaret's death.

"I didn't have the courage to put the letter about the dream in a post box, but I slipped it in the hospital mail. The next day Margaret said, 'I got your letter. Thank you.' And I said, 'You're welcome.' We didn't speak of what the dream meant, that I would be going on with my life alone and she would die."

Later Margaret said to Helen, "I want to go home. I hope it can be arranged that I can go home."

On Sunday, March 24, a group of worried people met after the service at Holy Trinity. Hilda Powicke remembers that they had heard I was determined that Margaret should go home and be cared for there. "The idea of a Holy Trinity team to help do that was born right then," she recalled. "Elaine Hall and Helen Gough were all for it. Joan Headley, who works at Nellie's, comes to Holy Trinity sometimes, and she happened to be there that day. She promised that Nellie's would help. There was a lot of hugging."

Margaret's collection of reading now included several gift books about diet and regimes that promised a cure for everything, about which I gave my unsolicited opinion that they were hogwash. She had other books about dying, notably the one by Elisabeth Kübler-Ross, about which I made no comment.

Margaret had been told of a Texas doctor, Carl Simonton, who was treating cancer patients by training them to concentrate on an image of their cancer cells and to direct their will power to the destruction of their tumours. That sounded good to me: non-intrusive and, who knows? maybe effective. I promised to buy the Simonton book, *Getting Well*, but on my next visit I saw that someone had already brought Margaret a copy.

Margaret, in fact, was experiencing a richness of advice about cancer cures. She consulted Bill Whitla in some distress. One person at Holy Trinity was insisting that she try a certain kind of diet. What did Bill think? And there was the problem of what would happen to her next. Should she go home, should she stay in hospital, should she go to a clinic?

She wailed, "I don't feel I'm in control of my life."

33

He soothed her. Don't rush it, he said. You have lots of time. All the time is now your own, you can control it. You can decide where it is you want to spend the rest of your life, and what therapy appeals to you. Take what you like of the suggestions people are making and go with that.

"Will it do any good?" she asked plaintively.

He said honestly, "I don't know."

I called her surgeon, who accepted me as the official next-of-kin. He didn't know how the idea of St. John's Hospital had started, but it wasn't "appropriate" and couldn't be considered. I spoke then of her return home and said there was an offer from Stephen Langmead, an architect and member of Nellie's board of directors, to supervise the installation of a toilet downstairs to spare her the need to climb the stairs.

The doctor discouraged this with an evasive comment. I asked quickly, "How long does she have?"

After a pause, he said, "We aren't talking years."

He went on to outline the home-care services available in Ontario to someone in Margaret's situation. A nurse from the Victorian Order of Nurses (VON) would visit on Tuesdays and Fridays, and twice a week someone from Visiting Homemakers would perform the necessary household chores. This generally was sufficient in situations where the patient was living with a family, he said. He was concerned that Margaret had no one.

"That's not true," I said. "Margaret has a huge family. You can make a discharge plan for her exactly as you would for someone going home with lots of people to take care of her."

He said he was impressed. It was quite unusual.

On my next visit I suggested to Margaret that a few of us wanted to stay with her when she went home, if she wished. She said quickly, in her musical way, "Oh, that's very kind I'm sure, but I don't think it's really necessary."

I said, picking my way carefully, "Can you picture yourself getting your groceries? Taking your clothes to the cleaners? Paying your telephone bill?"

She looked quite faint at the thought. "No-o-o-o."

34

"Well, we'll just hang around and take care of those chores until you're ready to do them yourself. We won't get in the way, I promise, but we want to settle you in."

She grinned at me and shook her head in a you-are-the-limit way. I put my arms around her, squeezed her hard, and said, "Thanks."

Joyce Brown, acting on the assumption that Margaret would want to go home to die, had already discussed with Elaine Hall the possibility of putting together a team . Elizabeth Greaves, of course, was convinced that it would work. Margaret shared her doubts with Bill Whitla. "I don't know how it's going to work," she said. "All those people in my house, falling over one another."

He was reassuring. It was worth a try. Margaret was already aware that the hospital, knowing she had no family, would not release her to go home if it were not for the quality and numbers of people who were promising to care for her. Hospital staffs, quite properly, worry about discharging seriously ill people to what might be a haphazard or negligent situation. Margaret had vouched for the team several times when her doctor and the hospital discharge planners had questioned the wisdom of the scheme. "This is a remarkable group of people," she had insisted. "I'll be fine."

Subsequently Margaret discovered our intention to have someone sleep overnight in her guest room. Bill Whitla was visiting on the afternoon when she took issue with me about the overnight shift.

"I really don't think I'll need anyone there at night," she began. "I do see the need for people during the day, but I'll be perfectly fine by myself at night."

"I understand, better than most, how you feel about being alone in your house," I said. "We're all very conscious of the fact that you've always had your domain to yourself and now you've got this horde of people sitting around being cheerful at you. But the night is often a difficult time for people who aren't well, and I don't want you to be alone then."

Margaret opened her mouth to protest further, but Bill Whitla

35

came to the rescue. "Margaret," he said with a disarming smile, "if June thinks you'd better have someone in the house overnight, then you'd better listen to her."

She conceded, but she wasn't convinced.

On March 19, a bitterly cold Tuesday, I visited Margaret for a few minutes after lunch. We were alone, and there was something bleak in her eyes. During the ritual walk the length of the corridor, she was withdrawn. As I helped her into bed she said, in a child's high wail, "I don't understand. The doctor says there is nothing they can do. No operation, no chemotherapy, nothing."

I hesitated over all the choices of response open to me and said, holding her hands, "That's right, Margaret. There is nothing they can do."

Her eyes filled and I put my arms around her. After a moment, she patted my shoulder to comfort me and said, "I've had a good life." I held her tightly and wept.

The idea of forming a family of friends for Margaret was gathering strength by a process of simultaneous combustion. What we could do for this beloved and valuable woman, clearly, was to organize a support group that would function the way the human tribe, the human family, had always done in such a crisis. We thought that at the least we could help her return home for a few days, or maybe longer; if possible, we might assist her to die there rather than in an impersonal hospital where doctors didn't have the time to learn her name and nurses didn't think it important that her room wasn't ready.

Joyce Brown, experienced and proficient at the maddening task of preparing schedules for Nellie's, was already drawing up a list of volunteers. My feeling, quite unrealistic, was that there were sufficient of us within the Nellie's network to cover shifts around the clock. One day when I mentioned to Margaret how well things were progressing, I learned for the first time that Holy Trinity was also involved. "Elaine Hall is taking care of everything at that end," she told me, looking blissful.

Suddenly, I knew we could do it.

Michael Creal, an Anglican priest and a professor of humanities at York University, brought Margaret Holy Communion and learned that a plan was taking shape. Margaret wasn't certain of the details, so Michael, a member of the Holy Trinity congregation, suggested to Bill Whitla that Bill should co-ordinate the parish's participation. Bill, scrupulously considerate, asked Elaine Hall if he was invading her territory, and Elaine assured him that she welcomed his help.

The first day of spring, traditionally a day when the oppressive Canadian winter begins to lift, was far from hopeful. Outdoors was miserable, and Margaret's movements were sluggish as she put her arms into the blue dressing-gown. I had to put her slippers on her feet. She walked unsteadily but chatted brightly about something she had been reading. As I made her comfortable in her bed afterwards, I noticed a beautiful poster of white gulls against a pure blue sky, a gift, she said, of her CAMMAC friends.

"They've signed the back of it," she said cosily, curling up under the patchwork. "Isn't that nifty?"

I thought: CAMMAC! More people for the team.

Two days later, a Saturday, Margaret announced joyfully that she was to be discharged the following Wednesday. I had a flutter of panic that it was too soon; we weren't ready. She didn't notice my consternation. She told me proudly that she had had a normal bowel movement that day. I was amused that Margaret, normally so private that I didn't even know her sister had disappeared fifteen years ago, was bragging about this triumph of her beleaguered alimentary system. There was more, she went on. Her stitches were out, and she was no longer taking sedatives for pain.

She bragged, "I find I can control the pain now by deep breathing."

Margaret's mood was almost frisky. I had a wild thought that maybe she *was* getting well. When she told me that she had refused to comply with the nurses' request that she get dressed in her street clothes, declaring that the elastic of her underwear hurt her tender abdomen, I cheered. Here was the old spunky and independent Margaret.

37

A few minutes later she went into the bathroom, where she remained a disquietingly long time, emanating gurgling, tormented noises. She emerged with a ghastly pallor. Neither of us made a comment.

On Tuesday I was confident that the network of Margaret's friends would be ready. We had a reprieve we welcomed because Margaret's friend Hope Hoey was coming from St. Sauveur des Monts in Quebec to stay with her for four days. They had tickets for the musical *Cats* for March 28 and, as Margaret had been telling her doctors decisively for the past two weeks, she intended to attend.

Remembering that she had sung a demanding concert with the Concord Singers only three weeks earlier, I was prepared to accept that this woman who could scarcely walk fifty steps in a hospital corridor would in three days get dressed in her prettiest, climb into a car, drive five miles to a theatre, and attend a musical.

I asked Margaret for a shopping list of the groceries that might appeal to her almost non-existent appetite. She dictated: ice cream (any flavour), homemade soups (not made with meat), fish, bland-tasting bread (not the good crunchy kind), bananas, skim milk, grapes, oatmeal porridge.

"Babying food," I concluded. She grinned.

Carmen Bourbonnais, a Nellie's staff person of uncommonly sunny disposition, would do the shopping. Diane Savard, a former resident and later a staff person at Nellie's, had volunteered to clean Margaret's house in preparation for the homecoming, but she was in hospital herself for surgery on an abscess on her arm. Margaret had been trying to contact Diane and was anxious. I assured her that someone from Nellie's would fill in.

She made a rueful face. "I haven't been keeping up with the housework lately," she said. "It's a mess."

"I'm shocked to hear that," I told her gravely.

On the morning of March 27, a windy Wednesday, I arrived at the hospital at eleven to take Margaret home. I found her in her room, dressed in the clothes she had worn three weeks earlier. They hung on her like a clown's costume. She was surrounded

38

by green plastic garbage bags stuffed to overflowing with the possessions she had acquired during her stay. At the nursing station I inquired about the obligatory wheelchair and was asked to be patient.

We waited like strangers in a bus station, talking desultorily. A cheerful young man arrived with Margaret's wheelchair and was aghast to see how much had to be transported. He noted the tiny patient collapsed in her clothes, the several green garbage bags stuffed to the top, her radio, the tape deck, the stack of books, the multitude of flowers and plants, the fleece, the patch-work quilt, the roll of posters, the silver balloon. He departed to find another chair.

Between us we loaded Margaret into one wheelchair, piling on her lap the blanket, the fleece, her handbag, and her antique luggage, and stuffed most of the accumulation into the other chair. Margaret supervised all of this, seated in her wheelchair in the doorway as I made a final inspection. I decided to leave behind several pots of dead daffodils. She protested indignantly. I argued back, pointing out that there was no room. She burst out, "They're *bulbs*! I might live to plant them!"

The young man and I were stunned by her raw courage. We bumbled around, getting in one another's way, to find space for three more flowerpots on top of the heaping disarray in the other wheelchair.

"I hate to tell you how small my car is," I told him gloomily as the elevator descended. Enchanted with Margaret, he paid me no attention. "We'll manage," he told me in the soothing tone of one reassuring a child about monsters in the woods.

With the aid of a kindly doorman and a passing nurses' aide, we managed to cram Margaret and her possessions into my tiny Fiat Spider, daffodils and all. The complexities of this put us all in a merry mood, and we departed the hospital driveway with shouts of good wishes on all sides.

Margaret's house was gleaming. Someone had left a basket filled with freshly made apple muffins, and there was a tin of her favourite banana muffins on the dining-room table. In the refrigerator I found everything on the shopping list, plus a dish of pasta someone had made and placed in the freezer. Margaret sat on a small green sofa positioned at the end of her living-room with its back against the latticed windows. She looked around with a quizzical expression. "Everything looks the same and everything looks different," she mused.

She fluffed up a small green velvet cushion and lay down with her head on it. The sofa was so short that she had to draw up her knees to fit. The house was cold, the thermostat set very low, and I asked if she wanted a blanket. She said there was one on a table in the front hall. As I went to get it, she called, "Not the plaid one. The one underneath, the green one." I found it exactly as she said, a lovely dark green mohair throw, soft as angelhair.

When Margaret died almost three months later, she was lying in almost exactly that position, on that small green sofa, under that green mohair blanket. She had taken up her battle station from the moment she arrived home.

Her tenant, Vincent Levesque, knocked on the door between the kitchen and the basement stairs. He was a dark young man, twenty-two, deferential and uneasy, with a rich French accent. He stood awkwardly beside the couch, expressing his best wishes for Miss Frazer's speedy recovery. He said Cleo was out of cat food and offered to get more. As he passed me, returning to his apartment, he gave me a look of naked anguish.

"He's the best tenant I've ever had," Margaret told me, snuggling deliciously under the blanket. "This winter when he saw I wasn't feeling well, he did all sorts of things to help me. Shovelling the walk, that kind of thing. He's just the kindest person imaginable."

A visitor came, a dark young woman with a lovely face and gentle manners, carrying a chortling baby boy. Margaret's face lit up. This was the next-door neighbour, Mary Hiseler, mother of three children whom Margaret adored. Margaret had had a photograph of them in her hospital room, two bright-faced little girls and the enchanting baby, and she kept it handy like a proud grandmother to show visitors.

I explained to Mary about the team. She said she already had met Carmen, who had cleaned the house, and found her charming. Mary wrote her telephone number on a scrap of paper that I taped next to the kitchen telephone mounted on the wall. In an emergency, she said, she would come at once to help. She also offered to assist the team with shopping or any other needed service.

The telephone rang. It was Dr. Linda Rapson, forty-three, Margaret's friend and the team's newest acquisition. We had no inkling at that stage of the process, naive as we were and new to the hazards of home-based palliative care, that what we were proposing to do would have been impossible without the intense commitment of a selfless, dedicated, expert, and resourceful doctor. When Linda volunteered herself, we had the team's essential ingredient.

Linda and I had been friends for longer than I had known Margaret. We first met in the early seventies when it was illegal to perform an abortion in Canada and women were dying of kitchen-table butchery. I was part of a new group called the Canadian Association for the Repeal of Abortion Laws (CARAL), and Linda was a founding member of Doctors for the Repeal of Abortion Laws (DRAL). I encountered then her warmth, intelligence, honesty, tenacity, stamina, and kindness. Also evident, even to a dim-eyed observer across a football field, are her gusto and love of life; she's not famous for dissembling about how she feels.

Linda graduated in medicine in 1965, when she was only twenty-three, and for nine years was in family practice. She left that because she was intrigued by the potential of acupuncture in the control of pain. Not many doctors are interested in pain, but Linda sees the relief of pain as a primary function of her profession. One of the earliest members of the Acupuncture Foundation of Canada, she is now in charge of the foundation's education programs and gives seminars on acupuncture everywhere in Canada. On these occasions she brings with her

41

such visual aids as slides, graphics, and videos, evidence of a fascination with gadgetry that might be in her genes. Her father, W. Howard Rapson, an ebullient and inventive retired professor in the engineering faculty of the University of Toronto, is devoted to electronic gimmicks.

Linda Rapson has a square-set build and the beaming countenance of a good-tempered child. She's optimistic, enthusiastic, intelligent, direct, and what a generation ago used to be described as "good-hearted". Her style is less than sleek. She prefers comfortable, even baggy clothes, keeps a minimum-bother haircut, avoids make-up, possesses a sense of adventure rare in an adult, and is devoid of any skill at subterfuge.

Occasionally her candour is startling. For instance, we were together in the fall of 1985 at a sedate dinner attended by lawyers and doctors in the august chambers of Osgoode Hall, chatting to a highly esteemed person Linda had known in school. I said to him, "Linda tells me you were quite a ladies' man when you were a student."

"I didn't say that," Linda corrected me. "I said he slept around."

At my urging in 1977, she served for two years on the board of directors of Nellie's, where she first met Margaret, and since then has been such a staunch supporter of Nellie's that she purchases tickets for her entire family – her husband, lawyer Morris Manning, her teenaged daughters, Kate and Rachel, and her parents, Howard and Mary Rapson – every time Nellie's has a benefit.

"My first impression of Margaret was of sweetness," Linda once told me as we sprawled on a breezy veranda at her cottage on Pigeon Lake, north east of Toronto. "Sweet in the way she talked to you and the way she paid close attention to what you said." Linda also remembers being impressed at Margaret's and Eileen Swinton's teamwork on Nellie's board, as both of them ploughed ahead imperturbably through all difficulties, from unexpected expenses to bureaucratic roadblocks.

"They did what had to be done without fuss, and nothing phased them," Linda said lazily as we sipped white wine and watched the fall of light through the summer trees. I reflected, amused, that those were qualities that Linda herself possessed in conspicuous abundance. Perhaps, I speculated, people admire in others reflections of themselves, or what they are becoming.

Linda's involvement in Margaret's case, so crucial to the outcome, came about as a bit of luck. Linda hadn't seen Margaret since the previous summer when they had lunched together to talk about Margaret's imminent trip to China. Margaret had become intrigued with China after hearing Linda rave about a trip she had made with other doctors interested in acupuncture, and when an opportunity presented itself for Margaret to accompany a group going to China, she signed up and borrowed the travel money from her credit union. Then she sought out Linda to ask what she should pack and what she could expect.

Linda next heard from Margaret in November. Margaret called to say she was having some difficulty with her health and was dissatisfied with her doctor. Could Linda take her case? Linda explained that she wasn't doing family practice any more but was specializing in the treatment of pain with acupuncture. Since pain wasn't Margaret's problem, Linda recommended a woman doctor in her building.

Linda saw Margaret briefly at Holy Trinity's Christmas pageant, where Margaret was one of the readers and Linda's daughters were in the Nativity cast, but she noticed nothing amiss. Later Linda acquired a new patient, Hilda Powicke. Hilda, sixty-seven, an attractive, lively, and intelligent person, is a member of the Holy Trinity congregation. Born with a mild degree of spina bifida, her body is tiny and slightly twisted. That winter she had suffered a series of misfortunes, among which were five serious falls, some surgery, and a shoulder that became temporarily immobile. Because of these afflictions, she had been obliged to get about in a wheelchair. When she developed a painful attack of shingles, it was the last straw. Her doctor sent her to Linda for acupuncture treatment.

43

Early in the series of treatments, Linda and Hilda discovered that they both knew Margaret Frazer. Hilda was having her regular treatment one day in March when Linda happened to ask, "How's Margaret?"

Hilda told her that Margaret was in Wellesley Hospital with inoperable cancer and that a team of people was preparing to care for her in her home when she was ready for discharge. That was a situation Linda knew about firsthand. The summer before, a young woman very close to her, Joan Partridge, whose family had lived near the Rapsons while all the children were growing up, was dying of cancer at her summer cottage in the Laurentians. When Linda learned of it, she drove there at once and found Joan in agony. With the assistance of a nearby Quebec doctor, Linda was able to administer treatment with liquid morphine that kept her friend almost pain free for the two weeks left in her life. Joan died peacefully with her husband, children, and parents at her side.

Linda learned from that, she says, that "you should just barge in when people you love are in trouble. You understand what to do better than you think. It's emotionally hard, but I would be more upset if I couldn't do something to help someone I care about."

Another lesson from that sad summer was that Linda discovered she is able to treat a patient with whom she has emotional ties. All her medical training had strongly advised otherwise; she had been taught that doctors should remain emotionally detached from their patients in order to keep their judgement cool and should never treat anyone dear to them. "Taking care of Joanie showed me that I could handle that kind of situation," she said. If she kept her head, her love for her patient didn't get in the way.

"If you ever don't know what to do," she observed thoughtfully, "you can always hug."

On the day she learned Margaret was dying, Linda hurried to Wellesley Hospital. She wrapped Margaret in a big embrace and asked her medical history. Margaret could talk about symptoms, such as bouts of hiccups that had annoyed her in China and were growing worse, or the weight loss, but she was vague about the extent of her cancer.

"Who's your doctor?" Linda asked.

"You remember," Margaret answered. "You recommended your friend. I've been seeing her."

"I'll talk to her, if that's all right with you," Linda said, plunging in. "I have some experience with palliative care, and if you like, and if your doctor agrees, I'd like to help."

Margaret knew exactly what "palliative care" meant – support to enable people to die as naturally as possible – but she didn't flinch away from the term we all had avoided. She said fervently, "I would love it if you would help me."

Margaret's face was heart shaped with a prominent brow, deep-set blue eyes, and an expressive mouth. She could wear her feelings all over it. During this exchange it was the intensity of her relief and gratitude that caught at Linda's heart. However tricky the ethical issue of one doctor moving in on another, even one who is a friend, she prepared herself to try.

She took Margaret's hands, gripped them, and promised: "I'll see you through this, Margaret. I'll make sure that you're comfortable." Margaret's eyes filled with tears.

Margaret's doctor was completely agreeable. "We'll share it," she said to Linda. "You do pain and I'll do after-care."

As the case unfolded, however, it was apparent that few doctors in the world would be prepared to do, or could afford to do, what Linda Rapson did for Margaret Frazer. Though Linda frequently consulted a colleague, a cousin by marriage skilled in cancer treatment, a second doctor on the premises was never needed.

Her telephone call only minutes after Margaret's arrival home from hospital gave the first indication of the depth of Linda's commitment to Margaret's care. She greeted me cheerily and wanted to know what prescription for pain Margaret's surgeon had given. I read it to her and she snorted "That's a silly drug. I think Tylenol No. 3 would be better, but what she's going to need eventually is liquid morphine. Get the hospital's prescription filled to tide her over tonight in case she has pain, but tell the pharmacist we'll be ordering liquid morphine. Druggists don't usually keep it in stock."

I told Margaret I was going to slip out to have her prescription filled. While I was at it, I'd pick up something for dinner for her and her friend Hope. Margaret thought the latter was unnecessary. "We'll just go out to eat," she told me placidly. "There are plenty of restaurants around here."

"You twit," I said fondly. "You're just home from hospital, and the weather is terrible. You're not going anywhere."

When I returned she was dozing. I put away the take-out casserole I'd purchased and put on the kettle. Margaret roused at the clatter and asked what kind of tea I was making.

"Someone's left you blueberry," I called from the kitchen. "It looks wonderful. Is that all right with you?"

"Lovely, but it will have to steep at least six minutes."

That's not how I make tea. Five seconds seems ample to me, whatever the brand, but I did it her way. As I checked the time, I thought: This is your house, Margaret, your kitchen, your tea, your teapot, your ridiculous crocheted tea-cosy. After exactly six minutes, I poured the fragrant brew into her blue-flowered mugs.

We settled for a chat, me in a vaguely Danish-looking armchair with a matching footstool, both pieces covered in a forest green like the couch, and Margaret propped up on the sofa supported by some extra pillows I had taken from her bedroom. She spoke of her family again. Her father, A.C. Frazer, known as Archie, was the English-born director of personnel for the Steel Company of Canada and much admired for his probity. Known as a "sincere and friendly man", according to the company magazine, he retired in 1953 after forty-five years with the company and was presented with a radio. Her mother, Phoebe Emerson Frazer, was a reader in the local Baptist church and the daughter of a stern Baptist minister.

The distinguishing features of Margaret's childhood in Burlington were those Baptist values. The three daughters were imbued with consciences that felt guilt if they were frivolous on a Sunday. Sex was a particularly dark and taboo topic. Young male

Bible students used to come for dinner at the Frazers, but when Margaret and her sisters reached their teens the young men were not invited again. Once, when Margaret was fifteen, her school was holding a tea dance at four o'clock in the gymnasium. Her parents refused to allow her to go, shuddering at the thought of a man touching her. She grew up with a sense of men as dangerous and revolting. She once told me, "By the time I realized that wasn't true, I had finished university and was teaching school. It was too late."

Even as a youngster, Margaret wondered if other religions were softer. "Once I went to an Anglican church with a friend who belonged to St. Thomas's in Hamilton," she said idly. The conversation was turning into a comfortable putting-in-time exercise, not so trivial as to bore us but economical of effort. "I took communion with her and I loved it. All that ritual. My friend's father was shocked. He took me into his study and explained that I was supposed to be confirmed as an Anglican before I could do that."

She sipped her tea. A banana muffin I had buttered for her was almost untouched. "It's difficult to shake off a Baptist up-bringing," she said with a grimace.

I said something about liturgical music, and she brightened. Music had a good deal to do with her choice of Holy Trinity as her church. She had been indifferent to religion for about twenty-five years, she told me, but she developed a longing to be in a congregation where people took an inquiring approach to theology. She went first to a Unitarian church, "but they seem so sure they're right". For a long time she worshipped with the Quakers because she liked their stand on social issues, but they had no music.

Next she tried Holy Trinity, which had just weathered a tumultuous period of internal discord and battling the mother church because most of the congregation wanted to allow American draft resisters from the Vietnam war to sleep in the church. Margaret grinned, "People there seemed concerned and, besides, there was glorious music. So Holy Trinity it was."

47

I cleared up the mugs and plates and she talked of music. Some of her friends could play two or three instruments well. "They are so gifted," she sighed. Just about her favourite thing was to get together with other musicians, put "something really gorgeous, like Bach" on the music stands, and play it together. She first did that when she was a young woman visiting musical friends at their summer cottages. On one occasion, she recalled, she was so intimidated by the company she was in, so much more skilled than herself, that she couldn't play a note. She vowed she would never do that again, would never let shyness spoil the pleasure of playing, and she never did.

I knew she had shown that same indomitable spirit in learning to play the flute at the age of sixty-four. She tried three teachers before she found one who made her work as hard as she thought she should. The teacher was later to say, "I have never taught anyone who didn't have her own teeth to play the flute, but Margaret was so *determined*."

Margaret glanced at her flute case on top of the piano. "I wonder if I'll ever have the strength to play my flute again," she said, her voice light.

On impulse she stood up and went to the piano. For a few minutes she tried to play the music that was open on the rack, but the chords were full of wrong notes.

I urged her to change into a nightie and dressing-gown to be more comfortable and she agreed, going slowly up the stairs, insisting I was not to help. When she returned we talked about singing. I reminded her that I am tone deaf, and she reminded me that this was impossible. We settled to enjoy ourselves. We had found our way to very familiar ground.

"There's no such thing as being tone deaf," she said indignantly, as she always did when I mentioned my disability. "You can be taught to sing on key."

I repeated that I was beyond salvation. To divert her, I told about the time five years earlier when my mother was dying of a stroke. As she lay in what seemed a coma, I hovered over her, stroking her hair and kissing her soft cheek. I felt the same tenderness as when I had comforted our babies. I whispered, "Mom, would you like me to sing to you?" My mother roused herself from the deep place her mind had been wandering and groaned, *"No!"*

My family thinks this is a hilarious story, but Margaret was appalled. The time had finally come, she told me firmly. She was going to teach me to sing in tune. I would be her fourth successful pupil. "Pick any tune you like and sing it to me," she commanded. I could think of nothing I wanted to inflict on her, but she was insistent. We finally settled on "O Canada", and I was singing our national anthem, at full voice and very badly, when Margaret's friend Hope Hoey walked in the door.

The Middle

Hope Hoey was all anyone could want in a friend. She burst in the door, radiating good health and common sense, and went at once to the couch to hug Margaret, not showing the slightest sign of shock at Margaret's appearance. She told me later that Margaret had admitted to her that her weight loss was close to forty pounds, so she had prepared herself for her friend's greatly altered appearance.

Margaret's face was shining. Hope kept up a cheerful chatter about driving conditions and the state of her car as she moved about the house, as familiar with it as the owner. She put a gift for Margaret, a two-quart container of maple syrup, in the freezer compartment of the fridge and hung her coat in the front closet.

Old friends they were. They had met at Girl Guide camp in 1933 when Hope, now a glowing sixty-six, was fourteen, and Margaret, then sixteen, had been hired as the nature counsellor. Margaret's luggage included nature books packed in a soap box on which she had altered the word "LUX" to read "BUX", which Hope thought witty of her.

"I decided then and there that this was someone I was going to like very much," Hope wrote to me after Margaret's death. "After four weeks of camp with her, during which she taught me the excitement of learning to identify trees and flowers and birds and stars, I think I loved her. Her own love for all the things of nature seemed to be passed on to me by some magical form of osmosis, and it's something I've never lost."

After that summer in camp, Hope frequently saw Margaret in the halls of Hamilton Central Collegiate, where Margaret was a year ahead of Hope, but they didn't have the same circle of friends. Margaret appeared a very serious person. She never had a date and didn't seem to be interested in boys, which set her apart; but she was devoted to music. Hope recalled that Margaret's entire family was interested in music. The mother played the organ, the father was tenor soloist in the church choir, and all three daughters were capable instrumentalists. Margaret went to McMaster University, paying her tuition in part by teaching canoeing at summer camps and by winning two scholarships. She graduated in 1938 with an Honours B.A. in English and history. Hope remembers that Margaret was keenly interested in the Oxford Group at that time. On graduation she obtained teacher's certificates in English, history, music, and guidance at the College of Education in Toronto.

The two women kept in touch over the years as Hope married an executive with Procter and Gamble and had four children. Margaret taught high school for three years in Kenora, where she led the school orchestra and ran the school library, in addition to teaching English and history to four grades. After that Margaret taught for a year at Central Collegiate Institute in Hamilton, but the school burned down and she was out of a job. In 1946 she was one of the first staff hired by Bloor Collegiate in Toronto. She started as an English teacher and a member of the guidance department, but in her first year rounded up enough students to start a school orchestra, which she led.

She never intended to stay. Her plans for her life were to study psychology at the London School of Economics and find work in Canada as a psychiatric social worker. In 1948 she wrote a wistful letter to the head of guidance in Winnipeg schools, asking for advice. "I am thirty-one now. Before too long I want to have done a bit of travel and study and have settled into what I should like to regard as my life work."

For years Margaret saved for that ambitious undertaking, but there was never enough money to do it. In 1957, her sights reduced, she took a sabbatical and spent a year in postgraduate study of English at Birkbeck College, University of London. After that she contented herself with an active role on the leading edge of change in education. She was on the executive of the Ontario Council of Teachers of English during its first three years and a member of the Department of Education's Committee on Grade

13 Curriculum in English in 1967.

Margaret was godmother to one of Hope's daughters, also named Margaret, who was born in 1944. In 1958 the Hoeys moved to Quebec, where Hope's husband headed Procter and Gamble's new offices in that province. When Margaret Hoey was married in 1965, Margaret Frazer attended her godchild's wedding in St. Sauveur des Monts in the Laurentians, where the Hoeys had a summer home. Margaret played the organ at the service.

The basis of the long friendship was their mutual love of nature. Margaret's letters to Hope were full of stories of bird sightings, and when they were together they tramped through the woods, birding. Hope was endlessly impressed that Margaret could identify birds by their sounds and knew the name of every wildflower and weed. They had other common ground after Hope followed a long-held ambition to become a teacher and found she loved it as much as she had expected she would. Like Margaret, she had a keen interest in learning how things work. She eventually became head of the teachers' union in Quebec.

When Hope was widowed in 1967, the two women began to see more of one another. Once they drove through the Maritimes in Margaret's elderly Datsun. Another notable trip was in 1983 to San Francisco. Thinking back, Hope wondered if Margaret had been ill even then.

"She wasn't the same person that trip," Hope recalled. "She didn't laugh as much, didn't find things as funny as she usually did." And there was a mysterious collapse in a restaurant, which Margaret dismissed as food poisoning. The next time they saw one another was the summer before Margaret's illness, when Hope came with her fourteen-year-old grandson on a visit. On that occasion Margaret was unaccountably crabby. Hope was puzzled; that wasn't like Margaret at all.

Around the spring of 1984 a few people at Holy Trinity had also noticed a change in Margaret. Nancy Whitla, for one, observed a testiness that had never been part of Margaret's nature. At meetings she was quick to anger, easily upset, and prone to long digressions on matters irrelevant to the issue being addressed.

Margaret confessed to her, and to others, "I don't have much energy any more. I've got to cut back. I can't do as much as I used to."

When Margaret and Hope talked on the phone at Christmas, they discussed going together to see *Cats*, the hot new musical that had just opened in a newly restored theatre in Toronto. Margaret purchased three tickets for the night of March 28 for herself, Hope, and a mutual friend, and in a letter confirming the arrangements mentioned for the first time that she wasn't feeling well. In her next letter she admitted she had lost forty pounds. Hope was deeply concerned, but the tone of Margaret's communications remained cheerful, so she put her worry aside.

Margaret called Hope just before she went into hospital. She said, with no special emphasis, that she was going to have a bit of surgery for a bowel obstruction. Hope said uneasily, "Do you think you'll be able to go to *Cats*?" Margaret responded, "Oh goodness, yes. Of course I will." At this point Margaret had known for two weeks that her cancer was terminal. Hope suggested that she should stay somewhere else in Toronto rather than at Margaret's, but Margaret wouldn't hear of it.

They talked again after the operation, and Margaret seemed in a fine mood. There was no mention of the seriousness of her condition. She was being discharged in time to go to *Cats* and would in fact be home in time to welcome Hope when she arrived. Which she was.

I left the two friends to their reminiscences and drove home through a bleak March twilight. Knowing Margaret's frugal nature I was certain the tickets she had purchased for *Cats* were in the last row of the final balcony. I couldn't picture how she would manage to get to the seats; so early the next morning, I rented a collapsible wheelchair upholstered in bright blue leather, stood it at a jaunty angle in the trunk of my Fiat, and delivered it to Margaret's.

My cowardly intention was to pop it into the front hall, give Margaret a quick hug, and run, leaving Hope to cope with the situation if Margaret was affronted. Instead I found Linda Rapson there, making her first house call and excited by a new gadget that she hoped would reduce Margaret's pain. Called a TENS machine, standing for transcutaneous electrical nerve stimulation, it looked to me at first glance like a Frankenstein torture implement, but Margaret, always open to possibilities and adventure, was loving it.

TENS is an application of acupuncture that patients can administer themselves. Margaret, wearing the blue dressing-gown, was stretched out on the sofa as Linda placed black electrode pads that resembled suction-cups on various acupuncture points on her thin limbs. Linda was happily explaining how the process worked. She loves to teach, and she's good at it. As Margaret listened intently, Linda explained that the brain normally produces a marvellous chemical, endorphin, which acts to block the flow of pain messengers coming from the parts of the body where damage has occurred. Acupuncture, in simple terms, is a technique to fool the brain so that it produces more endorphin.

"TENS is do-it-yourself acupuncture," Linda crowed. "These electrodes are connected to an electrical stimulator that will give you small pulsation sensations. That notifies the brain to send out pain-blockers." I thought, hogwash, but everyone else seemed so delighted with the apparatus that I contained my skepticism.

I was wise to do so. The TENS machine was replaced two days later by a Codetron, a more sophisticated, experimental version of the same idea. Although cancer of the pancreas can be one of the most painful ways to die, that Codetron machine kept Margaret almost drug free and pain free for the next three months. Margaret was the first cancer patient to use a Codetron, so its impressive benefits with her have attracted wide interest. The machine now is undergoing clinical tests on other cancer patients to determine if it can be recommended widely.

The Codetron consists of a small control panel on which is mounted a row of toggle switches, each paired with a light and a control knob. The switches operate rubber electrodes, flat black rubber patches on the ends of a spaghetti of coloured wires. One rubber patch, the grounder, was placed on Margaret's heel. Six others were fixed on one ankle, below each knee, on the inside on her right arm, and on the backs of her hands near the thumb joints. Margaret could regulate the intensity of the electrical impulses by turning control knobs.

Linda stayed with Margaret for an hour and a half, teaching her to use the TENS machine and making sure that Margaret wasn't faking her eagerness in deference to Linda's feelings. I lingered to watch, but my mind was on the Margaret team that would take over when Hope left on Sunday to return to Quebec. We had almost a dozen volunteers from Nellie's, and I was certain that Elaine Hall would provide a substantial number from Holy Trinity, but I hadn't really stopped to consider how the team was going to work.

"What kind of things do you want the team to do?" I asked Margaret.

She observed, with delicious irony, "Oh, so now you're consulting me?"

She raised her old objection to the overnight shift. She wasn't convinced it was necessary. "If something happens," she pointed out, "I can always call Mary Hiseler next door."

I said, "That might not be possible, Margaret. What if you're suddenly too ill to move? What if you fall?"

Linda was on my side. "Remember, Margaret, you told me that you've had a few falls." I hadn't heard about that and groaned aloud.

Margaret gave Linda a glance of the betrayed. She muttered, "I haven't fallen for weeks," but the matter was settled.

I called the next day, a Friday, to ask how the night at *Cats* had gone. Margaret was breathless and had no time to talk. The nurse from the Victorian Order of Nurses had just arrived. "Wait until I tell you about my entrance in the wheelchair," she enthused. "It was *gorgeous*."

Hope later informed me that the wheelchair had saved the day. The three women arrived in the lobby somewhat at a loss, she said, because Margaret "hadn't anticipated that she would be attending in a wheelchair" and had purchased tickets in the second balcony, to which there was no wheelchair access. The house manager noticed them and escorted Margaret to a choice seat down front on the aisle. He helped her transfer from the wheelchair and then whisked it away. Hope stayed with her until just before the performance began and then fled to her seat in the rafters. When it was over, the house manager appeared promptly with the wheelchair and saw them out.

"It was just a great night," Hope assured me.

The following day, the sun shone and Margaret and Hope worked together to do some laundry and tidy the house. Margaret was so full of energy that she even did a bit of work in her garden. But in the afternoon, the VON nurse came and turned out to be a disaster, subjecting Margaret to a harsh interview and reading her the hospital record, which contained the comment, "she looks older than she is". When Margaret described the team, the nurse sniffed that Margaret's "fancy friends" wouldn't want to do housework. Then she examined the arrangement of bedroom and bath and informed Margaret that it would do for a while, "until you get weaker".

Margaret was devastated. That evening she couldn't touch her dinner. She sat at the dining-room table sobbing.

Hope concluded that it must have been the first time that anyone had suggested to Margaret that she wasn't going to make it, but this wasn't entirely true. What the nurse had accomplished, however, was the temporary demolition of the small piece of hope that Margaret had been nourishing. Her refusal to believe totally in the reality of her condition was not unlike the denial that follows a death in the family. For a long time, the newly bereaved harbour in secret a desperate belief that someone has made a mistake. The beloved person isn't really dead. One day, any day now, the error will be found and that dear person will come through the door and say, "Surprise!"

That madness can't be sustained. Mourners eventually know that the beloved person will never come through the door. The second wave of grief, the one Margaret suffered that day, is in some ways worse than the first.

Hope tried to comfort her friend. She pointed out that it was natural for her to cry because she was weakened from the operation. It was to be expected that small matters would upset her a great deal. Margaret remained inconsolable. Her face streaming tears, she called to her cat, Cleo, who veered out of reach. Margaret cried harder.

"What can you expect?" Hope said, grateful to pretend the subject was the perversity of cats rather than the inevitability of death. "Cats are like that. That's why you like them. They're independent."

Margaret began to recover, but the ordeal had taken its toll and she was wracked by pain. Hope telephoned Linda and furiously described what had happened. "Those silly remarks the nurse made have stripped away all Margaret's courage and dignity," Hope told Linda.

"We'll get rid of that nurse," Linda promised.

She suggested that Margaret take a Leritine for the pain and a sedative for sleep. Margaret came to the telephone and admitted that her weeping had been caused by the VON nurse. "She thinks I'm going to get progressively weaker," Margaret said in anguish. Linda replied in a strong, confident voice, "But you don't intend to get weaker, do you?" Margaret rallied and responded, "No, I don't." That night Margaret took not only the Leritine but also a Tylenol No. 3.

The next day she had a drug hangover, but otherwise was cheery, behaving as if nothing had happened.

Margaret's style of dying was based in good part, Linda Rapson thinks, on her inability to grasp the time frame her disease offered. Her doctors believed she had only days to live, but Margaret talked of her plans for the summer, for the autumn, for the next Christmas pageant at Holy Trinity. At one level of awareness, she knew perfectly well she would die eventually of her many cancerous tumours, but she buried that knowledge as deep in her consciousness as she could. She concentrated instead on a bold Margaret-style plan to delay the inevitable. She resolutely believed that if she wanted strongly enough to live, she would.

What's more, she succeeded: by extending her life to three months, she accomplished a miracle. The victory goes to her stubborn intransigent nature and to her courage, but some small credit is also due to the unusually solicitous medical care she received and to the cushions of love that the team placed around her sore body and tenacious optimism.

In her desk I found a tiny leather-covered birthday book full of quotations from Charles Dickens. One from Nicholas Nickleby struck me as applicable to Margaret Frazer's spirit. It reads, "Don't leave off hoping, or it's no use doing anything. Hope, hope to the last!"

On the cold bright Saturday morning after the blizzard of tears caused by the nurse, Hope suggested a restorative walk in High Park. The two friends strolled the thawing grounds for a few minutes, admiring the colour of the sky and a grove of red pines and looking for signs of spring. When Bill Whitla dropped in for a visit later, he found Margaret in her garden exclaiming over green blades of tulips poking through the softening earth. He noticed a broken lattice, a casualty of Sunday's wild storm, and offered to bring tools and repair it.

Hope spent four days with Margaret, her friend of more than fifty years, but they never discussed the subject that mattered most to them both. Hope longed to talk openly with Margaret about her death, but Margaret kept that door firmly closed and Hope would not open it without permission. They skirted the topic in various ways, several times speculating how "the team" would work. Hope privately was apprehensive at the prospect of so many people tramping in and out of Margaret's home, but she was all for Margaret dying at home as naturally as possible. "At least she can die in her own way," Hope thought.

Joyce Brown had flu that week and spent a productive day in bed making telephone calls to Nellie's board and staff people, asking them if they wanted to be part of the Margaret team and, if so, what day and what time. She divided each twenty-four hour period into three shifts: overnight people would arrive about nine and depart at breakfast, day-shift people would start early in the morning and leave mid-afternoon, and evening shift people would cover the hours between. From Elaine Hall, Joyce obtained some Holy Trinity names and called them too.

Linda Rapson, meanwhile, convened a Saturday morning meeting in her office. She said Nellie's and Holy Trinity had to get their act together, which was certainly true. I arrived first and found her bustling in the reception area, hospitably laying out cheese and crackers, coffee, and herbal tea. In the next few minutes the Nellie's contingent – Jay MacGillivray, Elizabeth Greaves, and Joyce Brown – arrived, along with Elaine Hall and Bill Whitla representing Holy Trinity.

We sat in the waiting room, munching and trying not to get crumbs on Linda's carpet. She told us about the VON nurse, and I volunteered to have her shot. That settled, I suggested we pick a name for the group. How about Friends of Margaret? Everyone thought that was fine, but in fact it was rarely ever used. From beginning to end we were simple "the team".

Joyce reported that the schedule had gaps in it. Bill suggested a meeting at Holy Trinity the next day, a Sunday, after the service. We could go over the ground rules with everyone assembled, and people could volunteer to fill the spaces. Linda circulated a thirty-seven page monograph on the management of cancer pain that had been prepared in 1984 for the federal minister of Health and Welfare by the Expert Advisory Committee on the Management of Severe Chronic Pain in Cancer Patients.

We read it avidly, particularly the multiple references to the need for a team approach in cancer care. Under the heading "Utilize Team Approach", the committee had written:

> The complexity of pain demands a team for effective therapy.
> The patient and family, as the core of this team, will require
> the assistance of physicians, nurses and other profession-
> als.... Such a large team of many disciplines each with its
> own expertise and vocabulary requires co-ordination and
> communication – a working *with*. Careful written documen-

62

tation and frequent team conferences are necessary to provide logical, integrated and consistent therapy.

Under the heading "Use Environment in Therapy" was another paragraph of relevance to the Margaret team:

Environment has a dramatic impact on cancer pain. One of the goals of treatment is to create a supportive and therapeutic milieu in which to treat pain.

For many patients, the home is the ideal environment as long as sufficient physical and emotional support can be provided by the community. To achieve this goal, visiting nurses, homemakers, physiotherapists, volunteers and a physician may be needed to assist the family in care.

Perfect. Just what we planned to do anyway. I volunteered to make copies for everyone.

Linda talked about the importance of our attitude. Above all, she stressed, we mustn't dampen Margaret's enthusiasm. "We can't take that optimism away from her," she said earnestly. "Her situation is serious, but not hopeless. We just never know with this disease. Once in a blue moon, we see a miracle.".

Linda raised the critical matter of medical confidentiality. In most circumstances doctors are ethically bound not to reveal details of their patients' condition. Since Margaret's care would be shared by some forty people, this presented Linda with a serious problem. There would have to be complete two-way communication between Linda and the team on such intimate matters as the state of Margaret's bowels. When she explained her dilemma to Margaret, she was relieved that Margaret promptly and without hesitation gave her permission to discuss her health with the team.

Linda's reference to bowels was not a facetious example. As she explained, Margaret's bowel function was the key to her survival. Though the surgery had found no obstruction, there was always the danger a blockage would develop. If this happened Margaret would have severe pain, and if Margaret had severe pain Linda would have to prescribe heavy narcotics, and if Linda prescribed morphine, the narcotic would cause further constipation, which in turn would create more pain. The increased pain then would require increased doses of morphine, and so on. A bowel blockage would finish Margaret.

"So don't bung up her bowel," Linda concluded.

At this point Elaine Hall observed quietly that she was a nurse who specialized in colon therapy in an Alternative Health Clinic. Linda greeted this news with a whoop.

"I'll be prescribing a stool softener," Linda said. When she mentioned the name of it, Elaine nodded approvingly.

Linda told us she had a back-up cancer specialist she would be consulting regularly, Dr. Larry Librach, a cousin of her husband's, head of the Family Practice Unit of Toronto Western Hospital and also head of that hospital's palliative care unit. On the basis of what Linda was able to tell him, Larry had not been optimistic about Margaret's case. He thought she could live perhaps a few weeks, but not much longer.

Linda described the Codetron machine, a sophisticated version of the better-known TENS apparatus, that she was taking to Margaret that afternoon to replace the TENS. She pointed to the place in the federal government monograph on cancer pain where TENS was listed among recommended non-drug therapies.

Certain neurons in the dorsal horn, when activated through direct electrical stimulation or through stimulation of large fibres not conventionally associated with pain, (e.g., vibration, touch and pressure), inhibit the propagation of pain.

The gate-controlling physiology of the dorsal horn explains the ancient observation that gentle rubbing of a painful part (counter-irritation) or the application of ice, heat or pressure eases the discomfort. More specific techniques of nerve stimulation have been developed, including transcutaneous electrical nerve stimulation (TENS) and acupuncture. The TENS apparatus consists of a battery-powered pulse generator and electrodes which are applied to the skin at empirically determined trigger points, or acupuncture points. These may lie adjacent to the painful region or may be located some distance proximal to the pain. TENS is well tolerated by most patients, although skin irritation is sometimes experienced.

Several hours of pain relief may be achieved after as short a time of stimulation as 5 to 20 minutes. About two-thirds of patients obtain short-term relief and one-eighth realize some long-term benefit, although information on its use in cancer pain is only anecdotal.

Linda told us with relish that the inventor of the Codetron, Dr. Norman Salansky, a biomedical engineering physicist, had insisted on loaning the machine to Margaret without cost, since it had never been used for a cancer patient and he regarded this as a test run. "So the price is right," she grinned.

We turned next to practical matters. If Margaret's death was imminent, the matter of her will was pressing. Liz said she knew a lawyer who would "make a house call". She would see what she could do to urge Margaret to make use of that convenience to update her will. Linda asked that the team keep a medical record of medication, bowel movements, and whatever else seemed pertinent. I began taking notes. Someone would have to secure power of attorney so that Margaret's banking could be done and the bills paid. Bill Whitla was concerned for Margaret's sisters. He volunteered to speak with Phyllis and try to locate Lynn. I thought we needed an extra front-door key to be hidden outside the house in case of an accidental lock-out. And what about Margaret's funeral? someone asked. Maybe Margaret would want to plan that.

I remembered Judy LaMarsh, lawyer and one-time cabinet minister in the Pearson government, whose situation was something like Margaret's in that she too was a woman who lived alone and wanted to die at home. When Judy learned that her cancer was terminal, Barbara Frum of CBC television's *The Journal* put together a financial package that made it possible for Judy to have her wish. In addition to a housekeeper, several of Judy's friends provided such services as grocery shopping and, towards the end, Nancy Morrison, a Vancouver judge, moved into Judy's house and cared for her.

The point I wanted to make with Margaret's team was that I remembered Barbara telling me how much satisfaction Judy had derived from planning her funeral. Judy decided, for instance, that she wanted women pallbearers and took pleasure in selecting the eight women she wanted to perform that sad duty. I ventured the thought that Margaret might also be interested in designing her final rites.

We looked at one another unhappily. I had a sudden picture of Margaret, jaw clenched, declaring, "I'm going to get well!" I really couldn't compare her to Judy LaMarsh, an intensely pragmatic woman, who took profane glee in dictating the names of her pallbearers.

Bill Whitla, his expression reflective and sorrowful, observed that Margaret certainly would have some definite preferences about the music for her service. A silence fell. Liz cleared her throat and said, "She's a member of the Toronto Memorial Society." That meant that Margaret had prearranged a spartan funeral and, most likely, cremation. Someone said, drily, "Oh, good." Our voices dragged. We were hating this conversation. We disposed of it by agreeing that we would watch for an opening when we were with Margaret. Perhaps it was on her mind. We'd let her be the judge of when to discuss it.

We turned gratefully to the trivia of housekeeping details. Joyce volunteered to circulate a telephone list of everyone in the Margaret network so we could get in touch with one another easily if necessary. I said I would have more copies made of the monograph on pain. We wondered about the bedding overnight people would need and eventually reached the obvious conclusion that they should bring their own linen so that Margaret's sheets wouldn't have to be laundered seven times a week.

Daytime people, we decided, would be responsible for groceries and should monitor the schedule of visitors to avoid people coming in great numbers at the same time or staying too long.

"Most of all," Linda declared, "remember that Margaret is in control. We are guests in her house, and we must be respectful of her rights and privacy. She's not to feel that we have taken over. She must remain in control of what happens in her own house."

Respect for Margaret's authority and dignity seemed such an important point that we wondered how the team could be reminded of it from time to time. We talked about circulating a newsletter and decided it would be too slow and cumbersome. Instead we agreed on a telephone information post where team members could call before leaving for their shifts to get updates on Margaret's condition and pick up tips on what they could do to make her more comfortable.

Jay MacGillivray was beginning to squirm. She was distressed that the talk was reducing something as spiritual as dying to the mechanics of bed linen rotation. She was feeling claustrophobic on Margaret's behalf as details piled upon details and, moreover, was alarmed every time Linda mentioned the possible use of tranquillizers and laxatives. Her manner was polite and co-operative, but I felt her underlying edginess when she said quietly that she was concerned that Margaret might be over-medicated.

Jay is a medium-sized woman with sharp features, pale skin, blonde hair chopped short, and a notable wit. She has a fixed place in Nellie's lore because of her knack of being on the scene of every disaster. Jay is always the staff person on duty when lightning strikes, as it literally did one morning, or when someone has to be rescued from a fiery room full of choking black smoke, or when a resident runs amok with a butcher knife. Her presence of mind on such occasions is awesome; she is fearless.

When I praised her cool after one such episode, she told me bashfully, "I shake like a leaf afterwards." Afterwards doesn't count.

Because she has spent so much time in hospitals, sometimes the victim of misdiagnosis and malprescription, Jay has developed a lively skepticism toward the entire medical profession. She has combined her mistrust of the medical establishment with feminist principles honed during the years of working at Nellie's and the Margaret Frazer House, and has put them together in a decision to learn midwifery. At the time Margaret became ill, Jay was enrolled in a course of midwife training. What concerned her when she rallied to Margaret's support was that "the doctors will screw it up". She was relieved to discover that Linda Rapson did not plan any heroic intervention. Linda's rule in palliative care, as she announced at that first meeting, was "don't bug the patient". Relief showed in Jay's face.

Linda and Elaine Hall left to go to Margaret's to demonstrate the Codetron. Linda was more worried about Margaret's condition than she had admitted. Margaret's bowel had not functioned for four days.

Toronto's Holy Trinity Anglican Church isn't difficult to find. It lies in the crook of the elbow of the Eaton Centre, a Toronto landmark and tourist attraction that flows a wall of concrete and glass along Yonge street from Queen to Dundas. Inside this fortress is a lovely galleria filled with light, fountains, and living trees. Early in the development of this massive project there was an assumption that the beautiful but deteriorating Holy Trinity church, which was in the way, would be purchased from the congregation and flattened. This proposal came to nothing; in fact at one point it looked very much as though Holy Trinity would flatten Eaton's.

When the rhetoric of a thousand meetings, petitions, delegations, confrontations, and backroom deals was over, Eaton's was beaten. The department-store chain paid Holy Trinity a fortune for air rights and other concessions and made adjustments in the design of its proposed skyscraper to allow space for a park around the church and an ample fall of sunlight on Holy Trinity's glorious stained-glass windows.

Holy Trinity earmarked some of this windfall to build affordable housing for low-income people and used part of the rest to renovate and restore the church and to add a tiny, perfect park around its newly washed brick walls. This park was under construction on the wretched Sunday morning when the first general meeting of Friends of Margaret took place at the church. High hoardings protected deep pits that had been dug in glistening yellow clay, and a trailer used by the contractor's crews blocked the main entrance. Shivering in a driving rain of sleet, I walked almost completely around the church through what seemed a reproduction of a First World War battlefield before I found a side door that was usable.

Holy Trinity, only a block from City Hall and one of the most downtown of all Toronto's churches, might well have disappeared as Toronto began to sprout skyscrapers in the fifties. Instead it found a new purpose as a centre for social activists fighting to defend Toronto's urban core from wrong-headed development. In the sixties Holy Trinity attracted dissident clergy and a congregation of intellectual reformists whose brand of Christianity resembled that of the radical Methodists who had supported the "social gospel" of income redistribution on the prairies after the First World War.

Merylie Houston, a Holy Trinity parishioner for twenty years, recalls that the change from the traditional Anglican congregation was gradual. When she and her husband, Jim Houston, a former Jesuit priest, first joined the church, the most interesting activities were happening in the Sunday school. Out of that yeast of rebels against doctrinaire stiffness came a monthly family service in the church, during which art and dance and "moving around" were introduced. This proved so popular that the pews were unbolted from the floor and arranged in a circle. The choir was disbanded, and every service became communal and, to a great extent, spontaneous. When the spirit moves them, Holy Trinity's congregants rise and dance.

"Trinity is a lot of exploring people who love and support one another," Merylie explains. "That's how we express our spirituality. It doesn't have much to do with organized religion."

Holy Trinity's influence in the community was out of proportion to the size of the congregation. The services were a mixture of ecclesiastical ecstasy and hugs, but the social activism was bare-knuckle. One of their number is writer-historian William Kil-bourn, who is married to a former art critic, Elizabeth, who became one of the first women ordained in the Anglican Church in Canada. Bill Kilbourn served many years on Toronto's City Council as an alderman in what was called the reform group, which fought successfully to maintain the city's human scale in the downtown core.

I can recall noon-time lectures fifteen years ago that drew sandwich-eating office workers and clerks to hear speakers on unpopular causes. Holy Trinity not only gave sympathy and direct help to American draft resisters, but also provided a meeting place for Toronto's first homosexual organization. When the church allowed gay men to hold dances in the space in front of the altar, the archbishop was apoplectic. Most recently, in February 1986, Holy Trinity was in the news when parishioners backed two lesbian deacons, one of them pregnant, who had been disciplined by Archbishop Lewis Garnsworthy for regarding them-selves as married. Holy Trinity's priest, Rev. Jack Adam, said he "regretted" the archbishop's decision to suspend the two women.

When Margaret joined Holy Trinity, it was a little while before she caught on to the style. Merylie Houston remembers Margaret attending meetings of the Worship Committee soon after she retired from teaching. "She was very much the teacher then," Merylie smiled. "She sort of assumed the chair and ran the meeting as though we were children in her classroom. We were to speak one at a time, and that sort of thing. She got away from that later, of course."

During the caring for Margaret, Jay MacGillivray went to Holy Trinity the Sunday before Easter out of curiosity. She's a woman who has a positive religious faith, and her sister is a minister of the United Church. Afterwards Jay described the service.

"They had this ceremony they call the flowering of the cross," she explained. "Everyone in the church, even the children, fas-tened a real flower on this giant wooden cross. Then they walked the cross through Eaton Centre – I'm *not* kidding — meanwhile doing a lot of hugging. Holy Trinity is very big on hugging. And I noticed a number of winos and other street people in the church, apparently just as welcome as anyone else. At the end there were intercessions, where people called for a prayer for Margaret or whatever else was on their minds. At this point someone asked for a prayer for Nicaragua in its struggle against the Contras. I nearly fell over, but no one batted an eye."

"They've got quite a handle on Christianity," I observed.

"I'd say so," she agreed.

Despite my admiration for Holy Trinity, I entered the church reluctantly that Sunday. My family was approaching the third anniversary of the night a drunk driver killed our twenty-year-old son, Casey Frayne, our youngest child. Since his death I have been unable to avoid feeling edgy when people praise death as a gateway to immortality. I don't share that hope; death looks pretty final to me. I did not want to arrive until the Palm Sunday service was over.

When I stepped into the church, braced for a panoply of the ritualized escape from fear, I was enveloped instead in pure holiness. The congregation had just finished reading together "The Passion of Jesus by Mark", as arranged by Bill Kilbourn, and people were moving slowly in the dim light, embracing one another gently. Incense and awe hung in the air; even small children were dazed and solemn.

I saw a coffee urn and poured myself a cup, feeling uncomfortable, wistful, and very moved. Sis Weld approached me with tears in her eyes. She's a real-estate dealer and a member of Toronto's old-money Rosedale-based society. "I missed Margaret Frazer at the service," she said. "Someone just told me how sick she is. I can't bear it."

Elaine Hall spotted me and invited me to eat. Holy Trinity provides lunch after Sunday services, and she was serving macaroni and cheese. People carrying their meals on paper plates were making their way to the vestry, which had been stripped of its contents by the renovators. We gathered heavy chairs from the sanctuary and arranged them in a roomy circle. Nellie's women

71

were drifting in, looking around uncertainly. Linda Rapson arrived, beaming greetings.

When we were settled I counted about thirty people, far more than I had expected. Most were women, but there were three or four men. The Nellie's people were mostly young women who wore jeans and construction boots. Some sat on the floor. The Holy Trinity congregants were older, even white-haired, and most were dressed conventionally in stylish clothing of good quality.

Jay MacGillivray, seeing them as middle-class and "Rosedale", meaning affluent and safety-minded, was wondering, as she later admitted, "what loud-mouthed me was doing there". She told herself she would have to watch her language. She had two reactions. One was that the team was so diverse that if it worked it would be wonderful, but if it didn't it would be obvious why it failed. The other was that it was a statement about Margaret that so many different people were drawn together to care for her.

Only a few weeks later, she found it hard to remember that she had ever thought the group ill-matched. "It turned out we were all pretty much the same kind of people," she told me thoughtfully. "I don't know whether it was because Margaret was a common denominator and we drew our tone from her, or whether there really hadn't been much disparity in the first place."

I took the lead, using notes that I had prepared on the basis of the previous day's meeting.

"This is really Plan A," I began. "It is an attempt to perform the functions that a large caring family automatically does when a member is seriously ill. Essentially the Friends of Margaret is an urban version of the way the human tribe has always responded when one of its members is in trouble. The support system we're trying to put together today is probably as old as the human race. Our hope is that by working together we can see Margaret through this situation.

"If it doesn't work out," I went on, drawing a breath, "we'll have another meeting and look at Plan B, whatever it might be. Perhaps we'll take up a collection and hire a live-in housekeeper and pay for whatever other services Margaret requires. Something like that happened in the case of Judy LaMarsh, so we could study how that worked."

Checking my notes, I said, "The most important part of what we are undertaking is that we don't undermine Margaret's authority. She must remain in control of what happens to her and what is done in her house. We're going into her home to help her, not to take over running the place as we see fit."

I introduced Joyce Brown, who was seated on the steps near the door, a clipboard on her lap. Joyce would take names of people not yet on the schedule, I said, but we also needed what railways used to call a "spare board", people available to fill in the shifts if someone couldn't make it because of a conflict in schedule, or if they had picked up something communicable like a cold. In the event people couldn't do their shift, each would be responsible for getting his or her own replacement. When the list of volunteers was complete, everyone on the team would get a copy, with telephone numbers, to facilitate making such arrangements.

Someone asked about the gaps between the shifts. In some cases afternoon shift people would have to leave an hour or two before the evening shift was due to arrive. We agreed that these spaces were probably a good thing at this point, since they would give Margaret some time by herself, but that people should always inform one another so that Margaret would know what to expect.

The team would not be on its own. Besides Linda Rapson, who would be on call day and night, there were a Visiting Home-maker who would be doing housework chores and a VON nurse who would come twice a week to give such assistance as baths. That reminded me of the disaster of the first VON visit, and I described what had happened. There was a groan of dismay.

We talked of an information clearing house. Elizabeth Greaves thought Nellie's could act as collector for its network, and a dark woman with a quiet manner volunteered to perform the same function for the Holy Trinity people. She was Vivian Harrower, the parish secretary.

Hilda Powicke offered to be a central reference point for both

73

networks. She explained that though she wasn't physically able to take a more active part on the team, she wanted to contribute. "I've got a computer and printer," she went on. "I can help with the mailings as well." I learned later that she had purchased the computer in order to write a book about her experiences as a missionary's child raised in China.

We talked about record keeping and decided that a chore list would be useful so that such details as getting extra keys for the front door wouldn't be lost between shift changes. Also, I recommended a daily log-book (this being a Nellie's practice) so that everyone coming on shift could look back and see what had happened the previous week. For instance, it would be helpful to know how many visitors Margaret had been seeing, or if there was something special she fancied to eat. In addition, there would be a medical log.

"We have a number of specific tasks to sort out," I continued. "For instance, I'll make sure Margaret never sees that VON nurse again." Cheers. "And Liz Greaves will be nudging Margaret to revise her will. Bill Whitla is doing the missing-sister search. We all have to be alert if Margaret wants to talk about funeral arrangements. Margaret's banking has to be arranged. Day people will handle grocery shopping and laundry and such things. Overnight people, bring your own sheets. Day people should know there is a portable wheelchair at the house, so Margaret can go on outings in fine weather. And we should remember that Margaret doesn't have the strength to endure long visits or a lot of people coming at once. Somehow we'll have to find a tactful way to usher people out after ten or fifteen minutes if Margaret is tired."

We speculated about visitors. Because Margaret's house in north Toronto was less accessible than her downtown hospital room, we wondered if the problem might be too few visitors rather than too many. In any case, we hoped people would telephone first, rather than drop in unannounced. If Margaret's dance card was full that day, visitors could be asked to come another time.

"When Margaret has a visitor we'll get out of the way, of course," I went on. "People will want to be alone with her rather than spend the time chatting with us, lovely as we are. There's a cosy study upstairs where we can go when she has guests."

I cringe to remember that I was so pompous. In the realm of sensitivity and consideration, I had nothing to teach anyone in that room. My only excuse is that I didn't yet know most of them.

"Margaret isn't eating well," I said. "She's clinging to a diet of soups and, especially, desserts. She likes sweetness and positively adores maple syrup on ice cream. You'll have to resist your parental instinct to push nutrition at her. As long as she gets sufficient liquids, Linda says that's all that really matters."

One last item of business was a warning that we were all on probation. Margaret in poor health was not the same resilient person as Margaret in good health. As her collapse following the exchange with the VON nurse had demonstrated, Margaret could be shattered by a careless remark. Well-intentioned as we were, it might turn out that Margaret would find one or more of us difficult. In such a circumstance, Margaret would tell me, and I would approach that person to withdraw. There was no disgrace in this, because we were dealing with a very sick woman who was entitled to be unreasonable. The purpose of the team was to help, so we must accept that Margaret alone would be the judge of what was helpful.

When I mentioned this part of the plan to Margaret in order to reassure her, she brushed me aside. "It won't happen," she said complacently. "I know those Holy Trinity people."

The corollary of a team person being asked to withdraw was that some might wish to quit, finding the reality of death too painful. There was no shame in resigning, I commented sombrely, wondering myself if what lay ahead would be more devastating than I could manage. "You can help in other ways than being on the team," I said. "You can make banana muffins. What Margaret doesn't eat can be served to her visitors."

When I introduced Linda, the mood in the room brightened. Linda not only radiated confidence and competence but she was prone to funny asides. She opened by distributing the "FRIENDS OF MARGARET MEDICAL BULLETIN No. 1":

Margaret has given her permission for the details of her medical condition to be discussed with the "Margaret team". While other concerned friends will be kept informed of her status, it would be appropriate for those who will be taking part in her day-to-day care to be aware of the responsibility for confidentiality which goes along with the sharing of private information with caregivers by one who is ill. She is vulnerable and dependent.

OBJECTIVES OF TREATMENT
- remove fear
- give security
- prevent pain
- make her comfortable

NON-DRUG TREATMENT
diet:
- push fluids, especially fruit juices
- avoid gas-producing foods such as beans and cabbage; Margaret has gone off raw vegetables
- she can only take small amounts at a time
- sweets – why not?
- whatever she fancies

pain control:
- Codetron is being tied – it is a high tech electrical stimulator designed to stimulate her own painkillers; if it works we may be able to avoid the use of narcotics, all of which cause constipation, which may be the cause of a lot of her pain. Even if it can reduce the dose of medication it will help.
- Echo Pulse is also being used – it is a simple transcutaneous electrical nerve stimulation (TENS) machine used to stimulate acupuncture points.

DRUGS
bowel:
- Colace (Regulex) – a stool softener; started on March 28,

76

one daily, increased on 30th to two. Dose will be increased as necessary.

- Senokot – a stimulant laxative needed to compensate for the bowel-paralysing effects of codeine; now started as of today;* dose will start at one or two a day and may go quite high (ten a day).

anxiety:

Two drugs are at the house to be used on an "as necessary" basis only, such as when someone upsets her or she can't sleep. They are:

- Ativan 1 mg – a short half-life first cousin of Valium; dose is one every twelve hours as necessary;
- Halcion .25 mg – an excellent sleeping pill, usually gives good sleep without hangover; to be used only when asked for, not regularly.

pain:

At the present there are two drugs at the house for pain:

- Tylenol No. 3 (also labelled Exdol 30). If necessary we will start with this, one every four hours; at the moment we are feeling our way;
- Leritine 25 mg (Anileridine) – a strong narcotic prescribed by the hospital. At the moment it is only being used "as necessary" until we see if we can avoid narcotics. When and if it becomes necessary, oral morphine will be started. A training session for all Friends of Margaret will be held if we reach that stage.

The team was poring over this model of lucidity as Linda continued. "I'm going to be on a beeper, so you'll have lots of

---

*Actually, Margaret didn't take her laxative that day, or any day. When Margaret died, Linda found the bottle of pills was untouched.

back-up," she said. "You can call me any time, I stress *any time*. I'll be talking to Margaret twice a day and seeing her a few times a week, but if you notice anything that gives you the least concern, get right on the phone to me." There was a palpable sense of relief in the room.

"We've got to give Margaret confidence that we know what we're doing. So we've never done it before – so what? People at Nellie's have moved mountains, and so have people at Holy Trinity."

The monograph on pain was distributed as Linda, an expert, addressed this area. "Fear turns into pain," she explained. "That's what happened to Margaret when the VON nurse frightened her. Right away she had pain. We've got to cushion her against that kind of stress. Her days and nights have to be smoo-oo-ooth."

She described how the Codetron machine worked, making it sound sensible and less bizarre than it had looked to me. Margaret should use it twice a day for twenty minutes, Linda said. She explained that she had drawn circles with a ballpoint pen on Margaret's skin and numbered each circle, so it would be simple for the team to attach the electrodes in the right places. They had to be moistened to make them adhere, and maybe some elastic straps with Velcro fasteners would be needed to hold them in place.

"The bowel is critical. We're going to be talking a *lot* about Margaret's bowel. If it is obstructed, Margaret may have to go into hospital. Constipation will cause her great pain."

She asked how many people had been close to someone who died of cancer. I was amazed at how many hands were raised. "Margaret has had this cancer for a long time," Linda went on slowly. "It has taken maybe years to grow to this stage. Those hiccup attacks she had in China seem to suggest that. And you've all heard that funny gulping sound she makes when she's trying to avoid a belch. This disease didn't arrive overnight. We're not trying to save her life. We're helping her to die as comfortably as possible."

Noting the men in the room, she said she welcomed their

participation. "It might be that at the end, in order to spare Margaret embarrassment as her needs become more intimate, the men will have to withdraw, but for now it is wonderful that they are here."

A crowd of people formed around Joyce to select their shifts as I made my way to the church door. Linda caught my arm. "Help me walk Hilda Powicke to the parking lot," she said. "There's a terrible wind out there and I'm afraid she'll be blown away."

The weather had worsened. Sleet had frozen on the ground, making walking treacherous, and a banshee wind howling from the west was tearing shards of ice from trees. Holding tightly on either side of Hilda, who didn't protest, we escorted her across the slippery lunar landscape of the construction site. Linda said, bellowing against the wind, "The shifts have started, you know. Grace Ross slipped out of the meeting an hour ago to go to Margaret's."

"Who is Grace Ross?" I asked.

"A Holy Trinity person," Hilda supplied. "She's a nurse, and she's good."

Linda and I exchanged grins of delight.

Margaret wrote that morning in a journal she sometimes kept: "Hope has left and I'm alone with Cleo. How I need to be alone. Yet I need help."

A few weeks after Margaret died, I went to see Grace Ross to ask her what happened during that first shift when Grace set the tone for everything that followed. If someone less wise and imaginative had launched the team, we might well have floundered.

Grace is a small woman with a sumptuous country-girl body, a scrubbed face, a mop of curly hair, and a manner full of bounce and crackle. She's thirty years old and holds the important job of supervisor of public health nurses for the city of North York. She lives in a pleasant house near Toronto's High Park with her husband, Christopher Ross, thirty-nine, a doctor of psychology who has his own psychotherapy practice. He's English-born, a peace activist and, at six-foot-six, notably tall; she fits under his arm. Chris Ross is a grave, courteous, and thoughtful person and was one of the four men who were regulars on Margaret's team.

"I thought the team was a wonderful idea," he explained simply, "and I wanted to be part of it."

The Rosses had known Margaret for only three years. It was by no means unusual that people who for three months would devote a great deal of their time to help Margaret die were little more than acquaintances. A curious aspect of the team was that almost none of us had known Margaret before the date of her retirement ten years earlier. She was a gregarious, enthusiastic, attractive , interesting, easy-to-like woman, so it is impossible to accept that she made no close friends in all those fifty-eight years who would have wanted to share our vigil. We found in her effects scores of names and addresses strange to us; her personal telephone directory was studded with names we didn't know.

There must have been a great many people like Hope Hoey, with whom she had retained ties since adolescence, and team member Helen Cram, a member of Holy Trinity who had known Margaret for thirty years. Margaret would have made friends in her student days at McMaster University, among teachers with whom she taught in Hamilton, Kenora, and Toronto, with prize pupils who would have kept in touch, and with the neighbours from the several places she had lived before buying the house on Deloraine, with the two women who at different times were her roommates, and others met through travel, music, or social activities. Yet the life she chose to live after her retirement was so distinct and different from her previous existence that she seemed to have wiped the slate almost clean. Only one of those people – Helen Cram – was a part of the team.

We discovered, for instance, a small journal that Margaret kept in the winter and spring of 1945-46 when she appears to have been active on the Women's Salary Committee of the Ontario Secondary School Teacher's Federation. The language of the notes is stiff, but the spirit is contemporary. She writes on

November 21, 1945, that the woman chairing the meeting had "urged the women to get out and vote, and also to use their influence in helping to get good women candidates." Where were the comrades of that pioneer struggle?

Margaret kept a 1954-55 list of secondary-school music teachers on which her name appears near the top. That group must have meant a good deal to her at one time, but we saw none of them.

In 1957-58 she travelled in Europe. Her travel diary reveals many of her contradictions, providing a glimpse of the woman who was a romantic, open-armed to experience, and possessed of an erotic sensibility, but at the same time unable to escape the pedant in her nature and personal habits verging on the compulsive. One passage that illustrates the dichotomy describes the morning she attended Mass at St. Peter's in Rome with an Irish woman she met in her tour party. "We had both been needing companionship so were disposed to take a polite interest in each other. She delighted me because she responded to any subject," she explained.

Glad to find she was Catholic, I went off to St. P. with her at 9:45 a.m. To the Tiber, and then along it in the fitful sunlight of a soft morning, on the broad Via Colazione, a majestic approach to St. Peter's. There were just about ten rows of people when we arrived. When Mass began at 11:15 there were 85,000 packing the Square and the Via C., as far as I could see. I went in curiosity to watch the people and listen. Of greatest interest to me, the tall fine-looking German, his three sons and daughter thirteen to eighteen years old. The good strong male voices in responses and chants. The punctilious devoutness of the oldest boy. . . . The band played beautifully the soft and sectional bits, but, like any other competent band, with untamed cymbalists and drummers the rest of the time.

Later she went to see Michelangelo's paintings in the Sistine Chapel. "It is a work of art – one artist's mind. I sat down with my guide book and took long looks. Reluctantly I came to *The Last Judgement* – 'largest painting in the world', horribly vivid treatment of the subject. For one terrified moment, the first in my life, I wondered, Could it be true? And turned away."

Here was the quintessential Margaret: questioning, observant, impatient, practical, and a sensualist – a complex and valuable woman.

She lived in England for a time but decided to return to teaching. She kept a letter from J.B. Wylie, principal of Bloor Collegiate in Toronto, welcoming her back and saying that a place would be found for her in English and in Guidance, "particularly counselling". Later she was made head of the English department. One of the teachers in her department wrote to her in 1967 to speak affectionately of his "respect for your ideals of a democratically run department".

Apparently in 1968 she made a decision, later rescinded, to leave Bloor Collegiate. A letter from a colleague protests warmly. "I still don't know what to say, except that Bloor C.I. is losing an excellent head of English and a wonderful person for no good reason that I can see .... I looked up to you as someone who was not afraid to follow her own ideals, even if they were not expedient. And Margaret, believe me, young teachers need idealists."

Hundreds of people whose lives she touched over her long lifetime must have known the shine of her qualities, but we never met them. Two hours after Margaret's death, I had an insight into how that might have happened. I was standing by my car in front of Margaret's house, from which her body had just been removed. I was finding it difficult to drive away. A young woman came along the sidewalk, stopped, and asked, "How's Margaret?" When I told her Margaret was dead, she burst into tears.

"I live on this street," she said, "and a lot of us wanted to help. But there were so many of you, coming and going all the time, and we didn't want to intrude."

I was shocked and dismayed. It was true that the team, unconsciously, had been exclusive. We could have pulled in Margaret's old networks and her neighbourhood, but in our preoccupation we had left untapped many of Margaret's rich resources. Our selective recruitment was our one major failure, I think, but Margaret bears some responsibility for that. She accepted us as her only family and at no time asked that we contact anyone else.

Indeed, she seemed to have cut her ties to her life before 1975. What she had been was not the woman we knew. We found a box of pocket-size notebooks dated in the sixties and early seventies in which she kept such reminders as teaching aids, a recipe for lemon cheesecake, and advice on how to thank a speaker. Each of these fifteen tiny notebooks was sufficient in size to record the sparse activities of her life in those years. They contained names of people and organizations I never heard her mention. She appears in 1970 to have attended one or two meetings of a philosophers club and an art club, but most of her schedule that year is a blank, broken by such entries as "car wash" or "bring credit-union cheque".

In contrast, her spacious 1984 *Everywoman's Almanac*, a loyal purchase from Women's Press, is bursting with activities. In several places her commitments overlap; she must have hustled straight from one meeting to another. Here we found the Margaret we knew. In her neat school-teacher's handwriting, she reminded herself of the Tuesday rehearsals of the Concord Singers, the monthly meetings of Nellie's board of directors, her Friday flute lessons, the schedule of Holy Trinity committees meeting to decide about interior renovations, CAMMAC gatherings, the meetings of a group she described as "Jesus and Women" (we learned from the books on her shelves that she was studying the place of women in Christian doctrine), fund-raising events for *Broadside*, a feminist publication, and *Phoenix Rising*, a magazine run by ex-psychiatric patients, lunches with Eileen Swinton and concerts with me, the meetings of the garden committee for the Margaret Frazer House, her trip in May to China, a two-day trip to Stratford in June to see three plays, her two weeks at CAMMAC in Quebec in July and August, a party at the Whitlas in September, the East Area Mental Health Coalition meetings on Wednesdays, a pot-luck dinner she gave for the Margaret Frazer House board and staff in early November, the opening of the Jessie's residence on November 29, and choir practices erupting on the pages in the weeks before Christmas.

The notations made during the last months of 1984 are poignant. Margaret's writing sometimes is so shaky as to be almost illegible, and appointments with her doctor have replaced references to some committee meetings she attended regularly during the first part of the year. These changes are more marked in the 1985 *Everywoman's Almanac*, where appointments with doctors were augmented with visits to clinics for x-rays and to Princess Margaret's radiology and nuclear medicine departments.

The division of Margaret's life into two unequal pieces, the relatively quiet period of the first fifty-eight years and the intense involvements of the final ten, had not been apparent to me until that August evening when I talked to Grace and Christopher Ross. Knowing how devoted they had been to Margaret's care, I was startled when they told me they had known her for only three years, had never invited her to their house, and had been in her house only once. That one occasion was not an intimate one. The previous Christmas Margaret for the first time had included the Rosses in her annual Christmas party at which some thirty people gathered around her piano for serious carolling.

"We met her at Holy Trinity," Grace explained. "That's the only context in which we knew her, the woman who played the piano and the organ and also led the choir."

The Rosses joined Holy Trinity after a trial-and-error process much like Margaret's own. They attended several churches, looking for a place "to be comfortable, where we could express our religious beliefs and also our social beliefs, where we could be accepted and nurtured, where our children, when we have them, will learn about Christianity and not just be taught it". His background is Methodist, but the teachings of the Trappist monk Thomas Merton appeal strongly to him for their meditative quality. She was raised on a farm near Blyth, Ontario, one of seven children brought up in a fundamentalist faith.

Their first visit to a Holy Trinity service horrified Grace. The

sermon was delivered by a man wearing cut-off jeans. They perse-
vered, going back twice more, when they "fell totally in love
with it".

"People embrace you," Grace explained.

Chris noted, "They're an intellectual group. They ask the un-
answerable questions like, How come God isn't female?"

They saw Margaret Frazer as an amusingly quirky woman, a
character. That didn't make her unique; Holy Trinity abounds
in mildly eccentric people. Grace sang in Margaret's choir and
remembers Margaret's confident bossiness. "She would say,
'You've got the wrong note. We'll just try it again.' But it wasn't
a put-down. Her attitude was more like, 'You've got a good voice,
but we just have to whip it into shape.' Her criticism was never
resented."

The Rosses noticed nothing physically wrong with Margaret
during her annual Christmas party, but early in the New Year
Margaret's weight loss became apparent. Grace asked about it,
and Margaret explained that something was wrong with her pancreas, but it wasn't serious. Grace thought, *cancer*.

They heard about the team while Margaret was in hospital.
Grace was worried. When a few Holy Trinity people gathered
after the service one Sunday to talk about Margaret, Grace expressed her doubts. She had nursed the parents of a close friend, both
of whom died at home of cancer, a year apart, and she knew the
difficulties better than anyone there.

"I wanted to can the whole thing," she said. "I felt that some
people were pushing their own vision of what they wanted on to
Margaret. Patients often feel safer in a hospital than at home,
thank you very much. Did anyone ask Margaret what she would
like? I also hated Margaret becoming a guinea pig for everyone
on the team with a theory about curing cancer, including the
crackpot ones."

Joyce Brown called to ask if Grace would be on the team.
Christopher answered and agreed for them both. Grace's heart
sank. "I had been through it," she said sombrely. "I know how
ugly and messy it can be, and about the incredible pain. There

was a whole lot of talk at Holy Trinity about how wonderful it was to give to someone and not much consideration of, Do I want to be around Margaret that much? Do I want to go through the grief?"

"Besides," she added honestly, "I don't really know Margaret that well."

Because Grace and Chris signed up for Sunday afternoon shifts, a time most convenient in their crowded lives, it happened that theirs was the team's inauguration shift. Chris stayed behind at the meeting in Holy Trinity to make notes of Linda Rapson's instructions while Grace slipped away early, concerned that Hope Hoey already had left for Quebec and Margaret was alone. Grace drove to Deloraine Avenue and let herself into the house by Margaret's unlocked front door. She found Margaret, fully dressed and alert, waiting on the living-room couch.

"I had my own agenda to clear up, all that stuff about how Margaret felt about what was happening. I said plainly, 'We have these plans. Did anyone discuss this with you?' She had the strange idea that she was the hostess and she was responsible for our comfort. She wondered about changing the sheets on the guest bed and getting groceries to feed people. I explained that this wasn't the expectation."

Despite all the conversations about the team that Margaret had with me, with Linda, with Elaine Hall, with Bill Whitla, she seemed not to have absorbed that the team would administer totally to her needs.

"She flipped," Grace recalled. "She said that all her life she had been the one to give, give, give. She didn't know how she felt about people coming to her house to give, give, give to her."

No one on the Margaret team doubts that this was the crucial moment of the whole process. Margaret's pride almost certainly would have made it impossible for her to accept our help for very long and would have seriously inhibited our efforts to care for her as she required. Knowing how flustered Margaret became whenever someone did her a kindness, I had been greatly concerned about the burden of gratitude that we were placing on her, but had failed to address it. Instead, Grace Ross with her candour and wisdom dealt with it in a way that enabled Margaret to preserve her dignity and yet accept her dependence on our help.

"Margaret," Grace said, "the biggest gift you can make us is to allow us to give to you."

Margaret listened thoughtfully as Grace elaborated. People were feeling good about themselves, she said, because there was something they could do to help Margaret in the crisis she faced. Being on the team was rewarding. It was an opportunity for people to respond at their best. If Margaret begrudged the gift and resisted what people offered, they would feel a sense of loss. But if Margaret could allow them to help her, the team would feel enriched. A time had come to make the best gift she had ever given: to allow others to give to her.

Margaret, who had never backed away from truth, could see that what Grace said was unassailably true. She turned it over in her mind and slowly nodded.

Grace went on, "One of the ways you can help us most is to make sure that each of us has something to do for you. Everyone on the team wants to feel useful. You can do a lot for us if you make sure there is always some service we can do for your comfort and peace of mind."

When we learned at Margaret's wake about Grace's suggestion, we howled in recognition. We had each been puzzled that Margaret, far from being shy about asking for help, was something of a martinet about household duties, parcelling out chores like a pit boss. Bill Whitla became Mr. Fixit, for instance. When he arrived on Tuesdays Margaret would say, in her trill, "Bill, there is something wrong with the light over the kitchen sink," or "Bill, the garden hose is leaking." Elaine Hall was Housework and Garden, Fran Sowton, a Holy Trinity team member, was Mending and Garden, Wendy Farquhar, also from Holy Trinity, was Garden and Laundry. The evening people were Conversation.

Once close to the end, when Margaret was growing very weak, she asked Fran Sowton to cut her fingernails. Though Fran had been preparing to leave, she went upstairs to get the manicure kit, came back to snuggle against Margaret on the couch, and carefully cut her nails. Fran's replacement, Elizabeth Greaves, was in the kitchen preparing dinner. Margaret gave a worried glance in that direction, lowered her voice and asked anxiously, "Do you think Liz will mind that I asked *you* to cut my nails?"

Fran, amused, thought, "She is parcelling out the duties, trying to be fair to each of us."

Another item on Grace's agenda that first shift was to assure Margaret that the team would not be taking over her home. "If you want to be alone any time, you must feel free to tell us to leave."

Margaret protested. "How can people accept such rudeness?"

"It isn't rude at all," Grace told her. "We're here to make you feel better, and if you think you'd feel better with some privacy, that's all right with us."

The two women talked of something else for a moment, and then Margaret said, brightly and decisively, "Grace, will you go now?"

Grace admits she was flabbergasted. The next shift, Wendy Farquhar and Nigel Turner, was not yet due, and she was uneasy about leaving Margaret alone. But she realized that if she stayed she would negate everything she had just said. She got to her feet, put on her coat, gave Margaret a warm goodbye, and left.

Margaret, flexing her muscles, telephoned Wendy and Nigel to say she wouldn't need them. She said she wanted to be alone to concentrate on her Simonton exercises, which are based on the theory that cancer tumours can be reduced by a focus of will.

Linda talked to Margaret that afternoon and was excited to learn that the pain was minimal and Margaret had not required pain pills since starting the Codetron the day before. She dared to hope that the machine was working to block pain. However, Margaret's bowel still was not functioning.

Joyce Brown did the first overnight shift and telephoned Linda close to eleven o'clock. Margaret had been suffering from sharp hiccups for an hour and a half. Linda called her cousin, who suggested some measures that Linda conveyed to Margaret. The attack didn't subside until around one-thirty in the morning, when Margaret gratefully fell into exhausted sleep.

When Linda and I talked the next day, April 1, Linda was still euphoric that Margaret's pain was under control. "The hiccups are part of the cancer situation," she added regretfully. "We can't do much about them, but we're lucky that Joyce was the one on duty. I can't imagine anything putting her in a panic."

Linda said that Margaret had just realized what a formidable commitment the team was making. Joyce had brought a stack of mimeographed schedules, which Margaret perused with astonishment. The roster of twenty-one names listed for the first week (two shifts still vacant, but two covered by couples) touched her deeply. She would see Fran Sowton on Monday morning, Liz Greaves in late afternoon, and Vivian Harrower overnight. Bill Whitla had taken a Tuesday-morning shift, and Jan Hatch, a bright vivacious young woman on Nellie's board of directors, the Tuesday overnight. Wendy Farquhar and Helen Cram from Holy Trinity and Leslie MacDonald from Nellie's had signed for Wednesday; Elaine Hall, Ruth McKeown, and I were listed for Thursday; Merylie Houston and Helen Gough of Holy Trinity and Pat Capponi of the Supportive Housing Coalition would cover Friday; Nancy Whitla often did the overnight Saturday, and Buffy Carruthers of Nellie's the overnight on Sunday. Sunday was a couples day – Chris and Grace Ross after church in the afternoon and Wendy Farquhar and Nigel Turner in the evening.

Most of the overnights were filled by people with daytime jobs or other consuming commitments. Nancy Whitla, for instance, was caring for parents who weren't well that spring. The daytime shifts meant another kind of commitment. All of us busy people, we simply wrote Margaret into our schedule and honoured the promise. Fran Sowton said with a shrug, "It just meant that I didn't go to my studio on Mondays." Helen Gough came from work on Fridays. When Margaret asked if it was a bother, Helen gave her a radiant smile. "It just means that every Friday I have someone to eat my dinner with."

Merylie Houston picked the day shift on Fridays because on

Mondays and Wednesdays she teaches English as a second language to immigrant women in a low-income housing development. She sometimes rued her choice, because Friday had been a day when she consolidated housekeeping, banking, and grocery-shopping chores, and sometimes a committee she chaired would fix a Friday meeting date. Merylie let it all go.

"My husband, Jim, made it his contribution to the Margaret team to fill in whatever had to be done at home, and I cancelled everything else," she explained. "I felt clear and good about my decision. The feedback, the energy, the support of the group was very powerful. If only you could bottle and sell it."

As promised, I got in touch with the Victorian Order of Nurses and asked that the nurse who made the first house call to Margaret Frazer be replaced. I said Margaret was very sensitive these days, and with reason, and the nurse just happened to have a temperament that jarred her. The supervisor accepted this and said she would see what she could do, but Linda called soon after to tell me to cancel everything. She didn't believe it was necessary for Margaret to have either a VON or a Visiting Homemaker. So I made arrangements for Linda to activate their help as she saw fit.

I don't think any of us thought of them again. One bad experience was all we needed to convince us to become completely self-reliant.

On Tuesday Linda called in a celebratory mood. Our daughter, Jill, whose voice is much like mine, answered the phone. "Margaret pooped!" Linda told her. "I think you want my mother," Jill said. "So much for medical confidentiality," Linda groaned. But she had wonderful news: not only was Margaret still almost pain free, but her bowels were working for the first time in a week – and without a laxative. "Joy! Jubilation!" Linda wrote in her medical record. She said to me, "I think she's going to get well."

That day the person who arrived on the evening shift caused Margaret irritation for reasons that we never understood. Margaret became angry and upset over what she perceived as thoughtlessness and began to suffer pain. Linda was called and recommended that she take an analgesic.

The next day I was asked to deal with the sensitive situation. Margaret had asked that the person withdraw. Liz Greaves came to my rescue and made the unpleasant call for me, explaining the situation with consummate tact. She said that Margaret was irritable these days and probably would be increasingly so. By the end, Margaret probably would be able to tolerate very few of us. It just happened that this person was the first, but no personal criticism was involved and Margaret's respect and gratitude remained undiminished.

Happily, the person received the dismissal gracefully, but the lesson made a strong impression on us all. It was clear that Margaret, close to death, understandably was unduly touchy. In her physically and emotionally frail state, she was vulnerable to stress that under normal circumstances she would have ignored. If we truly wanted to be helpful, our behaviour would have to be consistently gentle.

We all reaped as much benefit from that enforced tempo and tenderness as Margaret did. Because we slowed down, kept our voices low, and avoided clatter and dispute, the environment in Margaret's house became so tranquil that we all felt rested and restored by being there.

Chris and Grace Ross spoke of "moving as slow as molasses". He described "a need to go at things with poise and centredness", with the result that he would leave Margaret's in a mood of serenity. Others spoke of the house being "a bower", "a refuge", and "a Zen experience".

At the centre of this peacefulness lay Margaret, curled up on her small sofa under the dark green blanket, attentive to us all, and dying very, very slowly.

Linda spent two hours with Margaret Wednesday afternoon, listening to the uproar in her bowels and noting that her abdomen was beginning to distend. When Linda made her usual morning call on Thursday, Margaret told her she had tired herself the night before by talking too long with Leslie MacDonald. "I'm discovering a few things," she said, putting zest into her voice, "and this is a beautiful experience."

91

Linda was having an attack of self-doubt, her first and by no means her last. Her fear was that she was causing Margaret pain by keeping her on the Codetron and intermittent pain pills instead of giving her morphine regularly. One night she talked a long time with Liz Greaves, who provided comfort, pointing out that Margaret was almost pain free and having a good time.

Liz cautioned me: "We've got two people in this situation who need all the support we can give. There's Margaret, of course, but there's also Linda."

At Linda's request, Margaret was keeping track of her bowel movements, which had become regular, and the medication she took as needed. Since Margaret sometimes experienced pain when she ate, Linda had suggested that she take a product called EN-SURE, a canned liquid that provides all essential nutrients. If Margaret drank three cans of ENSURE a day, it would not matter if she took nothing else but fruit juices. ENSURE comes in three flavours, eggnog, vanilla, and chocolate. Margaret had already decided that she liked chocolate least.

All of this, together with the Codetron treatments for twenty minutes twice a day, the voluminous mail that arrived in her rusty mailbox daily, the countless friends who telephoned, the half-hour spent in Simonton meditation twice a day, the stream of visitors who came with flowers and home baking, and the comings and goings of the team members, added up to an exceedingly busy day for Margaret. She said she welcomed the activity. When she was occupied and content she was scarcely aware of pain.

"The team has its drawbacks," she reported to Linda with a chuckle, "but it is very enriching."

She told everyone, jubilantly, that her house had never been so spotless or in such good repair. Wendy Farquhar had cleaned it from top to bottom, Fran Sowton had mended the drooping hem of her bedspread, and Bill Whitla had fixed the trellis.

When I arrived on Thursday at three o'clock for my first shift, I brought a cordless telephone. I think Margaret thanked me about twelve times for that gadget. It was indeed invaluable because it saved her the necessity of rising from the couch, walking through the living-room and dining-room, and standing at the kitchen phone to speak with friends who called.

She was wearing a plaid flannel shirt and a beige corduroy skirt, half unzipped to accommodate her bulging abdomen. Except for the ominous swell of belly, she was even thinner. Her head was balanced on a stick-like neck, and her wrists were as small as a child's. Her lips were dry and her eyes feverishly bright, but she was in a fine mood, bragging to me about her bowel movements. I knew she had expressed worry to Linda that morning because she had so little energy, but she was showing me no signs of flagging.

A woman called to say that she and her husband were in the neighbourhood. Could they drop in for a visit? I asked Margaret, who made a face but said, "Sure. Tell them to come."

I waited upstairs in Margaret's cosy book-lined study, rocking in a chair I came to love. The voices of the visitors were a low mumble, but I could hear Margaret distinctly. She was speaking sharply, an indignant tone in her voice, like the Margaret of old. From the snatches I heard, she was annoyed about ticket sales and was growing increasingly exasperated at the response she was getting. After twenty minutes, I was concerned and went downstairs. The people took the hint and departed. Margaret fell back on the pillows, shaking and in a state of collapse. The visitors had been from the Concord Singers, and she had allowed herself to get excited about the choir's shortcomings in the area of publicity and promotion.

"I shouldn't have done that," she gasped. "I haven't the strength. They won't do what I suggest anyway. I shouldn't have been so forceful. I've got to conserve my energy for getting well."

I held her hand and said in a dreamy voice, "Margaret, I have just created a wonderful motto for you. It will serve as a reminder whenever you feel obliged to reform the Concord Singers' box office. It will also be a helpful guide on all other occasions when you are tempted to save the world rather than let the world take care of itself until you recover your health."

She was breathing more evenly, watching me with interest.

"I'm going home and I'm going to get one of those needlework samplers, you know the kind? And I'm going to embroider this inspiring motto on it, and put some tasteful flowers and fruit in the corners. What do you think about the background? Would a soft green be pretty? And then I'll have this masterpiece suitably framed, natural oak I think, and we'll hang it right here in the living-room over the mantelpiece. Every time you get a bout of enthusiasm for other people's problems, you can look at it. It will read 'FUCK THE CONCORD SINGERS'."

She burst into laughter as I put on my coat to go out for some groceries.

I bought some yellow tulips while I was out and found in a book store the perfect log-book, a good-sized journal with flowers on the cover, titled *A Woman's Notebook: Being a Blank Book with Quotes by Women*. The first page had two lines from Sylvia Plath across the bottom: "I took a deep breath and listened to the old brag of my heart. I am, I am, I am."

The sentiment was appropriate, I thought. I wished the woman who wrote those indomitable lines hadn't killed herself.

In the blank space above the quotation I wrote:

April 4. Five visitors this afternoon (in three batches). We must work out a tactful way to ration visits. Dr. Linda says: Push liquids. Is someone getting more keys? Do we need them? Desk in den has receipt for ENSURE delivered today. Pharmacist thinks this can be covered by OHIP. There is chicken, tarts, pasta in fridge. *Wendy*: pls, will you repot the geraniums?

June C.

Margaret was proudly displaying her skill with the Codetron. The procedure had the fascination for me of witnessing an arcane ritual beside the fire in a Druid cave. Arranging herself comfortably in the green armchair, she put her feet on the footstool and removed the shoe and sock from her left foot. I saw ink circles drawn on her bare legs. She chuckled, "I'm not washing until I get this down pat."

Dipping her finger into a glass of water on the table next to her, she wet the flat surface of the black rubber electrodes and stuck them, one by one, on the circles Linda had drawn. Next she bound each electrode firmly in place with elastic straps, which Elaine Hall had shortened to fit her, fastened by Velcro tabs. In her lap was a tangle of wiring connecting the electrodes to the control panel. She fiddled with buttons and knobs and switches, her reading glasses sliding down her nose.

The lights on the control panel bounced off and on as she twisted the knobs, looking like Woody Allen in drag playing a demented scientist. When she had the voltage to her satisfaction, she leaned back placidly and surrendered to the machine's antic pattern of mild shocks.

She'd been having pain, I knew, and Linda had suggested that Margaret increase the amperage to whatever she could tolerate. It seemed to me, suspicious as I was of the gadget, that Margaret was being altogether too co-operative.

When she finished, she unwrapped the straps and gingerly pulled the sticky electrodes off her loose skin. She replaced their paper moisture seals and returned them carefully to a plastic bag to protect them from drying. We were ready for dinner.

We ate in the dining-room, lit against the early darkness by an overhead fixture. I produced pasta and some wine, which she touched almost not at all. She excused herself suddenly, apologizing, and returned to the couch, grimacing in pain. As I cleared the table, I saw her shifting position to find a comfortable one, first sitting up, then lying on her back, then turning on her side. She apologized again, this time embarrassed by the loud gurgling sounds her bowel was making.

I suggested a Tylenol to relieve her agony, but she hesitated.

"It takes energy to fight pain," I told her sternly, heartsick at her suffering. "Do you think that's an appropriate use of **your** strength when we've got all these lovely pain killers?"

She took the pill and gradually relaxed. She wanted to talk about the Simonton method of combating cancer. According to the book, the first step in the process required patients to identify five major stress points in their lives. To her dismay, Margaret could think of only one. "That night when Hope was here and I cried so hard," she observed. "That certainly was one. But I can't come up with another." She was quite agitated to think that the method might not work if she didn't find four more stress points.

Apparently Margaret did not consider a diagnosis of terminal cancer a stressful event.

"Three more," I said, trying to be helpful. "Look at the stress you're having because you can't find four."

She gave me a fond smile and asked me to put a record on her turntable. I found her equipment easy to operate because it was about the same vintage as a record player my family owned thirty-five years ago. We listened to something French and ticky-tacky, which she said always cheered her up. She was having musical hallucinations, she told me absently as we listened. Household noises aroused musical patterns in her brain. When the furnace started up, for instance, it created a tune in her head.

"It's very peculiar," she observed, closing her eyes contentedly, "but interesting."

At her request I had turned on but one light, a bronze figure standing on a side table with a pink shade on his head. The charming little lamp cast a restful pool of rosy light. I sat at Margaret's feet in a small rocking chair, feeling curiously suspended. I had no sense of time, though I had been with Margaret for six hours, and no awareness of the city or my own usually frenetic preoccupations. The pool of pink light enclosed all of reality, and I floated in a slow-paced conversation with a drowsy woman. Margaret lay on the couch, knees up, covered with the green blanket, her white hair rumpled against the pile of pillows at her back, and I rocked. We talked, listened to music, fell silent, smiled warmly at one another, talked some more.

She told me Bill Whitla had brought her Communion and how much that mattered to her.

"It isn't the ritual so much as the feeling that I'm still included," she said slowly. "I'm going to Easter service on Sunday in my wheelchair. Don't tell me I'm not. I want to be part of the singing, and I want to be with that remarkable collection of people at Holy Trinity."

I asked her bluntly, "Are you able to talk about your fears with some of us?"

She raised her head, gave me a level look that closed the subject, and answered, "Yes."

I called Linda when I got home to tell her about the pain. She sounded crushed. Margaret had been having too much pain, she said. The decision to put her on a regime of regular pain killers would have to be made soon because the "as necessary" system wasn't working. Margaret delayed taking pills until the pain was so established that it was hard to eradicate.

"Once we start regular narcotics, though, we'll bung up her bowel," Linda said gloomily. "And that will finish her."

Linda found the failure of the Codetron hard to understand. "It really *should* work," she said in despair. I told her staunchly that it had been worth a try, given the grim alternative, and might still prove effective if given time. The biggest selling point for me was that Margaret loved it.

After Margaret's death, I found a single sheet of paper where Margaret had tried to list five areas of stress. Headed "Getting Well Again – Simonton", it contained only three:

1. The first clue came in my crying jag as Hope and I sat down to dinner the other night. Both of us think of ourselves as strong, capable people, others think of us this way. In my case one cause of stress is volunteering to do something such as chairing the committee on work for mentally disturbed people – a daunting job in a time when there are many people out of work. I thought of ways of going at this and sources of information. *But* I never called the committee together. Instead I took these very tentative steps and *let*

the problem fester in my mind. That is *stress* caused by my not taking a firm first step.

2. I, a musical person, should have learned to play the flute long before this. I wasted time going to .... I don't think this is in itself a cause of stress. Here the important thing was that I got to Judy when I did. [This entry was crossed out.]

3. Publicity for the Concord Singers? Making things better. How to do it (not talking to ... as I did).

The next morning, however, Margaret reported to Linda that she was feeling better than at any time since her operation. "This experience is helping me to learn things about myself," she said with her old enthusiasm, and added gratefully, "Thank goodness you're phoning every day."

It was Good Friday, and Linda made a house call, arriving as Margaret blissfully was listening to the *St. Matthew Passion*, a favourite of hers. Linda tested the Codetron and discovered that it hadn't been recharged properly: in fact, its battery was so depleted that the machine was scarcely functioning at all. Margaret's pain therefore might be blamed on the impotence of the equipment rather than a failure of the treatment method. Elated because her confidence in the machine was restored, Linda decided she would borrow a newer and stronger Codetron from Nigel Turner, a member of Margaret's team who was also one of Linda's patients.

Linda called me that evening. She was in a buoyant mood and about to dive into Passover soup with her husband's family. She wanted to assure me that Margaret was eating better and had enjoyed a pain-free night on Thursday. With a new Codetron machine, she was sure Margaret wouldn't need drug therapy just yet. "She was so hyper this afternoon when I saw her that I had to tell her to calm down."

Ruth McKeown had written in the log-book that morning, "I am amazed at the lift in her spirits since coming home." Under that, Linda wrote, "It's working! Thanks to all." And Merylie

Houston, who cleaned the house that day, wrote, "A good day. Don't forget to feed the birds. Thanks to whoever made the celery with dill soup. It's all gone!" That night, however, Margaret was in great pain and took two Tylenols two hours apart.

Hilda Powicke also called me that afternoon. It was a moment before I could place her as the small woman Linda and I had helped across the parking lot at Holy Trinity five days earlier. She said some members of the team had been contacting her in her role as network co-ordinator. "I'm finding areas of confusion," she said.

That was tactfully put. The truth was that several people were upset. Grace Ross, still concerned about the volume of traffic in Margaret's house, wasn't yet convinced that the team was an entirely good idea, and Sheila Mackenzie, another Holy Trinity person and one possessed of a tart tongue, complained furiously that some of the team were acting as if they owned the place.

Hilda offered to circulate some guidelines to the Friends of Margaret network, which I thought a splendid idea.

A two-page list of sensible suggestions arrived in my mail a few days later. Included were such matters as:

Walk in: The door is always open during the day and evening. Be sure to pick up two lists – (1) list of volunteers; (2) schedule.

Log-book: Check this when you come in for information from those who have been in before you. Keep track in the log-book of what you have done, what needs doing, new instructions, number of visitors, and phone calls she has had. Dr. Linda Rapson calls morning and evening so you can record what you think she ought to know.

Daytime people: Margaret's appetite waxes and wanes. So far soups, very small quantities of simple casseroles, custards, and ice cream are about all she can manage.

Six p.m. tends to be a low time for Margaret. Linda

suggests that you see she has some ENSURE (in kitchen cupboard, back-up supply on back porch) around four.

Be sure her bed is made and ready for her.

Plants need to be watered every other day or so.

See that birdfood is out in the bird feeder each day.

See that Margaret's cat Cleo's needs are attended to.

At present Margaret is more comfortable during the day on the couch downstairs and takes naps there. Be sensitive to her need for rest and sleep and space to herself. She may ask you to go home early, and that's okay if you're sure someone else will be in before too long.

Five-to-nine people: If you are planning to bring in supper you might check with the person on day shift about what Margaret wants, and whether there is food already available. Remember, Margaret eats very little, so don't burden the fridge with left-over food.

Check whether she has had her five-o'clock Codetron treatment.

Night time people: Bring your own sheets and towels. (These may be left at Margaret's if you are on regular duty.)

Check with daytime person about arrival time. Be sure Margaret's breakfast is ready for her.

A brief chat before bed is probably enough. Save a good visit for morning.

Margaret has a bell, which she could have beside her bed if she needs it.

General suggestions: Margaret may need some help with the Codetron (neural stimulator). She knows where the electrodes are to be placed, but may find it difficult to get them on and off – especially the latter.

Note: Stress is what most often causes pain for Margaret. One needs to watch she doesn't have too many or too stressful visitors. If people phone and suggest coming in and she's had too many, suggest they come another day.

Give Margaret the time and space she asks for. She tires easily, but likes having you there and is eager to hear (briefly) about your doings. Always remember, this is Margaret's house.

Hilda lives with her husband, a professor, in a spacious house fronting a park in the east end of Toronto, an area on the lake known as the Beaches. Child of a missionary and raised in China, she joined Holy Trinity in 1957 because the congregation shared her view that churches should act as asylums. "It's a deep concept with me, coming from my years in China, that churches should protect people in times of trouble," she explained one afternoon when we talked on her broad veranda. "Holy Trinity always has had social concerns. It is interested in all sorts of issues and in helping people. There's always a willingness to be innovative. In the sixties when we made one-third of the church a space for Vietnam-war draft resisters to sleep, we lost a lot of church members, but I was all for it."

Hilda was there in 1973 when Margaret joined Holy Trinity, at a time when Margaret was still teaching school. Hilda took little note of her; Margaret was then a reticent, unremarkable-seeming person, even slightly stuffy. It was different after Margaret's retirement. Hilda watched with interest as Margaret unfolded her wings. "She became more and more experimental," Hilda recalled. "I didn't see that when I first knew her."

The two women, much the same age, found a common bond in their skepticism towards the fads that readily swept Holy Trinity's adventurous adherents. "We both resisted pressure to be enthusiastic about primal therapy, or hot tubs, or EST encounter groups, or whatever else was going around," Hilda grins. "We felt a bit guilty to go against the tides, but it helped that there were two of us."

They saw one another almost daily during the time Margaret was working in Nellie's fund-raising office in the basement of 10 Trinity Square, a heritage building next to Holy Trinity, and

Hilda was launching a distress centre that grew into a national organization, the Canadian Council of Crisis Centres, of which Hilda was president from 1978 to 1980. They lunched frequently, swapping suggestions for fund raising and fretting about the negotiations between Holy Trinity and the Eaton empire. Their relationship wasn't personal in the way of some friendships, but it had a sound basis of mutual respect and affection.

"I got a kick out of Margaret's enthusiams," Hilda told me fondly. "She would be all full of excitement one moment and full of indignation the next. When she first came to Holy Trinity she was quite dignified, but later there was a sort of bobby-sox glow about her."

Hilda was depressed that her physical difficulties made it impossible for her to be active on the team. When the first week of the shifts produced some concerns, she was grateful to find herself needed. Helen Cram called after every shift, distressed that Margaret wasn't entering into the acceptance stage of dying that she thought would be less stressful than denial. Linda called several times a week with encouraging news of Margaret's condition, though Hilda thought privately that Margaret was dissembling with Linda, keeping bad news from her out of polite concern that one shouldn't bother busy people. Sheila File, who drove Hilda to church on Sundays, also kept her informed. Hilda was one of the first to know that Margaret's abdomen was becoming distended. Sheila noticed it when helping Margaret into her bath.

On the Saturday before Easter, ten days after Margaret left hospital, Linda brought a new Codetron machine, a temporary replacement for the one Margaret had been using. Margaret was startled at the difference in the machine's power. Linda was convinced Margaret's pain the previous night had something to do with the inadequacy of the Codetron machine she had been using. Linda wrote in the log-book, "Please see that the machine in the living-room is plugged in overnight, using the charger in the little box in the leather case. Plug it into the wall, then into the hole at the back of the machine. MAKE SURE THE ON/OFF BUTTON IS *off* DURING CHARGING!!!"

She found Margaret in fine fettle. She was bragging to Linda about her bowel movements, now perfectly regular, and how her appetite was improving, when Joyce Brown and Jay MacGillivray arrived for the afternoon shift.

I remember when Jay MacGillivray was hired at Nellie's. It was 1979 and she was twenty-three years old, and stiff and prickly with defences that she had acquired after some searing experiences. Beneath the armour was a vulnerable, sensitive, softhearted person with an unerring ability to sense the pain of others. When she first encountered Margaret at a Nellie's board-of-directors' meeting, she was intrigued.

Few organizations have pleated together staff and board members as Nellie's does. The constitution does not permit the board to meet without staff being present in whatever numbers staff feels are appropriate. While staff members cannot vote, the respect for their judgement and knowledge is such that the board has almost never voted against the staff's wishes. One reason is that board members work in Nellie's on Sundays, cooking and serving a dinner for residents and ex-residents, and come to know firsthand how much human agony the staff must address.

Nellie's, named for Nellie McClung, the prairie woman who led the fight for women to vote, was established in the summer of 1974 by me and Vicki Trerise, a tall, sweet-faced young woman who had come to Toronto from Vancouver to head a hostel run by the Toronto YWCA. I had been active in Digger House, a hostel across the street from the Y hostel. In 1972 Digger House lost its federal funding after a stormy five years of housing young people who were described in those days as "hippies". Soon after the closing, Vicki invited me to visit her hostel, which was always so full that she was turning women away nightly.

Vicki and I shared concern at the lack of accommodation in Toronto for homeless women. The Salvation Army and others provided vast numbers of beds for homeless men, but the community seemed to feel that shelters for women were unnecessary. Vicki made a survey of the situation and documented that the city had close to a thousand beds for men and about thirty for women.

After a long struggle, we secured a fine old mansion situated

on a parking lot beside a YMCA in Toronto's east end. The Y
owned the ten-bedroom house but rented it to us in a paternalistic
agreement that required us to allow the Y to handle such funding
matters as our payroll. Vicki and I agreed that the staff should
be a feminist collective – that is, should have parallel salaries
and work collaboratively without an executive director. The collective approach not only would attract a staff of high-quality
women but would provide the distressed residents with a model
of women working together in an egalitarian structure, with the
possible result that they might feel more confident about their
own competence.

Because Vicki had parted from the YWCA in rather dramatic
circumstances, with the entire staff of her hostel fired overnight
and the residents taken away in taxis, we felt strongly that board
and staff should be integrated so that alienation and misun-
derstandings could be kept to a minimum. We therefore devised
a constitution providing that all committees of the board have
board-staff representation and that staff should attend all board
meetings.

We expected when we opened that June day that the residents
would be women of the type we both knew best — teenagers
with drug problems. With that in mind, we hired a young, street-
wise staff. The first women to use Nellie's, however, were middle-
aged alcoholics, followed by a succession of battered wives, homeless street women disparagingly known as "bag ladies", raped
women, women newly discharged from psychiatric facilities with
no families who would take them back, penniless women who
had been evicted, women hiding from violent pimps, runaways
from incestuous fathers and brothers, women fresh from jail,
women shattered in a multitude of group homes, Native women
lost in the city – a parade of human misery and degradation that
burned out the first staff like straw in a forest fire.

Months after we opened, Vicki called me with good news.
"Hey, we got our first teenaged speed freak." Under the circumstances, that was funny.

Jay MacGillivray's first encounter with Margaret, to recapitu-

104

late, was at one of Nellie's egalitarian board meetings, each one of which is chaired by a different board member in rotation. "I didn't know what she was doing there," Jay confessed. "She was so wee, and her heart was on her face. If someone was upset, so was Margaret."

The first time Jay saw Margaret at Nellie's, on an evening when Margaret bustled in with some donated clothing, Jay followed her around protectively. "I felt I had to watch out, to see the residents didn't take advantage of her." Instead she saw that there was a healthy degree of testiness in Margaret: she was nobody's victim.

When the two met at committee meetings, "we could raise one another's hackles in thirty seconds." They found they shared the same passions and commitments but saw solutions very differently. Jay's answer to the problems Nellie's was encountering with Queen Street's massive psychiatric hospital was to bomb it, while Margaret believed it was possible to negotiate differences without being co-opted by the system. Maddeningly, she would say to Jay, "Some day you'll mellow."

They even argued when their love of gardening drew them to the garden committee of the Margaret Frazer House, where Jay was the first employee; she had decided to switch from Nellie's because of her compassion for women who have been in psychiatric institutions. "Margaret wanted cow shit," Jay explains, "and I wanted bunny shit. Margaret thought bunny shit wasn't strong enough to do the job, but I disagreed hotly."

Jay grinned. "It became evident to me that the issues that divided us were becoming smaller and the areas of agreement larger."

I said, "You were mellowing."

She chuckled. "I was mellowing."

The two women didn't see much of one another in the fall of 1984, but one afternoon Margaret turned up at the Margaret Frazer House with a box of books. "These are wonderful books. Can you spare them?" Jay asked. Margaret gave her a significant look and replied, "I don't want my friends to have to go through too much stuff when I die. I'm cleaning some of it out now."

Later Jay said to Joyce, with whom she lives, "What's the matter with Margaret? She looked terribly ill to me."

Joyce said, surprised, "Nothing that I've heard."

Jay said, "There's something wrong. I know it."

One of the most painful periods of Jay's life happened about two years earlier, when she went daily for many months to be with her stepfather, who died dreadfully of cancer. Subsequently she volunteered to work in palliative-care units helping men dying of AIDS. Her style, gained in that grim crucible, is to look death in the eye. She describes a bizarre scene the evening after Margaret's surgery, when she visited the hospital. Liz Greaves was there, she remembers, along with Stephen Langmead, an architect who is a member of Nellie's board, and Eileen Swinton. They were occupying the three chairs, so Jay stood at the foot of the bed and had an extraordinary exchange with Margaret while the others, impervious, chatted over them.

"How's the baby business?" Margaret asked.

Jay, who was enrolled in a midwifery course, answered that it was intriguing. "It's a privilege to be there when someone is being born," she said.

Margaret gave her the same direct look as when she had brought the books. "What I'm doing is the other side of the coin, isn't it?"

And Jay, her gaze just as steady, said, "Yes, it is."

After that, Jay was one of the people with whom Margaret could sometimes talk about dying. Once Margaret asked Jay about her considerable experience with dying people. Jay answered, "It's different for everyone, but one thing they all have in common is that no one dies – except in an accident – before they are ready." She promised: "Margaret, you won't go until you're ready."

When the team held its first meeting, on Sunday, March 31, at Holy Trinity, many people had worried that Margaret didn't seem to realize that she was dying. They had done some reading about dying and knew that authorities had defined several stages, the first being this kind of denial. They felt Margaret's denial was lasting too long and therefore was impeding her progress to peaceful acceptance. While these views were being aired, Jay kept silent about her own frank exchanges with Margaret on the subject of dying. She assumed, she told me, that she wasn't the only one in the room to be in Margaret's confidence. She was grateful to note that these others felt as she did, that Margaret's trust had to be protected.

The Saturday morning of music with Margaret is a memory that Jay treasures. Joyce stayed out of the way, "endlessly watering the plants", as she told me with a grin, while Jay and Margaret explored their mutual passion for Bach. "Bach fills me like nothing else," Jay said simply, and Margaret totally understood. Jay told Margaret that she regretted she couldn't sing, and Margaret retorted, as usual, that everyone can be taught to sing.

"Hum something you like," Margaret ordered her.

Jay hummed bits of Bach fugues and Margaret, who was beginning to have trouble with her memory, was annoyed at herself that she couldn't remember the titles. Jay said she also loved *The Well-Tempered Clavier*, and Margaret, her face glowing at the thought, said she wished she could play it for Jay on the piano.

"But I can't, " she sighed.

"Why not?" Jay said, rummaging in Margaret's music cabinet. "Here, I've found some fugues. What about these?"

"I've tried to play," Margaret explained, "but it doesn't come out right."

"I'll play these one-handed and you try to guess what they are," Jay suggested.

After a bit of that, Margaret said, as Jay had hoped, "Let me try. See if you can guess what this is."

Standing at the piano, she played *The Well-Tempered Clavier* with one hand. Jay pretended not to guess it and asked her to play some more. Margaret turned to look at her, fully appreciating what Jay was trying to do, and they exchanged conspiratorial smiles.

Then she sat down and played for an hour and a half, occasionally making mistakes but tenaciously going back over the piece until she got it right. At one point Margaret began to weep. Jay, tears in her eyes, said, "Let's not cry. Let's keep on playing."

That night she told Linda modestly that she had played to her "satisfaction". To me, she said, still ecstatic at the memory, "It was musical! It was really musical! I played and played."

Jay and Joyce, applying some of the methods used to regulate the running of Nellie's by shift workers, announced in the log-book that there would be a chore list to make sure household duties were done, and another list of "Things to Do" where the team could enter those matters that shift people couldn't handle themselves.

For one, a railing was needed at the top of Margaret's stairs where they made a turn. Margaret was apprehensive at the absence of something to grasp when she had to climb or descend the four stairs between the upper landing and the second floor. I knew that Stephen Langmead would welcome an opportunity to help Margaret, and sure enough, in a day or two, a reassuringly solid railing was fastened to the wall.

To the dismay of us all, but especially Margaret, Nancy and Bill Whitla would be away for many weeks. He was working on some research in England, after which they planned to vacation in Greece. When Nancy did a final shift, on Saturday, April 6, she did not expect to see Margaret again.

Meanwhile, Margaret went to Holy Trinity for the Easter Sunday service and sang her head off.

Margaret's health that Easter weekend seemed better than at any time since her illness. Whether it was because of the new Codetron machine or one of the vagaries of her disease, she was almost free of pain, slept without a sedative, nibbled at three meals a day, and proclaimed her colonic regularity to all. She was bundled into her wheelchair and taken to Holy Trinity for the Sunday service.

The team, familiar with Margaret's gaunt appearance, saw only her dancing blue eyes and the grin, but those who hadn't seen her for a month or more were appalled. Her pallor was alarming, and her face had collapsed against the skull bones. Slumped in the wheelchair in clothes much too large for her, she seemed only half her normal size. The word was out that she needed to be cushioned against heartiness and too much stimulation, so people avoided rushing up to her at first. Hilda Powicke hung back with the others but noticed that the thoughtfulness had gone too far: Margaret seemed alone. She went to her, put her arms around Margaret's thin shoulders, and kissed her.

Part way through the Easter service at Holy Trinity there is a break, called "the peace", when people move around, talk, and embrace. "We're not like Baptists," Margaret told me with a sniff. "We don't have to wait to the end of the service to socialize." The teenaged children she had befriended over the years came up to her then. They could rely on her to remember their names and what interested them.

Margaret had come eager to join in the singing, but found she couldn't produce a voice. She mouthed the words in order not to feel completely left out, but towards the end of the service, in the midst of some alleluias, she heard her voice. "It got stronger and stronger," she told me happily, "until at the end of the service I was really *singing*."

Twenty people or more gathered around the church piano when the service was over. Margaret's wheelchair was pulled into the circle for some impromptu hymns. At times, she even conducted the chorus, flourishing her arms with her old vigour and insisting on yet another verse. Bill Kilbourn, worried that she was exceeding her strength, suggested at one point that the session should end, but Margaret reproved him indignantly.

Margaret later told Merylie Houston, "I know that Easter was the last service I'll ever attend at Holy Trinity."

Later that day, when Wendy Farquhar and Nigel Turner came for the evening shift, the glow had faded and Margaret felt her fatigue. She slept on her couch for an hour and a half while Nigel read and Wendy quietly tended the plants. Wendy wrote in the log, "Peace, joy, and love."

The next day, Monday, April 9, Margaret left a message for me to call her. When I did, Bill Whitla answered and said she was sleeping. A visit from Eileen Swinton had tired her, he thought, because Eileen has a hearing difficulty and Margaret was obliged to speak loudly. Margaret and I talked later, and her voice sounded hoarse and strange. The purpose of her call was to thank me once more for the wheelchair. She wanted me to know what pleasure it gave her. Because of it, she had been to church and Bill Whitla had just taken her around the block.

I wanted to see her. "I'm going to drop in for a quick hug," I told her. "I miss you."

She seemed weak when I arrived. She told me wanly that she had figured out how to manage her pain – she was taking the Tylenols at the first pangs, rather than waiting until the pain had taken hold. "It's easier to ward it off if I do something right away," she explained. Despite her exhaustion, she was radiant. The past three days of music had made her ache with joy. "It has been *gorgeous*," she said, rolling the word with relish.

"And it isn't over," she went on. "Bill and I have been listening to *The Magic Flute*. He knows it inside and out, much better than I do."

I picked up the log and noted that Bill Whitla had also raked the front lawn and oiled the humidifier. For an English professor and theologian, he was showing astonishing versatility.

That week Linda noted that Margaret's abdomen was becoming more distended. The tumours were growing. On Wednesday when she made a house visit, she felt that Margaret seemed sad. They talked about the Simonton method, in which Margaret was showing renewed interest, and Margaret approached the subject of death. She talked about out-of-body experiences reported by people revived from what seemed a death state. What did Linda think of that? Linda said, "You never know."

I dropped in later and found Wendy vacuuming while Margaret read contentedly on the couch. Wendy had taken charge of laundry, which had been neglected over the many months when Margaret was too weak to care. "It's a mess," she whispered to me. Margaret was amused when Wendy found a neglected hamper in the basement full of clothing that Margaret had forgotten she owned. "It's like getting a new wardrobe," she grinned.

Buffy Carruthers, a Nellie's staff woman, came Wednesday for the overnight and helped Margaret to have a bath, her first since her return from hospital. They agreed that Margaret needed a bar on the wall beside the tub to make it safer and easier for her to climb in and out, and a notation was made on the "Things to Do" list.

Buffy became a legend in the team because of the quality of her kindness and the bond that developed between her and Margaret. We all heard Buffy stories from Margaret, sometimes more than once, and it was easy to see why Margaret loved her. Buffy is Hollywood-perfect casting for the role of the warmest, most giving woman in town. Forty-five years old, with a beautiful, serene, and sane face, a soft body, a wealth of glossy brown hair pinned casually in a bun, and a melting smile, Buffy is what Margaret calls "gifted". She was one of the first Canadian University Students Overseas (CUSO) volunteers, teaching English and art in Benares. After that, she joined a dig for a fourteenth-century monastery in the Pyrenees.

She is separated from her husband, a York University professor, and lives with her teenaged daughter, Jessica, in a charming narrow house that faces a small park in mid-Toronto. After her marriage broke up she tried her hand at pottery and free-lance writing but found the work lonely. In 1981 she saw an advertisement in the Women's Book Store for a vacancy at Nellie's and applied. She was one of two women who were short-listed.

Nellie's believes in a baptism by fire and requires prospective staff members to volunteer for a night shift. When her turn came, Buffy got cold feet and called to say she wasn't coming. Gail Flintoff answered the phone. Gail is a black-haired, stubby, direct woman. Besides working at Nellie's, assisting with the sound equipment for a women's rock band, playing on a women's baseball team, and riding a motorcycle, she holds a graduate degree in social work and backs away from nothing.

Gail cut through Buffy's excuses and said, in a friendly, matter-of-fact way, "Oh, give it a whirl."

111

Buffy passed that test. The next hiring stage was to invite Buffy and the other applicant to a social gathering with the staff. "I didn't know which one was the other applicant," Buffy recalled with a chuckle, her voice like cream. "I didn't know who to chat up and who not to. It was quite a stunt."

She got the job and met Margaret four years ago at the first meeting she attended of Nellie's board. Buffy remembers that Margaret wore "an awful hat, tweed with a peaked brim, and an awful coat to match," and was beside herself with excitement over the Judy Chicago show, *The Dinner Party*, that was coming to the Art Gallery of Ontario.

As Buffy listened, she discovered that Margaret had travelled to Montreal to see the show, returning elated at the news that a last-minute decision had been made to bring the show to Toronto. To her dismay, however, the official guidebook to the show would be priced at about $25. Margaret indignantly approached the gallery management, pointing out that *The Dinner Party* was a celebration of women by women and for women, but most women are poor and cannot afford $25 for a guidebook. She prevailed upon the gallery to allow her to provide a short but serviceable guide, "The 39 Women", that would cost only two dollars.

Fran Sowton, a Holy Trinity team member, observed that Margaret's triumph at the AGO was "vintage Margaret". She said with a chuckle, "Look at the elements in it: the Scotch thrift, the anti-establishment approach, the feminism." Margaret had been saving for new teeth, but postponed the purchase so that she could pay for printing the guide. "That was vintage Margaret, too," Fran commented. "She had her priorities straight."

Even though she put off getting the teeth, her resources couldn't stretch to cover the printer's costs so Margaret borrowed $4,000. She had arguments with the New York publisher of the official guide over copyright but won them all. Then she wrote the guide, which is a model of sparse, brisk, and respectful description, and took charge of arrangements to sell it. At the Nellie's board meeting, she was brandishing the first copy off the presses with

112

such childlike glee that people smiled indulgently. Margaret in full sail was like that – her words tumbling, her hands gesturing, her whole self so fluttering that she seemed ready to jump up and down like a child.

"I thought right away that she was wonderful," Buffy remembered fondly.

When the meeting ended, Buffy found that Margaret had slipped a copy of the new guidebook in front of her, a thoughtful gift to welcome a newcomer. Buffy responded with a thank-you note.

"That's when we started looking at one another," she smiled.

The Judy Chicago guidebook was a triumph, selling 15,000 copies and earning Margaret enough money to repay her loan and make a royalty payment to the publisher of the other guidebook. Even so there was money left over. She never thought of the profit as her own. She made a donation of $600 to the Toronto Rape Crisis Centre and $400 to Interval House, a residence for battered women and their children.

Soon after the Nellie's meeting where Buffy and Margaret first met, Margaret invited the younger woman for lunch.

"I still felt like new staff," Buffy recalled, "and I was a bit strained. Margaret served an old-fashioned, three-course lunch; salmon soufflé I think. And then we sat in her garden for a bit."

When Buffy and Margaret met on subsequent occasions, their encounters were a pleasure for both. Margaret sought reassurance from Buffy that she should stay on Nellie's board, since the usual practice is for board people to serve only three years. Buffy assured her that she was needed for continuity and for her judgement. No one else was left from the early years to remember the history, and besides, she pointed out, Margaret was politically astute.

"She would leap into discussions focused on feminist or political issues in a very verbal way," Buffy recalled. "Margaret was opinionated, in the best sense of that word."

One Sunday the previous December when Buffy was on duty at Nellie's, Margaret arrived with her flute to play a concert for the residents. "She also ran all over the house trimming and watering the plants, scolding the staff for neglect of the horticul-ture while all hell was breaking loose somewhere in the house. I thought that was great."

Margaret stayed in the office a while for a chat with Buffy. She said she was tired and not eating well.

They talked on the telephone over the next few weeks about the purchase of a used piano that Buffy was contemplating. Buffy said, "I talked into her worry about her health. Like a good Anglo-Saxon, Margaret was trying to tuck it into her right boot."

Sensing that Margaret might eat better if she had company, Buffy invited her to lunch one day early in February. The younger woman gave the occasion a good deal of thought. She wanted Margaret to feel cared for, protected, cosied, so she prepared a simple meal, not too highly spiced, and served tiny portions. They ate in a sun-filled room off the kitchen and discussed old love affairs.

Buffy was working at Nellie's a few weeks later when Leslie MacDonald, thinking Buffy knew, made a reference to the fact that Margaret's cancer was terminal. "It hit me like someone had slammed a door. I went to the staff bedroom and had my weep."

Buffy's relationship with Margaret Frazer was obviously special. It was almost as close as her relationship with her own mother. Buffy would later say, tears in her eyes, "I found I was looking for a relationship with an older woman. I didn't know I was doing it with Margaret until I was doing it. There was something about Margaret I needed. And part of the reason I was special to her was that I really did need her, and she knew it. There was a terrific affection between us."

When she heard that volunteers were needed for Margaret's palliative care, she said, "Put me down."

On the first overnight shift, Buffy saw a side of Margaret that was new to her: the kindly martinet. Margaret was full of instruc-tions. Buffy was to open the basement door so that Cleo, her cat, could use the litter box located downstairs. She wanted her place set for breakfast on a certain placemat, with a certain size of plate, and a butter knife on the plate, not a dinner knife. Her

ENSURE was to be poured into a small glass, not a large one, and was to be served at room temperature not chilled in the fridge.

"And the tea ritual was a labyrinth," Buffy added with a grin.

"I know," I nodded. "Believe me, I know."

Margaret's thrift was another factor to be considered. "I wanted to leave a light on all night," Buffy said, "because I thought it would be comforting to Margaret, and helpful to me in a strange house, but she was horrified at the waste of electricity."

I reciprocated with a story of the time I wrote "foil" on the shopping list, to be rebuked by Margaret, who customarily washed and re-used foil.

Similarly, the team always felt that Margaret's kitchen was rather dim. Only after Margaret's death, when Ian and Fran Sowton were preparing the house to be sold, did we learn that the light bulb in the kitchen ceiling fixture, the main source of light at night, was a meagre 25 watts.

Buffy left her first overnight shift feeling discouraged. She went home glumly and was just stepping out of her shower when Linda Rapson called her. Margaret had announced to Linda that Buffy was her "favourite person" and Linda wanted Buffy to know she could come as often as she liked. Buffy was delighted. Later, when Buffy mentioned at Nellie's how she had felt a failure on her first shift, she discovered that nearly everyone had had the same experience. While Margaret was unfailingly appreciative, everybody felt they weren't doing enough, that what they did wasn't done properly, that they weren't solving the problem.

Buffy reflected, "Maybe that came from the fact that we weren't solving the big problem."

The team was writing notes in the log that sounded like the comments of satisfied restaurant critics. Dorothy Rogers, a long-time supporter of women's causes and active in Nellie's fund-raising, brought soups that everyone pronounced delicious. There were raves about someone's dynamite carrot cake. Jackie White-Hampton, a Nellie's member of the team, made a carrot soup that everyone adored. An anonymous person's beef soup was pronounced a big hit with Margaret, who had otherwise been avoiding meat. Someone announced that cream of broccoli soup had been stored in an ice-cream container in the freezer. Helen Cram of Holy Trinity advised the team that Margaret liked a chocolate dessert.

Other reminders concerned two of Margaret's favourite pastimes, bird watching and gardening. The bird-feeder outside the dining-room windows wasn't being refilled regularly. "Two cups of feed per day from the brown canister in the back porch," Buffy wrote sternly. On the same page she noted that the clematis needed pruning. "Project for a quiet day?" she inquired. And Sheila Mackenzie, a woman notorious for her indifference to punctuality, wrote in the log, "Would anyone have a clock to lend the upstairs bedroom?"

On Thursday, April 11, Margaret had a treat that she talked about for weeks. Jan Kudelka came and sang selections from *The Beggar's Opera* for her. "Not just her parts, but *all* the parts," Margaret told me, rejoicing. Jan is an amazing woman. She's a writer, and she's been a circus clown and an actress at the Stratford Festival. Her mother was prominent in theatre in Toronto, and her brother, James, solo dancer with the National Ballet and Les Grands Ballets Canadiens, is a well-established choreographer in Montreal.

The working of the team was not flawlessly smooth, of course. Each of us brought our own way of folding towels, our own way of washing a floor, our own way of doing dishes. Margaret, who had lived alone much of her life, had developed fixed household routines that often bore no resemblance to ours. In the spaces that sometimes occurred between shifts, when she was alone in her domain, she tried to restore order in her cupboards and shelves, though the effort left her wrung out.

She confessed to a few people, Liz and Buffy among them, that she was depressed to find dishes out of place, pots with scalded bottoms, the kitchen counter cluttered with dirty dishes and crumbs, plants over-watered, dusters that had been used as scrub cloths, and disorder in the utensil drawers and linen closet.

I asked her once how she was bearing up under the stress of

116

people cleaning – or not cleaning – her house in ways she didn't approve. She was becoming resigned. She said tranquilly, "It gets easier every time."

The clutter of leftovers in her refrigerater was harder to bear. Neighbours and friends brought great quantities of food intended to tempt Margaret's appetite, and this cornucopia of plenty went into the fridge along with the soups, custards, pasta salads, quiches, puddings, purées, scalloped potatoes, rice mixtures, and mousses brought by the team. Since Margaret ate little and people were reluctant to throw out remnants of food lovingly prepared, the fridge was bursting with tiny jars containing indeterminate ooze, saran-covered dishes of gloop, plastic bowls with lids, Styrofoam containers from take-out places, little bundles wrapped in foil, and sandwich bags filled with moulding green and orange puddles.

Once a week, Elizabeth Greaves dealt with this debris. "Here's some asparagus with cheese sauce, but it's kind of congealed," she would call to Margaret.

"Throw it out."

"How about these green grapes, slightly brown at the stem ends?"

"Out."

"And something with bits of cauliflower...."

"Out, *out*."

Liz also prevailed upon Margaret to discard some frugal accumulations, such as soured milk that had been waiting for weeks for someone to use in pancakes. "Some of the stuff she saved was really bizarre," Liz observed.

Elaine Hall also attempted to control the chaos. She printed in the log at large block letters: "PLEASE LABEL AND DATE ALL FOOD IN THE FRIDGE. LABELS IN DRAWER NEXT TO THE FRIDGE." A few days later, Fran Sowton wrote plaintively, "I pass along the suggestion that things that are put in the fridge should be labelled and dated. Labels are in the drawer nearest the fridge."

On the other hand, some foods were such a hit with Margaret

117

that they never lasted long. One of these was Merylie Houston's custard made with honey. Merylie obligingly wrote the recipe in the log-book and observed that Margaret liked it served at room temperature with maple syrup on top. Margaret also adored angel-food cake with a brown-sugar-sauce topping. The nutrition-minded on the team were appalled.

Margaret's crocuses were up, and on fine days she walked slowly in the garden behind her house, enjoying them. Linda, keeping her distance because of a heavy cold, talked to her on the telephone and learned that Margaret hadn't taken a pain pill for four days. Margaret wondered why she still felt so weak, even though she was trying to eat. To Linda's ear, she sounded weaker and "less bouncy".

One afternoon when I popped by, Margaret was reading a letter from a friend. She pushed her glasses down her nose and glared at me over the top of them. "This woman seems to think I'm dying," she said, offended. "Wherever did she get that idea!"

Jane Champagne, a Holy Trinity friend who had given Margaret the book about the Simonton method, came one day with an hour-long tape of a Simonton session. Her visit was at the suggestion of Sheila Mackenzie, who was concerned that Margaret seemed insincere in her commitment to Simonton. Sheila explained, "Margaret asked me in the hospital 'Is there something we can do to beat this?', so I felt responsible for that part of her that was fighting the disease. It was very frustrating for me that she would ask for help and then subvert it."

Jane's visit proved a tonic. She and Margaret listened to the Simonton tape, and Margaret's spirits soared. Her enthusiasm for "imaging" restored, she announced she was going to work hard on the method.

Linda meanwhile had learned that a doctor at Princess Margaret Hospital was using the Simonton method with a group of cancer patients. She talked with him and learned that he had a waiting list for his Simonton group and, besides, Margaret's was not the kind of case where the method had much application. Linda told him about Margaret's team. "That's the best possible way to prolong her life and enhance the quality of the time she has left," he told Linda.

Being with Margaret was doing a good deal to enhance the quality of life for us all. Wendy Farquhar wrote in the log, "It is so rewarding being here. I go home with a profound feeling of inner peace, joy, and love." Another time she wrote, "I give thanks for this opportunity to spend time with Margaret." Heather Sutherland, a Holy Trinity team member, wrote, "Peaceful night. All's well. Dawning a beautiful snow-covered morning." Jane Davidson, a Holy Trinity woman and former *Toronto Star* reporter, wrote, "Margaret commented on all the love surrounding her. I'm happy to be here and part of that." Arlene Parks, a Nellie's staff woman, wrote, "There is a very easy peace here. What a privilege to be with God and Margaret." Sheila File wrote, "She's resting now as I leave for church. What a special joy it is to be with Margaret." Linda wrote after a Saturday morning house call, when she found Margaret more relaxed than she had yet seen her, "Aren't we all lucky to be Friends of Margaret?"

Joyce Brown commented wryly, "In Margaret's place I would be a wreck, and God help the people coming in; but Margaret's dignity and peace throughout the whole process were steadying. After rushing around to meetings all day, I found that going to Margaret's was a rest. I would come away from her house feeling fine – maybe sad, but not devastated. That's what surprised me: that it was so easy to be there."

On Monday, April 23, two weeks after Easter, Heather Sutherland wrote: "Margaret and I chatted about 'Why it seems to take a disease to bring warmth out of some people.' Margaret feels surrounded by care and warmth. Occasionally she mentions the frustration of not being able to thank everybody. She feels surrounded by warmth she never knew was there for her. The lessons are many in being with Margaret. Indeed, why does it take a disease to make us show our core?"

Heather was carrying the burden of a life-changing decision. She's a beautiful woman with a mane of curling blond hair and

119

an expression that is affectionate and intense. Most of her life has been spent in education, teaching students from Junior Kindergarten to Grade 13, and she has also held an important job as a consultant for the North York school board. Her three children were grown, and she had fallen in love with a man who for twenty-two years had lived under vows of chastity and poverty. In order to be with him, she was thinking of taking similar vows for herself.

Margaret Frazer clearly was concerned. From others at Holy Trinity, Heather learned that Margaret was worried about her. When she discussed it face to face with Margaret, the older woman was hesitant. She'd start to say something and then she'd stop herself, pursing her lips.

"That was very powerful," Heather later told me. "If you know people well, what they are *not* saying comes across clearly. Her feelings were so strong she couldn't discuss them, and that had a profound effect on me. Just the fact that she was concerned that I was perhaps making a mistake made me pause and think it over."

Nancy Dodington was perhaps the least obtrusive person on Margaret's team. She's a very tall and very thin woman, thirty years old, who worked for many years at Nellie's and then moved to the Jessie's collective. Her voice is soft, her expression mild, her manner self-effacing, but she's a strong, competent, and resourceful woman – greatly admired and respected by her peers. To her belongs much of the credit for putting together the Jessie's housing component, which is a model of its kind.

Her introduction to Margaret was at Nellie's. "She surprised the hell out of me," Nancy recalled as we lunched one rainy day in a King Street restaurant. "She arrived at the door of Nellie's when I was working my first Sunday shift, and I didn't know if she was a volunteer, a board member, or what. I was still trying to get a grip on what was going on, and here was this white-haired woman who said she had come to help with dinner."

Margaret seemed to know her way around and greeted several

120

residents by name. Finding that she was too early to start cooking, she curled up on the couch in the office and fell asleep. Nancy was astounded. "No one else would do that. They would be afraid they might miss something, or else they'd find it impossible to sleep with the phone ringing every five minutes and people coming in and out of the office all the time. But Margaret just curled up and slept peacefully. I thought she was quite wonderful."

As she came to know Margaret better, her affection grew. "She said what she felt," observed Nancy, who finds it difficult to be assertive. "There was no making Margaret do anything she didn't want to do. She was her own person. She could be cranky, or high on a project, or in rapture over something like music. She was human."

Nancy believes that Margaret played a crucial role on the Nellie's board of directors. "And not only in fund raising, where her commitment was like other people's commitment to a career or a life work. She was the conscience of the board. There were a lot of good people on the Nellie's board, but Margaret was the consistent one; others came and went. She would lead us. She had the awareness of mental health as an issue and human rights in general, but especially of feminist issues and issues of sexual orientation. You could trust her."

Nancy joined the Friends of Margaret team as a relief person, available when Joyce Brown had a vacancy to fill. Mostly she worked overnights, but one shift was a Saturday afternoon. Margaret told her apologetically that day that she was too tired to talk to her. That was fine with Nancy. She told Margaret not to worry about it. Margaret needed the rest. Nancy went to another part of the house and sat quietly, wondering what would happen next.

What happened next was the Margaret called, "Yoo hoo. Where are you?" When Nancy came into the living-room, Margaret instructed her to sit down.

"Now," she said cosily, "tell me what's happening at Jessie's. And tell me what you are doing."

Nancy said, "I thought it was great when she could say that

she didn't want to talk. It's a relief to think that someone you're trying to help is able to speak clearly about what she wants. It would be dreadful if she was putting up with whatever everyone did for her for their sakes. It made me feel better about being there. I had hoped that this plan about the team, lovely in so many ways, wouldn't rob Margaret of her independence."

Our sandwiches arrived and we started to eat. Nancy said, "I would have been perturbed if she had been passive, if her attitude had been 'Anything you want to do is all right with me.' That would have meant to me that she really had lost the will to live."

She took a sip of coffee and grinned. "Anyone capable of having a nap in Nellie's in the middle of a busy Sunday afternoon is capable of being in charge of her dying," she said.

Liz Greaves and I had paired on the shifts, a useful idea for busy people. Normally her day was Monday and mine Thursday, but we switched around as our schedules required. On Monday, April 15, the first warm day, I arrived in late afternoon and found sticks tied neatly in bundles waiting at the curb in front of Margaret's house for the next morning's garbage collection. Frances Sowton had been doing yard work.

I found her inside, getting ready to depart. Fran Sowton is a beauty, with thick, lustrous grey hair worn in a twist that she lets down when making herself comfortable, velvety dark brown eyes, and an oval face full of repose. A former nurse, she's a gifted artist. She has a studio where she does ecclesiastical needlework, but she is switching to painting because "it's faster".

She explained once that she'll never leave stitching entirely. "Fibre is close to women," she observed. "Women swaddle their babies and swaddle the dead."

She and her husband, Ian Sowton, a professor of English at York University specializing in Renaissance and contemporary literature, live only a few blocks from Margaret's house. They have raised five children, one of them an adopted son so grievously damaged in a succession of foster homes and group homes that he spends a good deal of time in prison. Ian Sowton is a stocky man, steady and gentle, with twinkling eyes.

122

The Sowtons joined Holy Trinity about five years earlier, drawn to it by its inclusiveness, its non-establishment views, and the strong element of congregation participation.

"Margaret slowly revealed herself to us," Fran said thoughtfully during a chat one hot July day in the Sowton living-room. "She had looked like an ordinary person, which she *ain't*. Then we began to find all the things she had thoughts about – women's theology, non-sexist language in the church, and her passionate interest in music."

The Sowtons were members of the small choir that Margaret insisted on gathering together and rehearsing for such occasions as Christmas and Easter. Merylie Houston remembers that when Margaret joined Holy Trinity, the church had just got rid of "pews and choirs". Margaret didn't mind the loss of the former, but the absence of a choir was intolerable. From time to time she would conscript Holy Trinity parishioners into a temporary choir. The Sowtons laugh at the memory. Not everyone in the choir could follow the tempo or carry a tune. Ian chuckled, "Margaret's love of precision and accuracy used to struggle with her sense of charity."

Their first intimation that Margaret was ill came one Sunday when she was helping to lay out the food after the service. Margaret told Fran that she wasn't feeling well, an unusual admission. After that her weight loss became noticeable, and she no longer was volunteering to do church jobs that once she had taken on gladly. Fran began to suspect cancer.

When Margaret was in hospital and people at Holy Trinity talked of a team for palliative home care, Fran expected that what they had in mind was a temporary measure to tide Margaret over until her condition deteriorated to the point where she would be returned to hospital. Fran volunteered promptly, though she didn't know Margaret very well. As she later explained, her response to Margaret owed something to the fact that her own mother had died of cancer, and she had always felt guilty that she hadn't spent more time with her, not realizing how quickly the death would come. She saw in Margaret's dying an opportunity, at some level, to make a peace.

123

In one of the team meetings, Fran Sowton put her finger astutely on a motivation within us all. "You know what we're doing," she grinned. "We're boning up for our own finals."

That warm day in April had drawn Margaret to her garden, where she sat in the sun and watched Fran rake the flower beds. Five-year-old Gwen Hiseler, a charming and bubbling little girl, hung over the railing of her back porch and sang. Gwen was attached to Margaret, as children usually were, and never approached her without bringing a child's gift, the tiny flowers of weeds picked with one-inch stems and gripped in her sweaty little hand. Margaret listened enthralled as the child sang verse after verse of an English folk song, getting every one right, her voice sweet in the soft April air.

That same afternoon Margaret heard a cardinal, a piece of luck she took as a gift. She told Fran that every bit of her time in the garden was memorable. The sun gave her a headache, and she was obliged to take a Tylenol, the first in six days, but that didn't matter. "It was worth it," she told me that evening. "By the time I came in, I could smell the earth."

When Linda called, Margaret sighed, "It was been a day full of pleasures."

No one talked any more about whether helping Margaret stay in her home was a mistake. Clearly, she was rejoicing in the sight of spring coming to her garden, the hours of listening to Glenn Gould play Bach, the morning meditation in the lovely old rocker in her study, climbing into her own bed at night. Every day she performed a fastidious toilet and dressed for visitors, concealing the gaping zipper of her skirts under cardigan sweaters. After breakfast, her best meal of the day, she would assume her action station on the couch, arranging beside her a folder of papers and letters, a few books and magazines, the state-of-the-art tape machine Nigel Turner had given her, the cordless telephone, and a stack of tapes, mostly of classical music, that visitors and the team had brought her.

People came with flowers, which she appreciated intensely,

exclaiming over the colour and fragrance, fussy about which vase was most suitable for their charms and where they would be placed so she could see them best. For three months there were always fresh flowers in the living-room. Except for the two times a day when she moved to the reclining chair for Codetron treatments and those times when she climbed the stairs to the bathroom, she spent the day on the couch.

Her cat would nestle beside her in the folds of the green mohair blanket. While she talked, Margaret absently stroked Cleo's back. Every conversation with Margaret had a quality of reflection. When she asked what we were doing these days – and she always did – we replied by putting our activities in a context to avoid the suggestion of purposelessness. In Margaret's presence, it would have been blasphemy to speak of time frittered, mobility unappreciated, or energy used thoughtlessly.

In telling her of ourselves, we learned who we were. We saw the patterns.

She often said, making a cosy gesture with her shoulders, "I'm learning so much about all these people. It's such a rich experience to have the time to really talk."

Her responses to what she was told were thoughtful and perceptive. As everyone on the team noticed, she paid us close attention, which is rare enough in most social exchanges. She gave us back a better self; she always saw us as wiser, more sensible, more gifted, and more generous than we are.

When we stepped through her door, we were sure of welcome. "It's so good to see you," Margaret would say fervently. The goodbyes were unfailingly poignant and tender. No one left without kissing her.

Through the day, she received visitors, dozed, read, listened to music, chatted on the telephone, talked to the team person, watched the pale green buds on maple trees outside the window unfold into delicate leaves, and planned the spring planting of her garden. Most days she was the picture of contentment, a fulfilled woman whose expression grew sweeter and more pure every day.

Her position on the living-room couch represented control, the best and bravest she could manage in a deteriorating situation. The couch, placed with its back against the front windows, was close to the front door and gave her a view of the front hall. No one could go in or out without her knowledge, and she was also within hearing distance of the activity in the kitchen.

If she had remained in her bedroom she would have been spared the ordeal of the stairs whenever she used the bathroom, and the struggle to get into ill-fitting clothes every morning. Her bedroom, however, was situated in the back corner of the house. While it commanded a view of her beloved rear garden, it was remote from the daily traffic of housework and chores.

Dressed for the day and positioned in her living-room, she wasn't an invalid. She was a woman in charge of her household who happened to be lying down.

I was slow to understand the strategic and psychological importance of the fully dressed woman on her couch. I fretted because the couch was so short for her that she could never stretch out, and I wished she would wear her comfortable pyjamas instead of the thick skirts that got twisted under her and blouses with a million small buttons.

Around ten at night, after the final Codetron treatment, with a Mozart-inspired flute on the tape machine and the room saturated with repose, I would suggest that Margaret change into her night things and climb into bed. She always refused, looking at me in amazement at such a silly proposal. However tired she was, however much pain she was in, she would insist on waiting so that she could receive the overnight team member graciously.

I came to realize that in Margaret's mind only *sick* people are in bed when a guest arrives. She was not, of course, sick.

Margaret no longer made an effort to sit at the dining-room table for dinner. I made a space amid the clutter on the coffee table next to the couch and set it with a placemat, plates, a paper napkin, and cutlery. She was embarrassed and defensive about her weakness. "I last longer this way," she explained as I bustled between the kitchen and the couch. Sitting up with pillows behind her for support, she slowly ate some cream of leek soup with a teaspoon. A soup spoon, she said, was "too big and heavy".

She had a new and disquieting habit of swallowing strangely, like someone struggling not to vomit. Also, the noises from her abdomen mortified her. As I helped her to her feet so that she could move to the chair for her Codetron session, the gurgles were so pronounced we couldn't pretend they hadn't happened.

"I'm told I should rejoice in these sounds," she told me ruefully.

During the twenty minutes of Codetron treatment, Margaret would read a book, an aid to shutting out distractions so that she could open herself to the electrical stimulation. Accordingly, a preparation-for-reading ritual had been incorporated into the ritual of the Codetron machine. It began with Margaret being helped into the chair across the room from the couch and her feet lifted to the footstool. Then the Chinese black cloth slipper and thick sock would be removed from her left foot. Next we took the electrodes and tangled wires out of the plastic bag and patiently unscrambled them. Margaret would wet each electrode with a finger dipped daintily in a glass of water and supervise closely while they were placed on her foot, legs, arm, and hands, after which the elastic straps would be fastened over the electrodes.

Next her legs would be covered with the green mohair blanket, which was tucked around her, and the green velvet cushion from the couch would be placed on her lap. The final touch was to bring her book, which she placed at a comfortable reading distance on the pillow. Margaret was finding it too tiring to hold the weight of an unsupported book.

As I was preparing for about the fourth time to assist her with the Codetron, she looked at me sharply and asked, "Have you done this before?"

Such signs of mental confusion were becoming more frequent. One day she introduced to each other two women who had served together for years on the Nellie's board with her.

While she placidly read in the light of the tall lamp beside her, I would work on papers I brought in a briefcase. The peace

127

between us was so natural it felt as though we had been friends for fifty years.

One of the first books she read this way was *Willie*, Heather Robertson's prize-winning biographical novel about former prime minister William Lyon Mackenzie King. Margaret was shocked that I hadn't yet read it. She gave me a severe reproving look and pronounced it "fascinating".

On this shift in mid-April, Margaret was preoccupied with Simonton. She said patients were supposed to picture their cancer tumour as an enemy and imagine the body's immune system attacking that enemy ferociously. To do this, Dr. Simonton suggested that patients invent an image to represent the cancer and another image of appropriate attackers. Margaret had decided to imagine her cancer cells as a swarm of insects and her immune system as voracious birds descending on the bugs. "Birds are so quick," she explained earnestly. "I have to get rid of the cancer in my pancreas in a hurry so I can eat again and get my energy back."

Fran Sowton had suggested that the birds be swallows. Margaret wanted to know what I thought of that.

I had no opinion about the relative appetites of birds. I smiled at my friend and saw how much thinner she was. Her upper body was a skeleton and her face so shrunken that her teeth no longer fit properly.

That week Margaret had difficulty with a second member of the team, a generous-hearted woman with a rushed way of speaking and a booming voice. It was the noise level and the breathlessness that bothered Margaret, though she was deeply pained that her complaint seemed lacking in charity. She hated criticizing this kind woman, she went on, but loudness fell on her like blows, and quickness of speech made her reel. She couldn't stand it. I said I would deal with it. I telephoned Liz Greaves and Liz talked to the woman, who withdrew understandingly.

Margaret told Linda that same week that a new overnight person also had been jarring. The woman, apprehensive and too anxious to please, created a mood of tension that had the immediate impact on Margaret of a flare-up of pain. Margaret, horrified that this was the third "dismissal" and she was causing problems, insisted that Linda keep the information to herself. She would wait, she said; maybe the woman would be calmer next time. Instead,. the woman sensed that her nervousness had infected Margaret and removed herself from the schedule.

One Saturday afternoon in April, when Margaret and Linda Rapson were together in the garden, Margaret said, "I think I can beat this cancer. What do you think?"

Linda replied without hesitation, "If anyone can, Margaret, you can."

Margaret thought that a splendid comment. She told everyone on the team about it. "Linda said a perfect thing," is how she put it to me. What pleased Margaret was not so much that her doctor thought she might recover but that Linda had saluted her spunkiness.

Spunkiness was Margaret's long suit. When Nigel Turner visited her in hospital soon after the bad news of the futile surgery, he advised her that people can go a long way on hope. Margaret took that suggestion wholly to heart because it fit her nature. The optimist in her was ever victorious over the realist. Margaret's public face was one of confidence that the fundamental composition of all obstacles is sand. "I'm sure it will turn out all right," she used to assure me when I groaned about a shortfall in fund raising, an inter-agency dispute, or bureaucratic resistance. That positive side of her accounted for Margaret's tenacity in attending a hundred fruitless committee meetings about the homeless, while other people would give up in frustration. In the face of her own disaster, Margaret reached in her closet of ideas and put on the comfortable habits of a sanguine lifetime.

Linda, however, was beginning to believe quite sincerely that Margaret was improving. Margaret now weighed ninety-six pounds, a gain of four, and not much of this increase appeared to be abdominal fluid. Her feet weren't swollen, which was another sign that the fluid level wasn't rising. When Linda examined her for what she called "shifting dullness", the indication of the presence of fluid, the sign had disappeared. "It's spooky," Linda said. "She was supposed to be dead by this time. It's crazy to think along the lines I'm thinking, but I can't help it. I think she's getting better."

Margaret's progress came at a time when Linda was desolated by terrible news. Her close friend, Barbara Tait Scullion, forty-four, a woman dear to her and to her husband, Morris Manning, had just received a diagnosis of cancer of the liver and was dying, swiftly and in savage pain, in Princess Margaret Hospital. Barbara and Linda had known one another from the time Linda was twelve and Barbara was thirteen. The friendship was renewed when Morris and Barbara's husband, Charles Scullion, then a lawyer and later a judge, worked together in the office of the Ontario attorney-general. The Scullions purchased a cottage across the lake from the Rapson family compound, and the adults spent long lazy afternoons and evenings together.

Linda and Morris visited Barbara every day, wracked by their grief and the horror of witnessing the dying woman's agony. Morris was in the final stages of preparing arguments for his client, Dr. Henry Morgentaler, whose jury acquittal on abortion charges had been appealed by the Crown. The Morgentaler submission, a massive effort of 235 pages, would be made before five high court judges, but Morris was finding it difficult to concentrate. As he worked, he sometimes wept.

Linda's despair was complicated by frustration. She was convinced there were ways to manage Barbara's case so that her friend would not suffer such torment, but she was unable to interfere.

When Linda and I talked about it, she said her visits to Margaret had become her life raft. "I go from Princess Margaret where my friend is in the most awful pain and drive to see Margaret, and there she is, pruning roses in her garden. She's my respite, my inspiration."

Margaret beamed, "I'm a lucky woman. I'm getting better every day."

Despite the brave words, Margaret was never far from exhaustion. A garrulous neighbour who dropped in for ten minutes left

Margaret limp for the rest of the afternoon. Two cousins turned up one day, a visit that Margaret had been anticipating with keen pleasure, but when they left her face was ashen and she fell into a deep sleep. Sometimes she dozed off after breakfast and slept most of the morning. A new symptom had developed. When she bent over, she experienced sharp pains in her abdomen.

Toward the end of April, she asked Linda, "Do you really think the cancer's smaller?" Linda, who had been on her knees beside Margaret, examining her while she lay on the couch, sat back on her heels. "I'm sure it's not bigger," she said reassuringly. "It does feel softer and smaller."

We had decided on another team meeting after the April 28 Sunday service at Holy Trinity. Everyone else changed their clocks to daylight saving time that morning but I forgot. I arrived promptly, according to my watch, but was exactly one hour late. I found the Friends of Margaret in the vestry, some thirty people on chairs arranged in a circle. Hilda Powicke was chairing the meeting and Linda was talking as I found an empty chair and apologetically joined them.

Linda was replying to a question from Sheila Mackenzie. Sheila thought Margaret's diet was lacking in nutrition. "Anyone would be ill who ate what she does," she said sharply. Linda pointed out that the ENSURE provided all the protein Margaret needed. Sheila plainly wasn't satisfied. Hilda noted uneasily that Sheila had Linda on the defensive; she worried about them both.

Almost nothing about the meeting, in fact, appealed to Sheila. In the first place, Sheila blamed Linda for Margaret's *laissez-faire* diet and was angrier about it than she had indicated, out of deference to the congeniality we were trying to maintain. The quantities of sweets that Margaret was consuming seemed to her responsible for a hyper quality in Margaret's behaviour. She was appalled that people brought meat, even though it came in soup, and she thought goat's milk preferable to cow's milk.

More important, she had been looking forward to the meeting as an opportunity for team members to speak of their tangled feelings. For her own part, for instance, she was deeply troubled. Her mother had died of cancer of the pancreas, her grandmother

131

probably died of cancer of the pancreas, and Sheila fully expects that cancer of the pancreas will kill her one day. Nursing Margaret with cancer of the pancreas was freighted with dark meaning and memories for Sheila. As a precaution against collapse, Sheila had arranged to see a therapist every Friday morning, following her Thursday overnight shift with Margaret.

The mother of Jan Kudelka, the writer-actress, had died less than two years earlier of cancer. Jan too had been hoping that the meeting would help her deal with the surge of fresh grief that Margaret's dying was causing in her. Hilda Powicke was in a depression so severe that she was seeing a psychiatrist. She suspected that her mother's death from cancer at almost exactly the same age as Margaret had much to do with triggering her despair.

Fran Sowton touched on what was in the minds of many when she suggested that the team should try to separate personal pain from the situation, and not relive some previous death in Margaret. She was thinking of herself as well as the many others in the room who were sorrowing for mothers.

Sheila Mackenzie, her blue eyes sharp with annoyance, said after the meeting, "I thought it was going to be about *us*. Instead it was all about Margaret!" Her indignation wasn't selfishness. She worried that the team would not survive emotionally without acknowledging and dealing with the complex burdens many were carrying.

However, Linda's style, and mine too, is that one sticks to the agenda and waits until the crisis is over to sort out the mess inside. Sheila Mackenzie has a point of view on this, as on most things. She calls it "killing yourself with good works". She explains: "All the good ladies of Holy Trinity die of suicide or cancer, while the rotten people like me are perfectly healthy because we go to therapists and deal with all the emotional baggage."

Despite the awareness in the room that Sheila was quietly fuming at Linda, we went on with practicalities. Someone I didn't know asked if Margaret shouldn't be getting vitamins. Linda said that she was switching Margaret to ENSURE PLUS, which had more vitamins and other nutrients than ENSURE. "Besides," she added, "I like to follow Margaret's inclinations. I got the impression early on that Margaret wasn't interested in a diet program as a solution to her illness."

Jay MacGillivray caught everyone's attention when she said that she was experienced in palliative care. From what she knew of dying people she found Margaret curiously indifferent about doing more than to go through the motions of fighting the disease. It had been noted by us all that her initial warm response to Jane Champagne's advocacy of the Simonton method had waned. Jane had written in the log-book that Margaret should be encouraged to meditate three times a day, before each meal, but Margaret asked Linda to cross out that entry. She said she would meditate according to her own timetable, which turned out to be a few minutes before breakfast most days and occasionally in the evening before bed.

Jay observed after Margaret's death, "I was intrigued that Margaret wasn't really interested in alternative treatments. Other people with a diagnosis of terminal cancer are frantic to find out about wonder cures like peach pits and macrobiotic diets – whatever is going. But Margaret, who knew of such things, never mentioned them. She didn't show a genuine attachment even to the Simonton method. It made me nervous when people on the team would say, 'We've *got* to put her on vitamin therapy.' I thought the indications were that Margaret knew perfectly well that she was dying and that nothing would change it."

Only a few days earlier Margaret had been expecting someone else when Jay turned up for a shift. In a burst of crabbiness that happened every now and then, she said belligerently, "What are *you* doing here?"

Leaning against the door jamb, Jay folded her arms and replied, "Well, I guess I've come to watch you die. What are *you* doing here?"

Margaret's annoyance vanished. She said quietly, "Well, I guess that's what I'm doing."

"Okay," said Jay, "what do you want to do while you're doing it? Shall we have some music?"

Jay explained to me that she had decided when caring for her stepfather that people shouldn't accept mistreatment from the dying. "I used to say to Jack, 'I won't take that shit.' Essentially, that's what I was saying to Margaret."

They listened to Vivaldi for a while and then Jay explained how the mix-up on the schedule had happened. Margaret was contrite. "I have to be careful," she said. "I have to try not to get angry but just to accept the richness of it, that so many people want to come."

The consensus of the Friends of Margaret meeting in the church was that Margaret was ambivalent about her condition, torn between allowing herself to die and her fight to get well. One woman observed thoughtfully that Margaret was using her illness as a way of learning something about herself that she needed to know. She said, "She'll let go when she is ready." We were struck by the wisdom of that. We could each recall Margaret saying, with her eager little-girl expression, "I'm learning so-o-o- much."

Hilda Powicke's opening remarks had dealt with the contradictions within Margaret. "Some of you report to me that Margaret is in great form, and others tell me she's sad and fretful," she said. "Some see her as growing stronger and others find her deteriorating. Those fluctuations are indications of the different times of the day that you see her, the different moods she experiences, and the fact that each of you is different too." She praised the team. "Certain things stand out. Most of you have been to Margaret's at least twice, and you're more relaxed. You're working out little schemes that will make life more comfortable or more interesting for her. You're using your ingenuity, bringing your own talents and gifts to her."

She said it was becoming easier to identify what would throw Margaret. For instance, Hilda said, she got upset if there was a shift change she hadn't been told about, as when Jay arrived the night before, or when people came later than expected, or when visitors were talkative and stressful.

"The impatient or indignant Margaret, it seems, was a surprise to some of you," Hilda grinned as the team gave an appreciative groan. "That isn't true for those of us who have served with her on boards or committees, but let's not forget she was a highly respected teacher at Bloor Collegiate for twenty years and head of the English department."

She finished on a triumphant note. "It's working. You're enjoying it. You've told me it's an enriching experience, learning to know Margaret better and being part of a team effort. Incredibly, and largely because of the excellent scheduling work of Joyce Brown, it's worked with fewer bugs than one would ever have expected."

Someone chuckled that we ought to put together a book of Margaret recipes. We were learning to cook delicious food for invalids. Someone else commented that Margaret always spoke of the food in terms of the person who made it, as in "Jackie's carrot soup", or "Buffy's broccoli soup", or "Wendy's muffins". That reminded another person to caution us against too much enthusiasm when Margaret expressed delight in a new food. When she said she liked pineapple juice, the team had pushed pineapple juice with such zeal that in a few days Margaret detested it.

Jay talked about the serious pain Margaret had experienced the night before. Linda, who had checked Margaret that morning, thought it might be adhesions from the surgery. It might not, but the explanation was possible and Margaret was relieved to accept it rather than contemplate the possibility of decline.

The pain had frightened both Margaret and Jay. It began abruptly, in contrast to the slow build-up of pain to which Margaret was accustomed. Jay learned that Margaret had missed taking her Codetron treatment and suggested that Margaret take a Tylenol No. 3. Margaret agreed and swallowed it with difficulty. Her face remained contorted.

"Do you want to try some relaxing?" Jay asked.

Margaret nodded. With Jay's help she sat upright on the couch and Jay knelt in front of her, taking her hands. She told Margaret to close her eyes and breathe slowly and deeply. Then she asked softly, "Where in your body do you feel healthy?"

"In my hands," Margaret responded.

Jay said in a lulling chant, "Imagine the warmth in your hands

135

on the point of your pain. Feel that warmth move to the pain. Open yourself to the Tylenol because the codeine is starting to work. Breathe, breathe, breathe." In a few minutes, Margaret was calm and out of pain.

I complained about Margaret's uncomfortable clothes, which fit her nowhere. I suggested that if she was going to insist on getting dressed every day she needed something like a jogging outfit, something soft and loose. Jay told me about a store that stocked all-cotton jogging suits with drawstring waists and I noted the address.

The team had noticed how Margaret loved to be touched. Fran Sowton had observed to her one day that people can pass energy through their hands. She demonstrated by cupping Margaret's chilly feet in her hands. After that we all learned what pleasure it gave Margaret to have her feet rubbed. "Oh, that feels so-o-o-o good," she would say, closing her eyes. Some of the team knew how to give her legs and body gentle massages; some rubbed her back with lotion. When we hugged her, as we all did, we held on longer and longer.

Anne van Egmond, a CAMMAC friend on the team, mused after Margaret's death, "I wonder if she was touched, physically touched, as much in her whole life as in those last three months. I'm sure she was not."

At the end of the meeting in the church, the final question to Linda was, "How much longer will Margaret live?"

She replied sombrely, "I don't know. She's already on extra time."

Margaret had bouts of being vague and confused. One morning Nancy Dodington telephoned, identified herself, and said she was on her way. She asked if there was anything Margaret wanted her to bring. Margaret replied, "Tell you what, dear. You call in about two hours. Nancy Dodington will be here then and she'll talk to you."

Kathleen Metcalfe, a friend of Margaret's from both Holy Trinity and CAMMAC, volunteered for the back-up roster. Called on short notice one day, she was unable to get a sitter for her two-year-old. She brought the child with her, and Margaret was delighted.

Wendy Farquhar wrote in the log one day. "Margaret's illness has helped me in so many ways. So often when I love someone or have something done for me, I acknowledge my love and appreciation – and yet I did not truly let the other person know how much I valued what they did, or for just being them and being there. Margaret has made me aware of this and also how valuable our own health is, how vulnerable we all are. Another area is leaving the worldly daily stress behind as you walk up the path to the house. I have begun to handle my daily life differently .... So today I talked, we talked, about these areas of our lives. It was good. It is good."

Wendy did two shifts a week, one with her husband, Nigel Turner, on Sundays and the other by herself on a weekday afternoon, during which she cleaned and gathered up soiled clothes and towels. She and Mary Hiseler, the next-door neighbour, shared the laundry chores.

Wendy and Nigel are an arresting couple, both attractive, intelligent, complex people. Each had been married before and hurtfully deserted by the spouse. They have near-grown children from their previous marriages whom they have pleated together within a tall house in the Toronto Beaches area.

Wendy is intuitive, funny, and sparkling, while Nigel has the brooding, stormy disposition of a blond Heathcliff. Wendy, forty-four, was for many years a teacher of Grades 2 and 3 in an elementary school. Linda Rapson's daughters, Kate and Rachel Manning, were in her classes for two years, and Linda credits Wendy with imbuing them with a love of learning. "Wendy's classes were always noisy, busy, and bright," Linda recalls.

Nigel is also forty-four, an oil broker, who smiles smugly when accused of male chauvinism. Nigel was the surprise element on

137

the Margaret team, a restless, impatient man inexplicably volunteering to help an old woman die. But Nigel's visits late on Sunday
afternoons delighted Margaret almost most of all.

It was Nigel's Codetron machine that Margaret used while the
one on loan was having its battery recharger repaired. Nigel had
purchased the machine after a visit to Linda Rapson. His blood
pressure had been high for more that a year, and his own diagnosis
of his condition, arrived at in the absence of medical opinion,
was that stress was the cause. Though Linda expressed doubt that
the Codetron would relieve Nigel's high blood pressure, which
she correctly suspected was caused by an organic condition, he
insisted on trying it.

The symptom had alarming implications for him. Seven years
earlier Nigel's life had been saved by an open-heart operation
during which surgeons implanted a plastic valve. Though his
elevated blood pressure was reason to inquire if his heart might
be malfunctioning, Nigel stubbornly refused to submit to tests.
He is loud in his admiration for people who resist doctors and
refuse conventional treatment. I took this to be a manifestation
of Nigel's terror and his fear of helplessness.

Instead of having his heart checked, he kept to a regimen of
punishing physical activity that would have staggered a well man.
He engaged in work at his farm that involved lifting huge stones,
and on several occasions he rode his bicycle to Margaret's, a
distance of about ten hilly miles.

I visited Nigel in Sunnybrook Hospital one July afternoon, a
month after Margaret's death. He had been taken there, protesting, when his blood pressure dropped by half. The plastic valve
in his heart was leaking blood, but the apparatus was making
such a noise the doctors couldn't tell by listening what had happened. The next morning he would have a test, a tricky one for
someone in his precarious condition.

Wendy met me at the door of the cardiac unit, her eyes desperate but her smile glowing. She had brought some knitting with
a complicated pattern to help distract her.

Nigel, sedated and connected to a monitor, so that nurses in the cardiac station could watch his heartbeat on a screen, was pacing in the confined space beside his bed.

Wendy brought me tea in a Styrofoam cup and reminisced about Margaret. "She told me many times that she had always believed her importance and value lay in what she could do for others," Wendy said. "She never thought she mattered for herself alone. She had never really allowed people to give to her."

"I totally understand that," Nigel said curtly, still pacing.

Wendy smiled. "I know you do." She resumed, "Margaret was overwhelmed by the love and giving that came to her. For the first time in her life, she had a sense of being loved for herself. There was nothing she could do for us, really. People came to her house with no expectations of receiving something back, so she had to believe we loved her."

Nigel said, a stillness in his face, "I'm in the same spot. No one knows until you go through it how moving it is when people support you in a time of trouble."

Wendy withdrew, and Nigel answered my questions about Margaret. He had joined Holy Trinity, he said, because his wife "ran away with the vicar" of the church he had been attending and he needed to find another church for his children. When he went into hospital in 1978 for the valve implant, he was astonished that people from Holy Trinity rallied around to visit and show affection.

"Margaret was the lady who did the hymns," he went on. "I didn't like a lot of her choices. She liked experimental hymns, and I'm more comfortable with traditional ones. There are lots of women of her generation around Holy Trinity. They're all first-class persons, but I didn't know any of them especially."

He heard that Margaret was dying at a time when he must have had doubts about his own survival. He found himself thinking that he was too much occupied with business, that he should contribute more to helping others. "So I went to that first meeting at Holy Trinity and grabbed the Sunday-evening vacancy in the schedule."

Jay MacGillivray complained to me about a man at that meeting who read a newspaper throughout the discussion. She didn't know who he was, she said, but she had to control an impulse to kick him. The man, of course, was Nigel.

Nigel took a business-like approach to the responsibility he had assumed. Since he had little in common with Margaret, he had to find a territory that they could occupy together. "On Saturdays I'd sit down and think through what I could bring her. It was like a teacher preparing for a class. It was Margaret's time, so it was important that she get as much out of it as she could."

Once he took material about Greece and another time something to do with art. One Sunday he brought an illustrated book about birds and was enchanted that she was touched. For an hour she turned the pages, exclaiming over the birds and recalling times when she had seen each one while birding. He soon settled on Margaret's favourite subject, music. He played her some tapes he had in his car. A perfectionist, he was critical of the sound reproduction on her inexpensive hand-size radio and tape machine, so he replaced it on his next visit with a big and expensive one that provided splendid sound. He refused her offers to repay him, making it clear that he wanted to make her a gift. Margaret was thrilled with the machine and kept it beside her on a table pulled up to the couch. Eventually she mastered the intricacies of its operation.

After that, Nigel brought tapes from his home collection, "trying to get a sense of where she was at". When he thought he had it, he purchased Vivaldi's *Four Seasons* in a classical rendition and then a jazz version by Moe Kauffman, the Canadian flutist. Nigel and Margaret enjoyed a spirited discussion of the merits of each. "I thought she might be interested in classical jazz, and she was," he told me with satisfaction.

After that his weekly goal was to bring her something outside her normal realm of music. "I found I was thinking a lot about what to bring Margaret on Sundays. I didn't want us to just fill in time, I wanted what we talked about to be relevant."

That sense of the preciousness of a dying person's time came from Nigel's experience with his father, who died in hospital of brain cancer. Though his father often was so confused that communication between them was poor, there were a few lucid moments when the two men exchanged awareness. Nigel treasures these as "the high points". Valuing mental alertness and communication as he did, he was determined to give Margaret the pleasure of having her brain fully in gear.

"I learned with Margaret that you didn't have to know someone very long to know them well," Nigel reflected. "It doesn't take years of history. When people are dying, the bullshit disappears. I learned that with my dad. You can talk without trying to impress."

Margaret Frazer and Nigel Turner could not have been farther apart in their views on politics, on the economy, or on feminist theory and practice, but they talked animatedly about all those topics. A lot was happening in Ontario at that time: the Tory government that had ruled Ontario for two generations was coming down, and funding had been extended in the separate-school system. "She was knowledgeable and had historical perspective," he said. "We also talked about equal pay for work of equal value, about disarmament, about U.S. President Reagan. She was left wing, and I have more of a businessman's approach. She would put out a point of view I hadn't considered. I got a lot out of it."

While Wendy moved around the house doing the cleaning, amused and pleased for them both, Margaret scolded Nigel, and he scoffed at her. "Typical male," Nigel admitted. "I did the good stuff, and Wendy did the chores."

Nigel found Margaret full of surprises. He had expected that she would have an ecclesiastical view of Christianity, but he found her faith, like his own, embodied in a personal sense of God.

"I looked forward to Sundays at four o'clock," he said, hitching his dressing-gown around his thin body and pacing again. "It was a very giving relationship for me. By and large, I'm a taker. It felt very good that what I put out for her was accepted. It sounds a bit like the joy of giving, I know, but I've never gone through that before."

His face was intent as he explored how he felt about Margaret.

"It wasn't a chore, it took no effort. Intimate relationships take no effort. Whatever comes is okay, it flows. And it happened so quickly. Here in the middle of my life I was suddenly devoting five hours a week of my life to a lady I hardly knew."

He thought a moment. "It was mysterious. There were no expectations, nothing to get in the way. We both understood where she was. She didn't have to put on airs. If she wanted to go to sleep in the middle of the conversation, she was free to do that. I would wait until she came around." He paused again. "For me to be in a hundred per cent giving environment and feel good about it, that was new."

Margaret was again losing weight. She confessed to Linda the morning after the second meeting in the church that she wasn't eating as well and her abdomen was sore. Many of the team's entries in the log-book opened with "Margaret was very tired when I arrived...." Fran noticed when she gave Margaret a foot-rub that her right ankle seemed puffy. Linda made the same observation and concealed her distress. She had been checking from the start for swollen ankles, which could be an ominous sign, and was sorry to see them appear.

On Tuesday, April 30, Heather Sutherland, a Holy Trinity woman with an eager, arms-open style, came for her shift, driving a considerable distance from a cottage where she was holed up to write her doctoral thesis on industrial management. It was her inspiration to put Margaret and the wheelchair into her car and drive to Edwards Gardens. She wrote in the log-book: "Edwards Gardens was wonderful, complete with wheelchair routes. Margaret just loved being out and seeing, seeing, seeing."

That same day the award-winning novelist Joy Kogawa dropped in for a visit. Joy is a congregant at Holy Trinity and had shared with Margaret her pain over the failure of the Canadian government to make apologies or reparations to Canadians of Japanese descent who lost their possessions and freedom in the Second World War.

After that busy time, Margaret seemed remote and in pain. The next day, Linda brought Hilda Powicke for a visit, since

Hilda was unable to make the trip by herself. The three of them had a great talk, Margaret later reported to me, about birds and flowers. Hilda had been feeling left out, despite her usefulness as an information post, and was grateful to see Margaret and the setting she had been hearing so much about. "What a lovely, peaceful place," she wrote in the log. "I feel more a part of the whole thing now."

For Linda, the euphoria of Margaret's apparent improvement was over. She noted that Margaret's feet and legs were swelling. On the good side, the Codetron seemed to be effective. Counting up the medication in the month since Margaret left hospital, Linda noted in the log that the daily dose of Tylenol No. 3 averaged a mere 0.6. "Yes, I have a calculator," she informed the team cheerfully.

The next day Buffy wrote, "This morning the birds and Margaret are bathing; the lawns are being tended front and back, and we need more milk. I would like to have more time here. Will anyone give me some?"

Elaine Hall noticed on Thursday that Margaret's legs felt cold. That day, election day in Ontario, Anne Grasham took Margaret's proxy and voted the New Democratic Party candidate for her. It had taken three telephone calls to the campaign office of her candidate before the proxy was delivered, but Margaret was horrified at the suggestion that she not bother voting. She wasn't going to let dying interfere with the responsibilities of citizenship.

I hadn't heard of the ominous new symptoms and arrived that afternoon expecting to see Margaret in a bouncing mood. I brought some yellow tulips and some chicken soup I had made, and also a bright pink jogging suit. Margaret was asleep as I quietly let myself in the door, and I was shocked that her face looked so ill and even bonier. On the floor beside the couch and on the coffee table next to Nigel's stereo set were stacks of tapes. The house was sparkling clean (Elaine Hall), serene, and full of flowers. A bouquet of pink tulips stood on the hall table, a pot of yellow mums was in the window, and a sheaf of forsythia was glowing from the table near the piano.

143

Margaret opened her eyes and life poured back into her face. I complimented her on her new haircut, cropped at the back where it had been matted from lying against pillows, and smooth and short in front. She said her favourite hairdresser had made a house call. She told me about the visit to Edwards Gardens and two trips around the block in the wheelchair, talking in a rush of enthusiasm that didn't blind me to the fact that she was squirming in discomfort.

I helped her use the Codetron and noted that her swollen feet were icy cold. I suggested a heating pad and some down booties from a shop specializing in camp gear; she was willing to try both. She settled down to read Isak Dinesen's *Out of Africa*, and I warmed up the soup. Two small girls knocked shyly – Gwen and Jenny Hiseler, Gwen with tiny flowers she had picked and Jenny with a big piece of warm pound cake on a plate. Margaret beamed at them and gave me specific instructions where to find a tiny vase that would fit the flowers.

As spring darkness began to fall, I lit the rosy lamp and took my place in the rocking chair. I found a curious lethargy about Margaret, a sadness and stillness that had not been there before. I wondered if she was going to die like that, a gentle drift into passivity. She told me she had abandoned the Simonton image of birds eating insects for her meditation sessions. Instead she was picturing gardeners getting rid of cutworms and grubs.

"Mostly I think of Fran fighting the cutworms and grubs because she's such a good gardener," Margaret said, with a flash of her old spirit.

After a moment she said, "Linda always says the right thing." I thought she would tell me again about Linda saying "If anyone can make it, Margaret, you can," but this was another occasion. Margaret and Linda had been talking about the Simonton method and Margaret had confessed she was feeling discouraged. Linda had turned to her, eyes blazing, and said, "You've got to keep it up, Margaret. We *need* you."

I held her cold feet. She closed her eyes and said, "I love you." I said, "I love you too."

That night I dreamed about my friend Stoney Jackson Robinson, who died of a stroke at the age of forty-nine. We had shared an apartment in wartime Toronto before either of us was married, and we remained close afterwards. She and I used to joke that we would spend our old age together as full-blown eccentrics in red wigs, drinking sherry. In my dream, Stoney died again.

I popped by Margaret's the next day with an electric heating pad and some down-filled booties the colour of violets. Merylie Houston, a small, vivid, perky woman from the Holy Trinity network, told me she was just about to go shopping for a hot-water bottle. Margaret was on her couch under the green mohair blanket, dressed in the pink jogging pants, a pink T-shirt, and a pink sweatshirt. She assured me she loved her new clothes. We both knew she never in her life had worn the colour pink, but she didn't mention it. I apologized, nevertheless, explaining that the shade of blue available in that outfit was dreary.

Margaret told me Sheila Mackenzie had noticed that she was having difficulty with the two-cushion surface of her small couch. The space between the cushions had become irritating to her skin. Sheila's sublime solution was to order a one-piece futon. She had taken the measurements of the couch, and a mattress to replace the cushions would be delivered in a few days.

Margaret said with a smile of bliss, "I feel so pampered by you both that I may never get up." Then she realized what she had said, and she stiffened. "Yes, I will!" she cried, and we laughed.

Margaret told Linda that day how much she liked her new track suit. "I knew I was uncomfortable," she said, "but I didn't know what I needed."

Nancy Dodington was there when the futon was delivered. Margaret made a great fuss, Nancy said understandingly, about it fitting just right. "It was her special place for her final months, so it had to be the way she wanted it. Very clearly, Margaret had chosen her place by the front door where she could peek out the window when she wanted to, on top of everything that was going on."

145

One morning when Jay was helping her dress, Margaret referred to her growing collection of multi-coloured jogging clothes as "June's noble attempt to get me into contemporary clothing".

Sheila Mackenzie's entry in the log-book showed a different interpretation of Margaret's new mood. Where I had seen resignation and sorrow in Margaret, she described her as "calm, relaxed, and *grounded* – more natural than I have experienced before. She is getting used to us being here and doesn't have to rise to the occasion so much."

Mary Hiseler came from next door with news that depressed Margaret. The family was selling the house, and she wanted to warn Margaret before the real-estate agent's sign was posted on the front lawn. In fact, the house was sold the day it was offered. The Hiselers and their three children would be moving at the end of June. The log entries for days afterwards reflected Margaret's distress. She asked Pat Capponi, who came Friday nights, "Where can we find a four-year-old who asks her mother for gloves so her fingers won't fly away, and a hat so her thoughts won't spill from her head?" That was Gwen.

Margaret's house was ready for the summer. A handyman had come to remove the heavy wood-framed storm windows and replace them with screens. Deck chairs stored in the garage had been washed and were arranged on the lawn near the roses. Fran Sowton had planted flowers in the window-box on the front steps. Cleo had been shorn of the knotted fur on her belly and took to preening herself on the window-sill of the living-room's bay windows. Bluebirds had nested in a maple behind the house. Violets and a huge jack-in-the-pulpit were blooming at the end of the garden. We awaited the unfolding of a death amid abundant signs of life.

On May 6, a Monday, Linda's friend Barbara Scullion died. Linda hesitated whether to tell Margaret, but concluded that Margaret would sense her desolation and think it had to do with her own state. When Margaret heard the news, she reacted with a depth of compassion that touched Linda to the heart.

Margaret's capacity to empathize with Linda and with all of us was astonishing and gallant in one so gravely ill. She used the private time she had with team members to ask what each was doing with an interest that wasn't superficial. The concentration of attention she brought to bear when she asked, "What are you doing these days?" was such that people poured out confessions and fears. The conditions for confidences were ideal: the transactions with the woman on the couch could not be overheard and would not be interrupted, and the woman on the couch was a good listener – sympathetic, supportive, intelligent. Moreover, the imperative of her dying relieved everyone of the burden of concealment.

Somehow Margaret retained everything people told her. Though she grew confused about many things, she never mixed up one person's pain over a difficult marriage with another person's despair about a disturbed teenager. Weeks after Grace and Chris Ross confided that they wanted a child, she said to them during a sweet parting, "I hope you get your baby soon." She remembered trivia as well. She never forgot that I was writing a book about emotions against a tight deadline. "How is it going?" she would ask anxiously. "Did you finish the chapter on hate yet?"

Her determination to preserve her healthy self – the one that had been a growing person involved to the hilt in activities of the community – was nowhere more apparent than in her interest in a Nellie's fund-raising project. Patti Welsh, a member of the Nellie's fund-raising committee, did her first shift on the team in May and told Margaret about plans to sponsor a theatre benefit in June during the run of a highly successful play, *Trafford Tanzi*. Margaret knew the play, a comedy about a woman wrestler that carries a strong feminist message, and was pleased. After that she wanted progress reports whenever she could buttonhole a Nellie's fund raiser. When one such person, Jackie White-Hampton, paid a visit that same week expecting to find a pale invalid, Margaret was full of sharp questions and copious advice about promotion and ticket sales.

Wednesday, May 8, was the day of the funeral of Linda's friend Barbara Scullion, and the next day Linda gave a tribute at a memorial service attended by seven hundred mourners. She found it difficult to speak, but she got through it. She went to see Margaret afterwards, bringing a copy of the eulogy she had written. They sat in the sunshine in the back yard and Margaret read it. She told Linda, whose face still bore the marks of tears, that the words were beautiful. Linda was inconsolable. She explained that she was grieving not only over the loss of her friend but also over her failure to be able to relieve her friend's agony.

"Seeing you so comfortable with your disease gladdens my heart," she said.

Margaret burst out, "Linda, where would I be without you?"

The medical record that Linda was keeping about Margaret's condition shows the decline that began that week. The first signs were the swollen legs and feet and the enlarged abdomen. Linda listened to the sounds in Margaret's belly with growing anxiety. "Shifting dullness?" she wrote on Sunday, May 5. The next day she noted an incident indicating a slight loss of bowel control; Margaret's pattern had changed from constipation to diarrhea. On May 8, she wrote, "Shifting dullness for sure." The fluid was increasing and the tumours were growing.

The next day, a Thursday, was my shift. Though the breeze had an edge of chill in it, the sky was cloudless and the sun bathed the new-green lawns and trees with lovely light. Margaret's house was empty. Her pillows and blanket were arranged on the couch, but the downstairs was vacant. I looked in her bedroom and the bathroom. Cleo was curled on the guest bed where people on overnight shifts slept, but had no information. I even searched the basement, recently vacated by the tenant. Then I made myself some tea and sat down to wait.

If I had looked in the log, there would have been no mystery. Buffy Carruthers had telephoned the night before to arrange to take Margaret to the Toronto Islands for an outing. They returned about an hour later, glowing, and we helped Margaret up the porch stairs, out of her coat, and on to the couch. "It went very well," Buffy assured me as we hauled the wheelchair out of her car trunk.

It went much better than well. Buffy had planned carefully with the object of reducing stress on Margaret to a minimum. A small act of thoughtfulness, but one that Margaret noticed and commented gratefully to me about, was that Buffy didn't initiate conversation during the long drive to the Toronto ferry docks. She felt, correctly, that the impact of traffic, noise, and buildings was all that Margaret could handle.

"I wanted her to feel coddled so she wouldn't be anxious," Buffy explained later. "I took the corners smoothly and tried to brake without jarring her. I had checked the parking lot in advance, so I knew just where to go. I brought a down-filled sleeping bag to keep her warm, and I thought a lot about our picnic lunch: a sandwich for me, but soft cheese, yoghurt, and strawberries for Margaret. And a thermos of tea."

While they waited for the ferry, Margaret got out of the wheelchair and curled on a bench in the fetal position. Buffy didn't fuss over her; she felt that Margaret was conserving energy. The men of the ferry boat crew behaved like courtiers to the white-haired ill-looking woman in the wheelchair, rushing to help Buffy push her up the ramp and to find her a snug place on the protected deck.

Once on Centre Island, Buffy pushed the wheelchair in the direction of Hanlan's Point until they saw a small church. It drew them, and they found behind it a hidden rise of land overlooking the inland waterway. Buffy spread the sleeping bag under the trees, and Margaret stretched out and was enfolded in its down. They ate their lunch and found that the tea in the thermos had cooled. It didn't matter.

"It was bizarre, in a way," Buffy reflected. "We strangely felt very close, very connected. Like lovers almost. There was so much tenderness between us."

Margaret's mood after Buffy left was so soft that it reached me and took out the prickles that had developed over a hectic week. "I saw a black-and-white warbler climbing a tree, eating grubs," she said, her voice like music. "I'm sure it was a black-and-white warbler. Would you mind bringing me my bird book? It's over there, on the ledge by the dining-room window. That's it, thank you. And yes, *yes*! Here it is! It *was* a black-and-white warbler."

She said she felt wonderful – "all that freshness in me" – and marvelled at "the sense of distance, seeing so far" after a month of rarely leaving her living-room couch. I thought she would be tired and in need of sleep, but she preferred to bask and reflect. "Buffy brought all the right things for me to eat," she said at one point. And at another, "I'll remember this day a long time. I've stored up so much beauty."

Sheila Mackenzie found us that night in semi-darkness in the living-room, afloat in peacefulness. Sheila wrote in the log the next morning, "M very contented.... She has taken in much good energy through her eyes. They are rich in colour and retain some of that this morning. The sun on her face gave good colour – pink nose. *Ave* Buffy Carruthers!"

Days later, the log was still resonating with praise of Buffy. Pat Capponi wrote on Saturday morning, "*Buffy*! Nice going. You've done something very important – very neat."

I didn't meet Pat Capponi until Margaret's wake, when she stood out from the team members milling through Margaret's house because of her quality of stillness; her face a watchful mask, she wore a straight-brimmed black Peruvian hat level over her eyes. A few weeks later I went to talk to her about Margaret at a Queen Street West storefront called PARC, for Parkdale Activity and Recreation Centre.

She greeted me at the door and conducted me through the place, a former bowling alley that now serves as a drop-in centre for ex-psychiatric patients. It was plain that Pat Capponi is loved there. Men with twisted faces and tattooed arms joshed with her, small children ran up for hugs, wary-eyed women gave her radiant smiles and wanted to see her when she had a minute.

Pat is a staff person on PARC, but there is no distance between her and the people who use the centre. She knows all about emotional hell. We sat in her upstairs office where she could keep an eye on a mongrel puppy, Rufus, as he circled the newspaper she had spread for his comfort station. She's thirty-six, a small lean woman with long dark hair straight on her shoulders. She wears soft jeans and shirts and a Yasser Arafat PLO scarf, and walks with the easy loping gait of a Native person, though her heritage is Italian.

Her father was abusive, "so we all grew up a little strange", she explains with a grin. Whenever she wasn't in hospital for psychotic depression, she attended community colleges in Montreal and excelled in creative arts and English. Though a volume of her poetry was published, she didn't have much time for an education. She's been in hospital seven times for depression and suicide attempts, once for five months.

"I don't generally trust people," Pat said to me, noting approvingly that the puppy had urinated on the newspaper, "but Margaret was at ease with me, and not everyone is. For some reason, I trusted her." They met when a story about Pat Capponi was printed in the *Toronto Star* early in 1980 because of Pat's work to organize ex-psychiatric patients whose housing was deplorable. Margaret telephoned to invite her to a meeting at Nellie's and she went.

"Jay MacGillivray was there, and Liz Greaves, and some other people," Pat recalled. Margaret persuaded Pat that she was needed in the Supportive Housing Coalition because it was top-heavy with agency people, some of them at the removed level of executive directors. Pat's direct experience and intelligent judgement would be valuable assets, Margaret said. Pat accepted, though reluctantly; she knew the sessions would not be pleasant for her. She finds jargon and patronizing professionals hard to take, but Margaret Frazer was the redeeming factor.

"She always supported me. If there was a dispute, she backed me up. That was always there with Margaret, the loyalty. You go through tons of meetings when you do advocacy and see lots of people who are interesting, but you only touch base with them. It's only with a few that something clicks and you know everything is cool. That was Margaret."

Pat was stunned to hear in the fall of 1984 that Margaret had resigned from the Supportive Housing Coalition because of poor health. The next report was that Margaret was in hospital. Pat called her and learned that Margaret would be having surgery for cancer. Pat's first impulse, which she termed "cowardly", was to stay away. She has been handling her depression on her own for four years, without therapy or drugs, and she feared that exposing herself to Margaret's illness would put her back in hospital.

Nevertheless, she went. "When I got to Margaret's room she was just coming out of the anaesthetic and she was confused. She took me for her doctor. When she saw that it was me, she apologized. She knew that the last thing I'd want to be taken for was a doctor."

Pat asked about her plans, and Margaret said, "I want to go home."

Later, when Pat heard about the team, she called Joyce Brown and said, "Put me on the list." The risks for her mental health were enormous, but she weighed them against her feelings for Margaret, and the risks lost. She picked Friday overnight shifts because that's one night when committees don't meet. Pat is on numerous committees dealing with the difficulties psychiatric patients face, and she doesn't like to miss a meeting because usually she's the only consumer representative.

"I was really spooked the first time I did a shift at Margaret's," Pat remarked, her eyes on the puppy, who had fallen asleep at her feet. "I thought she had accepted that she was dying, but she kept saying things like, 'When I get rid of this cancer ...' I felt really sad, because there's no dignity in not facing death, in pretending you can beat it. But after a while I came to believe, too, that she could beat it."

Margaret showed her the Simonton book and explained the theory. Pat thought it couldn't hurt to believe in it, but she wondered why Margaret was struggling. "Being a crazy," Pat explained, "I wondered why she would fight it. There was no victory possible." She grinned, "For me, it would have been an exit ticket."

She lit a cigarette. "I had something to learn from her, that's for sure. I wondered how many people would wait around, fighting it."

Pat never overcame her fear that being with Margaret would flip her into another psychotic depression. "It's hard to see someone hurting and not be able to help them. It sets up an agony." Yet Joyce Brown said that Pat Capponi was one of the handful of shift workers who were the most willing to come in an emergency. Pat cheerfully offered, several times, to stay with Margaret for an entire weekend if she was needed.

Getting the hang of Margaret's kitchen and fixed habits was embarrassing. Pat felt inept and alien in Margaret's regimented environment. "I'm such a klutz, Margaret, you'll have to bear with me," she would say as she struggled with some of Margaret's artifacts, like the tea cosy.

"She was very patient with me," Pat recalled. "She probably knew that I would wither away and die if she lost her temper. I wouldn't know things, like what to do with sheets, and she would say, 'Pat, we all come from different backgrounds.'"

In the beginning, Pat recalled, Margaret fretted about people doing so much for her. "I'm so used to taking care of myself," she complained. Pat said to her what Grace Ross had said, only more economically: "There are two ways of giving, Margaret, and one of them is taking."

Margaret and Pat found a lot to discuss. They talked about birds. Pat adores birds and was amazed that there are different birds in the suburbs from the ones she saw in Parkdale. They talked also about the Supportive Housing Coalition, with Margaret avid to keep abreast of developments. Margaret worried about coalition documents in her possession that she thought the committee might find useful. One day Pat sorted them out and delivered them to the committee. "Margaret was so relieved when I did that. It had been pressing on her mind."

Pat adjusted her habits to Margaret. Though she usually retires late, she sensed that Margaret wouldn't sleep if she wasn't upstairs, so she went to bed when Margaret did. "I read," she explained.

Pat doesn't eat breakfast, but she managed to down a muffin every Saturday morning because it was clear Margaret didn't want to eat alone.

The routine changed in mid-May, when month-long Ramadan begins, because Pat is a Sunni Muslim. She was obliged to fast every day from four in the morning until nine at night. The fast is total: not even water is permitted. To survive the long parching day, Sunni Muslims eat and drink at about 3:30 a.m. Margaret assured Pat that she wasn't disturbed when Pat went to the kitchen, but Pat always felt that Margaret was only being kind and kept her movements to a minimum.

To Pat's amusement and the surprise of other team members, Margaret had abandoned modesty as a hopeless cause, despite the Baptist upbringing and a lifetime of reserve. She would emerge mornings from the bathroom naked and still dripping from her shower, a towel draped jauntily over one shoulder, and stand unabashed in the doorway of the guest bedroom. "She had more energy in the morning," Pat recalled. "She was so proud that she could do it, standing there like a fighter. She would say, in that trilling voice of hers, 'Good morning, Pat.' It blew me away."

Margaret mentioned Pat's name when we talked in our lazy fashion on the evening of the trip to the Toronto Islands. She said she appreciated the time she had with people because she was learning how remarkable they really were. She named a few examples. First, Linda Rapson. "What a privilege to have time to know her." Fran Sowton was another. And Jackie White-Hampton. And Pat Capponi. "You don't know Pat? Too bad." Buffy Carruthers, "especially Buffy". Wendy and Nigel; "I have great talks with Nigel." Diana Wedlock. "Do you know that Diana Wedlock changes her life every ten years, as a matter of policy?" I didn't, though I had served for years on a Nellie's housing committee with Diana. Margaret was full of information about Diana that I didn't know: that she is a biologist, that she teaches science environmental studies and women's studies at Seneca College. I marvelled and Margaret grinned at me.

She put back her head and let out a long breath. She said, "I'm so happy."

That next day, Saturday, May 11, Margaret fussed about how thin she was. Except for her distended abdomen and swollen legs, it was true she was a skeleton. Sheila File was there and gave Margaret assurances on the spot, which she reinforced in the log-book. We all knew Margaret read the log. "Margaret complained about being *bony*," Sheila wrote, "but to me she is cuddly and loveable and so appreciative and easy to love."

Linda, visiting the next day, noted that Margaret's legs were becoming grotesque. Not for the first time, she suggested a diuretic, but Margaret was adamantly opposed. Linda made some adjustments in the Codetron schedule and changed bowel control measures. She noted, with pleasure, that Margaret had not needed a Tylenol No. 3 for a week. All of this was written in the log, which Linda concluded by printing in big letters, "BUFFY: YOU'RE GREAT!!!"

Christopher Ross, nervous without Grace, did a shift the next day. It was his first time alone with Margaret, but he was not the first man to solo. Besides Bill Whitla, who was in Greece, there had been Ian Sowton filling in for his wife. Fran Sowton had been delayed an hour or so by the need to finish stitching eucharistic garments – a chasuble, and stole – to be shipped to a priest in England, so Ian agreed to stay with Margaret until Fran could get there. He spent the time mostly working in the garden.

Chris confessed acute embarrassment. "A friend from Kingston visited Margaret, and I found my situation ambiguous. Was I the maid, or the nurse, or the gatekeeper? I couldn't very well say, 'By the way, I'm a doctor of psychology.' I decided I was the educated servant and offered tea. Then I dithered around in the garden."

Chris avoided the meetings of the team, where he knew other men would be scarce. The preponderance of women reminded him of his discomfort as a boy when his mother would entertain her friends and he found himself in a room full of women talking about the women's world where he had no place. He often wished there were more men among the Friends of Margaret.

It was Christopher Ross, however, who used the expression

155

that caring for Margaret was like a Zen experience. "I was always reluctant to go to Margaret's, dreading it," he admitted, "but once there I never felt any pain. It was a real affirmation of my spirituality in the sense of what I've come to believe in, and a plumbing of the intuitive depths."

The physical changes Linda had noted were beginning to be reflected intermittently in signs of a weakened body. Margaret was climbing the stairs more laboriously, though she still refused help. It seemed to take her longer to get to her feet from the low couch. On Monday, May 13, Fran Sowton noticed that Margaret had difficulty supporting the heavy book she was reading. Fran suggested that she read it to Margaret and Margaret agreed. That same day Margaret said she was bothered that she wasn't answering her mail. Fran wrote several notes of reply while Margaret dictated.

Margaret had a bewildering capacity to bounce back from such lows. Two days later when Helen Cram was with her, Margaret seemed full of vim. Twice she went to the piano and played. She announced ebulliently that she intended to practise every day, "so I don't get rusty". The next morning, she went purposefully to the piano before breakfast and played finger-independence exercises, but was discouraged that she couldn't make the notes sound the same. When she stood to return to the couch, she fell. Buffy was there and helped her to her feet. Margaret, luckily unhurt, maintained stoutly that her fall happened because she didn't get up slowly enough. After that she slept for a long time. There is no further mention in the log of piano playing.

When I arrived at Margaret's for my Thursday shift on May 17, Merylie Houston had just left after a day of gardening. Margaret insisted that I see the jack-in-the-pulpit and slowly escorted me to the end of the garden, proudly calling my attention to the fact that she wasn't using a cane. The flower was indeed impressive, the largest I'd ever seen. Margaret was full of enthusiasm for her "three gifted gardeners", Merylie, Fran Sowton, and Elaine Hall, and took me on a tour of the newly pruned and sprayed rose bushes, the newly staked delphiniums, and a newly planted clump of violets.

She was calling the team "my people". She stopped, steadying herself on my arm, and exclaimed, "And they are all knitting together beautifully! I can't get over it."

I said, "You don't think it might have something to do with you, do you?"

She made an impatient gesture. Then she looked at me sharply and said, "I hope someone is going to write about this. It really is remarkable."

I was uncomfortable. I had decided to write about her and the team in a weekly *Globe and Mail* column I do, and to that end I had begun to keep notes. Part of me viewed my Margaret diary as ghoulish and an abuse of friendship, and part of me saw it as important social history, a record of an extraordinary person and the human tribe at its functioning best.

"If I ever meet a writer," I promised Margaret, "I'll mention it." She gave my arm a squeeze, and the bargain was sealed.

Back on her couch, she chatted on the cordless telephone, and I heard her tell a friend, Jean Burnet, a former professor of sociology at the University of Toronto with whom Margaret had shared a flat in the fifties, that she was planning to join a Simonton healing group for cancer patients. "There's nothing the doctors can do for my cancer, so I'm going ahead with the Simonton thing," she explained.

She was appalled that the healing group had no plans to meet until after the summer. "How can they wait?" she said to me indignantly. "If you've got cancer you want to get rid of it as soon as possible." I said we would try to find another group with more interest in survival. The team did try, but without success.

That evening, after listening to some Mozart, Margaret talked a bit about her years at Bloor Collegiate. "The kids were so intriguing," she mused. "We had thirty-three nationalities in that school, and I was supposed to teach them English literature. When I assigned compositions I always marked them on their ideas rather than the way they expressed themselves. I felt I had no right to judge them by the way they expressed themselves in a language that wasn't their own."

She grinned. "It was quite a challenge to teach Chinese kids

157

about the indefinite article. It baffled them, and it baffled me how to do it."

The next day Linda called with a truly wonderful idea. She had heard that Margaret's great idol, the flutist Jean Baxtresser, would be playing with the Toronto Symphony Orchestra in Roy Thomson Hall the following Wednesday. She had four tickets. "How about us taking Margaret? You and me and Buffy and Margaret?"

I had an engagement that night and so did Buffy, but we cancelled them.

Margaret was in a dither of preparations. She decided on a new dress made of a piece of silk she had purchased in China. With the belt removed, it was soft enough to fit over her tender abdomen. She arranged to have the hairdresser come the day before the concert to wash her hair. She had it all worked out, she told Pat Capponi on Saturday. She would do nothing but rest on Wednesday so she would be sure to have her strength for the evening.

When Linda made her Sunday house visit, she examined Margaret's legs and noted with dismay that they were growing more bloated. Her feet were so puffy she could wear nothing but the down-filled booties, and one of her toes was blackened with a bruise. Linda had consulted the specialist, her cousin-in-law, Larry Librach, who recommended a drug to reduce the fluid and a contraption called a Jobst pump that would squeeze the fluid in her feet and legs.

Michael Creal, an Anglican priest and member of Holy Trinity, came that day to bring Margaret Holy Communion, as he had been doing since Bill Whitla's departure. Glenys McMullen, a humorous, sensible woman from Holy Trinity, was there for the rite and made a note in the log-book: "Michael Creal is giving M communion wearing Fran's beautiful stole. We all enjoy bringing what we can here, but I always end by taking more home with me in the way of peace and lovely memories."

Ian Sowton came with Fran the next morning, Monday, May 20 – the Victoria Day holiday. He was "learning the drill", as Fran put it, because he would be replacing her when she went to London the following week to take an embroidery course. They worked in the garden and, when Linda called, Margaret reported gaily, "It's so nifty. Getting all this gardening done."

I arrived as the Sowtons were leaving, disappointed that a heavy cold rain prevented them from putting in the remainder of the annuals they had been planting. Margaret had finished reading Susan Crean's fine book *Women and the Media*, and was engrossed in the thick book Fran had been reading to her, *Holy Blood, Holy Grail*, a history of medieval religion. Three times she struggled to her feet and, with me holding her arm tightly, climbed the stairs to the bathroom. "Three bowel movements," she told me wearily. "I like to think they're full of cancer cells that I'm getting rid of."

We dined in the living-room on leek soup and a bit of salmon mousse that I had purchased at the take-out counter of Fenton's, one of Toronto's most beautiful restaurants. The young man who weighed the mousse asked if I was one of the people taking care of Margaret Frazer. I was startled. "I live a few houses away," he explained. "We watch you people going in and out. The whole street is talking about this gang who's helping her. We think it's wonderful. If I can help, like mowing the lawn or something, let me know."

I told Margaret about him while we ate. She was puzzled for a minute, trying to place him, and then her face cleared. She recalled him well. During the last few years that she was a teacher, and just after her roomer left, a number of youngsters on the street used to drop in regularly. Most of them were ten to twelve years old. "I think they were concerned for me because I was alone. Sometimes I'd get out some instruments, harmonicas, bongos, and other things, and they would play. Sometimes we'd sing around the piano. Sometimes they just sat in the kitchen and groused about their teachers while I prepared my dinner."

She was reflective. "That was very nice. I never fed them, so I knew they didn't come for that. They just ... *came*." When they became teenagers, the visits stopped, which didn't surprise her.

With the concert only two days off, she was full of expectation.

159

Looking at her feet, inflated with fluid to twice their normal size, she wondered what shoes would fit. I urged her to wear the down booties, but she was shocked. One didn't wear booties to a concert. "We'll put a blanket over your lap to hide your feet," I said.

"Hmmm," said Margaret, head to one side, picturing it. "Which blanket?"

I searched her linen closet, but there was nothing suitable. "I've got a light-weight white cotton blanket, the kind with a thermal weave," I remembered. "It will be perfect."

We listened to an Irish singer, Mary O'Hara, on a tape that Margaret had received from Helen Gough. Margaret told me about Mary O'Hara. She said the singer had been overcome with grief when her husband of only one year, a handsome young poet, died. She entered a cloistered convent and for twelve years was a nun, after which she returned to her profession as a folk singer.

Mary O'Hara's sweet pure voice filled Margaret's living-room. We listened, enchanted, while the soft spring night fell, loath to stir even to put on the lights. The last song on one side was the Paul Simon classic of the sixties, "Bridge Over Troubled Water". The words had not meant much to me; I thought the lyric was pretty but too sentimental and lacking in the power and idealism of the protest songs of the same era. Now I heard them in the context of Margaret's dying, and their meaning sprang clear:

When you're weary,
Feelin' small,
When tears are in your eyes,
I'll dry them all;
I'm on your side.
Oh, when times get rough
And friends just can't be found,
Like a Bridge Over Troubled Water
I will lay me down.
Like a Bridge Over Troubled Water
I will lay me down.

When you're down and out,
When you're on the street,
When evening falls so hard
I will comfort you.
I'll take your part.
Oh, when darkness comes
And pain is all around,
Like a Bridge Over Troubled Water
I will lay me down.
Like a Bridge Over Troubled Water
I will lay me down.

Sail on silver girl,
Sail on by.
Your time has come to shine.
All your dreams are on their way.
See how they shine.
Oh, if you need a friend
I'm sailing right behind.
Like a Bridge Over Troubled Water
I will ease your mind.
Like a Bridge Over Troubled Water
I will ease your mind.

When the song was finished, Margaret and I were in tears. I bent over and kissed her, and we held hands tightly.

The Ending

On the evening of the symphony, Linda Rapson, Buffy Carruthers, and I met at six o'clock in a Japanese restaurant around the corner from Linda's office. Linda had learned that the flutist Jean Baxtresser had been forced to cancel and was being replaced by a child prodigy who played the violin. It didn't matter. The concert in any case was largely symbolic: for Margaret, a clinging to life; for us, the ineffable pleasure of taking part in something irreducibly right.

In the restaurant we ate sushi and drank sake in an excited mood that contrasted with the subject matter. Linda was concerned that Margaret was still refusing hints from Liz Greaves that she should make a new will. "There isn't much more time," Linda said, dipping a morsel of fish and rice in some soy sauce. "It is eight weeks today that she came home from hospital, and no one expected she would last so long. It might have something to do with how happy she is to be at home, but Larry Librach tells me that Margaret could go really quickly at this point. She's got to think about her will."

I suggested facing the problem head-on. I would say bluntly, "See here, Margaret. For a woman in your condition not to have a will is dumb."

The others winced. Maybe the direct approach would be needed, they agreed, but they thought it should be a last resort. And what about funeral arrangements? Margaret should be asked what she wanted at her funeral service, but how could such a subject be raised with a woman who liked to believe that her bowel movements were disposing of her cancer?

We were noisy as we climbed into the comfortable Mercedes that Linda had borrowed from her husband for the occasion. Buffy, listening to the din, had a moment of silent alarm as she pictured "these three forceful women, lubricated with sake, swooping down on Margaret".

165

Driving to Margaret's, Linda told us that Sheila Mackenzie believed Margaret was suppressing great anger.

"I do too," I said quickly.

Buffy was silent. Then she said, "So do I."

When we arrived, Margaret was ready and on her feet. She had dressed with the help of Helen Cram. She looked exhausted. Her freshly washed hair had a wild look, and her clothes, the printed silk dress under a tweed coat and the booties on her feet, gave her the addled appearance of a woman whose address might be a bus shelter. She sat in the front seat beside Linda and didn't speak as we drove downtown. Linda and I chattered gaily out of apprehension. As Buffy later put it, chuckling, "There was quite a howl in the car."

Linda's preparations had been impeccable. She knew exactly where to park her car in the underground garage of the Roy Thomson Hall where it would be handy to the elevator reserved for disabled people. We made Margaret comfortable in the wheelchair with the white blanket covering her lap and legs, rose to street level in a mirrored jewel of an elevator, and swept grandly into the pearly lobby. The ticket-taker instantly left his post to escort us to another elevator and along the upper hall. Our seats were in the last row of the first mezzanine balcony, where there was space behind to store Margaret's folded wheelchair.

I had not realized how wasted she looked. Seeing Margaret regularly as we all did, I had adjusted to her pallor, to the sunken face, to the eyes deep in the sockets of her skull, to her mouth stretched thin by the too-large dentures. Whenever I looked at her, I simply saw Margaret, my friend, a gutsy, smart, perceptive, astute, quirky, valuable human being. In Roy Thomson Hall, filled with people who seemed in the prime of health, moving quickly and easily as people do when they are free of pain, hailing one another, having a drink at one of the many glittering bars, Margaret was suddenly, like Banquo's ghost, a shocking sight.

The guest conductor of the Toronto Symphony Orchestra that night was Pinchas Zukerman, the violinist, who proudly was introducing his thirteen-year-old pupil, Mi Dori. The youngster wore a little-girl dress with puffed sleeves and a sash tied with a bow at the back and played with the breath-stopping flawless brilliance of an adult genius. She was accorded a protracted standing ovation, which she received with endearing shyness, standing with her glossy head down as the tumult of applause poured over her.

The first half of the program was a Rossini overture, followed by Mi Dori and Pinchas Zukerman performing a J.S. Bach concerto for two violins, and then a lovely Mendelssohn violin concerto. It was a long program, and I leaned forward a few times to see how Margaret, seated between Linda and Buffy, was bearing up. Her eyes were shining with tears and her face was rapt.

We had expected that she would be ready to leave in the intermission, but Margaret was astonished at the suggestion. She strolled slowly between me and Buffy through the crowded, noisy mezzanine lobby, her frail arm tiny in my hand. We kept to the quiet corners, and then Buffy guided her back to her seat. I watched them as Buffy protected Margaret in a cocoon of calm, neither speaking. Buffy later reflected, "Margaret inspired that nurturing role in me. I must say I loved getting between her and the confusion."

I remembered that Grace Ross had said almost exactly the same thing. Speaking of her anxiety to please Margaret, she commented, "She brought out a physical tenderness I never knew I had. I couldn't be careful enough how I would place the Codetron on her legs, or arrange the blanket over her." I saw that same gentleness in Linda one day when Linda was replacing Margaret's sock after the Codetron treatment. She went to infinite pains to stretch the sock to smooth out wrinkles, and she folded the top neatly, evenly, and lovingly.

We settled for the second half of the concert, Mendelssohn's romantic Italian Symphony. When it ended we all were moved to rapture. As we unfolded Margaret's chair in preparation for leaving, she murmured, "That was better for tempo than the first half."

Margaret broke down and wept for a long time after Linda and

167

Buffy drove her home. The strain of the evening contributed to the tears, because she was tired and her control was weakened, but crying was caused by more than fatigue. As Buffy and Linda massaged her cold feet, she told them that the Italian Symphony was a favourite of her sister Lynn. The sisters had listened to the passionate score dozens of times together and, hearing it again, Margaret was swept by a sense of loss and knew truly that Lynn was dead. At the deepest level, of course, she was weeping for herself.

When Buffy and Linda helped her undress, she broke into tears again and clung to Linda. "I'll remember this night for the rest of my life," she said.

Linda, reflecting that Margaret had at most two weeks to live, felt a stab of pain in her heart.

Buffy was staying overnight but was so tired and emotionally drained that she feared she would sleep too heavily to hear if Margaret stirred. She found an antique bell, which she placed on Margaret's bedside table, and it proved a prudent precaution. Margaret had an unsettled, unhappy night and rang three times, once to ask Buffy to massage her feet, once to ask her to rub her back, and again for help in turning over.

"A very busy night," Buffy commented laconically.

The next morning, for the first time in Buffy's experience, Margaret slept until almost eleven. When Linda called, Margaret observed ruefully, "I'm paying for the intense pleasures of last night. I'm grumpy."

Kathy Johns, who works at the Margaret Frazer House, arrived for the day shift when Margaret was still upstairs. "Is that you, Kathy?" Margaret called sweetly.

She said she needed a few minutes to meditate. After a time, she called again and asked Kathy to help her dress. Kathy went upstairs and found Margaret in an exhilarated mood. "She was tired," Kathy reported, "but she was in seventh heaven."

Buffy pronounced the night "a triumph". Over the next weeks, Margaret often spoke of the music, but rarely the tears. "A rich and wonderful experience," she told everyone. "A night to remember." We had a new log-book, the first having been filled with entries that had grown more discursive and detailed every day, and Pat Capponi noted in it on May 25 that "the symphony outing sounded very neat".

Saturday mornings Pat Capponi would make Margaret's bed, fold up her own bedding, and wash the breakfast dishes, while Margaret, wearing a fresh jogging suit, stretched out on the couch under her mohair blanket to listen to Mozart and watch the trees moving against the springtime sky. When Pat had finished her chores and they had visited for a while, Margaret would say, "Pat, you can go now."

Pat would kiss her and go down Margaret's walk, taking long, loping strides, her hair bouncing on her shoulders under the flat black hat. It is one block, but an uncommonly long one, from Margaret's house on Deloraine to Yonge Street, where Pat would turn toward the subway station. She always hurried under the spread of tall trees through which dappled light fell on the beautifully kept lawns bright with dew, the perfect flower beds, the houses with their sparkling windows open to the sounds of people preparing for the weekend's grocery shopping.

Pat Capponi hates Margaret's neighbourhood. She felt an alien there, an intruder the street tolerated like a toad in the garden only because of Margaret. She thinks the residents are smug within the safety of their brick walls and paid-up bills and intact families. She was always relieved to turn the corner of Yonge Street and head back to Parkdale on the subway. On Saturday mornings in Parkdale, angular men lurch along the sidewalks, their faces blurred by anti-psychotic drugs, bruised women in need of rent money put on working clothes for a spot of prostitution, and children at play are as profane as oil drillers. Parkdale is Pat's home; the people there are kin.

Elizabeth Greaves and I had been switching shifts to suit our own agendas. Mondays and Thursdays were designated on Joyce Brown's neatly printed schedule as "Liz or June", so it wasn't difficult to make arrangements for the six days I would be away at the end of May attending a writers' conference in Italy. If Liz couldn't cover for me, Elaine Hall said she would do it. It was much more of a problem that Linda Rapson would also be away. She had been booked months earlier to present a training program in acupuncture in western Canada and had arranged to be gone from Toronto for nine days.

"I could skip Calgary," she said to me, very worried, "and go right to Vancouver. That would save two days."

I urged her to keep to the original plan because it allowed her some leisure time. Linda had suffered the deaths of two close friends within the year, the grief of which was still very much with her, and she was carrying an enormous workload in juggling daily attendance on Margaret with a full medical practice and time with a husband and children she adores. She agreed reluctantly, but only after Larry Librach offered to attend Margaret if he was needed.

"I thought Margaret would be in crisis by this time," Linda admitted, "but she's really quite well, except for the swollen legs." Linda's gamine face lit up. "I'm so touched by Margaret's sweetness, by how *interesting* she is, how interested she is in everything. And there is such peacefulness in her face."

I was away on May 26, when the team met at a hastily called meeting at Holy Trinity after the Sunday service. Vivian Harrower made some notes, which were distributed to the team. Margaret's increasing weakness was the first topic, after which much of the discussion centred on whether the role of the team would change as a result. Some who thought the team should be more directive, asked Linda if she thought it advisable to set up a schedule of medication, food, and rest instead of allowing Margaret to pick her own times for things. Others thought Margaret might accept tranquillizers more readily if they were presented under some other name, such as "muscle relaxant".

Helen Cram was concerned that Margaret still talked of "getting well" and "getting rid of this cancer". She felt the team was unwittingly allowing Margaret to remain in a state of denial instead of helping her prepare for death. Rather than take action to enrol Margaret in healing sessions scheduled weeks away, perhaps the team should simply listen sympathetically when Margaret talked about her future activities, and do nothing. Others agreed that it might give Margaret energy if she faced the fact of her dying instead of presenting a facade that must be exhausting to maintain.

Others were appalled by all the suggestions. They argued fiercely that Margaret should be allowed to choose her own way of dying, regardless of whether others thought it was the so-called best way. Linda supported the free-Margaret movement. "We have to respect Margaret's way of handling her illness," she said, all her usual merriment gone and her eyes stern. "We can use an appropriate opening to talk about death, but only if that's what Margaret wants. For myself, I would be honest if Margaret asked me about her prospects, but she hasn't."

The call for more volunteers to fill the holes left by people going on vacation was answered by three more Holy Trinity people: Pauline Bradbrook, Marjorie Perkins, and Barbara Webb.

Linda announced she would be away for a few days and left the home and office telephone numbers of Dr. Larry Librach. She said she would be calling Margaret once a day, in the morning, a time to which Margaret had grown accustomed. I called once from Italy when I was feeling bereft because it was Thursday and I was missing my shift. I slipped away from a PEN International session on writers and censorship and placed a call to Margaret.

"Are you back from Italy so soon?" she asked.

"I'm calling from San Marino," I told her. "You'll be interested to know it is cold and raining."

"Here it's lovely," she said, her voice weak. "I walked to the end of the garden. I think the boot is helping a lot. The swelling in my legs is down."

"The boot?" I asked, wondering if I had heard correctly.

"Oh, yes, Linda got it for me." The connection was poor, and the bells of a clock tower were clanging outside my room. I dimly heard Margaret say happily, "Linda just called a few minutes ago from Vancouver."

I was baffled, but on the morning after my return I had an

urgent errand at Jessie's Centre for Teenagers and ran into Liz Greaves in the nursery, a baby on her shoulder. She had been the first one to give Margaret a treatment with the boot, "It's called a Jobst pump. It's very strange looking," Liz said, "but it works. You'll see."

Elizabeth Greaves had been working at Nellie's ten years earlier when Margaret first took me up on my suggestion that she might be interested in helping that beleaguered emergency shelter. Because the staff a week later told me about a sweet, well-dressed, grey-haired woman who had drifted in, looked around a bit, and then tucked up her skirts and scrubbed the stairs, I always had assumed the person was Margaret. Elizabeth straightened me out. Margaret had come to volunteer at about the same time, but the woman who scrubbed the stairs was Margaret's friend from Holy Trinity, Joan Robinson.

Peter Gzowski interviewed Margaret in February 1984 on his wonderful CBC radio show, *Morningside*, soon after I wrote a column about the opening of the Margaret Frazer House. He asked about the stair-scrubbing incident, which I had attributed to Margaret.

"That's part of June Callwood's mythology," Margaret corrected him reprovingly.

Liz told me, that Margaret's introduction to Nellie's was somewhat less dramatic than Joan Robinson's but more persistent. She simply turned up one day, saying, "June asked me to help." The staff didn't know what to do with the pleasant but prim-looking school teacher. Nellie's was full of its usual mixture of battered woman, berserk children of battered women reacting to the violence and upheaval they had witnessed, penniless women discharged from psychiatric facilities with one streetcar ticket and a prescription for stupor-inducing drugs, women fighting alcohol addiction, women whose welfare had been cut off because a man moved in with them to comfort them, women prone to epileptic seizures, women coughing, women talking to themselves, women crying, women shouting, women on crutches, women in every stage of despair.

"Margaret was tentative, not a bit pushy, but it was clear that she didn't intend to leave," Liz Greaves recalled. "We could see she was determined to make a place for herself at Nellie's. She was much wiser than we were. She knew there was a place for her; we didn't."

Margaret joined Nellie's board of directors, of which I was the titular president. Attendance was haphazard and relations with the underpaid and overworked staff were not the best. The main problem was that no one on the board was an effective fund raiser. Hostels for women in crisis now are accepted as necessary in most communities, but Nellie's was one of the first and ahead of its time. We were fighting the apathy of governments, found-ations, corporations, and the general public, all of whom seemed to believe there was no need for a women's shelter. As a result, the morale of staff and board often sank to abysmal lows.

Margaret Frazer, however, newly retired from teaching, had the time and the devotion to come regularly to all meetings of the staff and the board.

"There wasn't much we could do about Margaret always being around except tolerate her," Liz recalled, her green eyes merry. "She even turned up when we were hiring new staff, which no one else on the board had time to do. We were very good in those days at turning people off instantly, but she hacked away at our reserve. And she kept finding tasks for herself, such as reorganizing the kitchen or folding laundry."

In the summer of 1977 the staff took matters into its own hands. With the nervous agreement of the board, Nellie's declared what was called an "occupation". Health and fire department regulations restricted occupancy to thirty people, but Nellie's announced it would stop turning women away when the limit was reached. All summer, homeless women slept on Nellie's liv-ing-room couches, on makeshift cots, and on the floor. By au-tumn, the dramatic stunt had proved that Nellie's was filling an urgent need. Metro Toronto made a small upward adjustment in the *per diem* payments provided to all hostels, but the increase was still inadequate to meet Nellie's overhead, and private dona-tions did not follow.

In the fall of 1977 the YMCA sold its Broadview Avenue property to a developer. Included in the package was the house Nellie's was renting. We took the Y to court, charging a violation of our agreement, but we lost. The developer announced plans to demolish Nellie's but was persuaded against it at an emotional meeting of the neighbourhood. People rallied to our support and told him furiously that Nellie's must be spared. The developer then offered to sell the building to us for $100,000. The price was a bargain but beyond our means. We owed the YMCA $18,000, and the Nellie's bank account stood at $300. We learned that dinner for the residents one evening had consisted of tomato soup, which the staff purchased out of its own pockets. The staff salaries hadn't been paid that week.

The board was optimistic in authorizing a purchase offer of $70,000. To pay for food and salaries, we put in what cash we could spare: a total of $6,000. Margaret's donation was $500.

The board and staff gathered the evening of November 2, 1977, around a battered table in a community storefront not far from Nellie's. The developer had lowered the purchase price to $75,000, but we computed the mortgage payments and concluded this was still beyond our means. He awaited our decision at seven o'clock that night.

The staff was recommending a tactic much like the occupation just concluded. They wanted us to close Nellie's with a bang, drawing media attention to the serious shortage of beds for women in Toronto and the poor financing of hostels. I thought it would work. I was sure that there would be such a public outcry that we would be able to open again very soon on a better financial footing. Also, I was reluctant to exploit our dedicated staff by asking them to continue when no one knew if they would be paid regularly or have money to feed the residents. As Margaret noted in her diary of the event, "Staff confidence in our ability to raise money, in the very viability of the hostel, is now constituted at zero."

Everyone on the board felt the same, with three exceptions. One was a teacher, Carol Kowbel, a sombre, thoughtful young woman whose style is cautious and deliberate. Another was Margaret Bryce, who was in charge of Nellie's financial affairs. And the third was Margaret Frazer.

"Where will the women go if we close?" she asked plaintively. "What will happen to the women who need Nellie's?"

The discussion went around and around, weighing the hard truth of our impoverished condition against the profound question that Margaret was asking about moral responsibility. We drank sour coffee in Styrofoam cups and intermittently phoned the developer, who was waiting in his lawyer's office, to apologize for the delay.

A collective doesn't proceed on the basis of majority vote, so numbers didn't count. The two Margarets and Carol had disrupted the consensus. Because they refused to change their vote, they stopped us cold.

We reached a compromise that makes no sense now, but on that harried night was the only way out of the impasse. We decided that if the developer would lower the price to $70,000, we would give ourselves a month to raise the down payment and try to stay in business. If he insisted on his asking price of $75,000, we would fold. We didn't have a penny, either way, but mortgage payments for the lesser amount would approximate our current rent, and we might be able to struggle along. Jackie White-Hampton and Margaret Frazer had been active at city hall of late, and hoped for a breakthrough from the politicians.

It was decided that Carol Kowbel and I would do the talking to the developer.

The developer, his lawyer, and his son were waiting with more patience that we deserved (we were two hours late) in a handsome boardroom. We sat at a gleaming mahogany table, feeling little hope. We thought it highly unlikely that the developer, a sharp-eyed, brisk person, would drop the price. Why should he? Nevertheless, I explained how poor we were. I told the story of the unpaid staff, our debt to the YMCA, and the tomato-soup dinner. I talked about the women who used Nellie's. Also, I cried.

Carol Kowbel, sitting beside me, lit a cigarette with hands that trembled. The developer watched, fascinated, as she fought to control the quivering match flame. He said he had to consult with a partner. He left the room, came back in two minutes, and announced he would sell at $70,000. As we cheered, he said it was Carol's shaking hands that convinced him.

When we got outside the lawyer's office we felt like a mountain-climbing team that had just planted a flag on Everest. All of us, laughing and crying, realized that we hadn't really wanted to close Nellie's. We hugged Carol and the Margarets and pounded their backs and rejoiced.

We held a press conference the next week to publicize our plight, and several thousands of dollars were donated in a few days. Then we called a public meeting in the Quakers' handsome Friends' Meeting House and made an appeal for support. Eileen Swinton, a stranger to us, was recruited by Elizabeth Greaves to attend. When the speeches were over she approached me quietly and said she would head a Nellie's fund-raising campaign.

We had never seen anything like the way Eileen Swinton operated. She persuaded the proprietors of the Eaton Centre to donate an office there, put together an attractive package of material, coaxed someone to pay postage costs, and mailed the appeal to a judiciously selected list of corporations and foundations. Then she secured a bank loan for $69,000 to buy the house. In February, Don Harron and Catherine McKinnon gave a benefit for the hostel, paying all the expenses themselves. The event resulted in a profit of $8,000 and gave Nellie's a social lustre and public acceptance that it had never before known. That summer the Toronto Rotary Club, after extensive backroom meetings, made a handsome gift of $70,000 so that Nellie's could own its house. In less than a year Eileen Swinton's committee raised about $200,000, and Nellie's has never since been in serious trouble.

Margaret Frazer, dazzled as we all were by Eileen's pyrotechnics, was her devoted assistant and brought into the fund-raising office women from Holy Trinity, Anne Grasham, Joan Robinson, and others, who had been hoping to find a way of helping Nellie's.

Nellie's then underwent a handsome renovation with the help of Canada Mortgage and Housing Corporation, and the staff was enlarged and given a decent wage. Nellie's, with its satellite long-term residences, is now one of the most respected women's hostels in the country.

When Liz Greaves left Nellie's a few years later, in need of a change, she worked with Margaret for a time in the Holy Trinity soup kitchen for downtown office workers. It was Margaret's idea to open the kitchen as a low-cost lunch place for people in need of a convivial, homey drop-in spot, and she decided Liz should manage it. Liz discovered that managing the kitchen also included making the soup and pies, the chili, and the sandwich fillings.

"Margaret would bustle in cheerfully in mid-morning to help, complaining that I was putting too much filling in the sandwiches," Liz recalled fondly. "And she did cut the littlest pieces of pie. Then she would fling open doors and windows, chattering a blue streak. Next she would water the plants. All of them deserved a decent burial, but Margaret kept them going. Always there was music – sometimes the choir or organist practising in the church, sometimes Bach and Beethoven on a radio. Margaret, playful and funny, was the hostess, sort of."

In four months the lunch room in Holy Trinity's vestry was showing a profit. The operation then was taken over by a community college to enable it to provide practical experience for students in restaurant and chef courses. Margaret concentrated once again on fund raising for Nellie's, and Liz took a job at Jessie's, as the centre's first counsellor to teenage mothers and fathers.

The relationship between Liz and Margaret had weathered well over the years. By the time of Margaret's illness the two women were entirely comfortable together, each sure of her place in the affection of the other. Margaret felt less need to be brave and self-reliant with Liz than with most others on the Friends of Margaret team. As Margaret's strength declined, Liz was always the person with whom she gave in first. Liz was there the first time Margaret decided to eat her dinner on the couch rather than at the table, and Liz was the first to be allowed to help Margaret on the stairs.

"That's new," I said when Liz told me that Margaret needed support to climb the stairs. Liz nodded. She told me I would see in the log that Margaret had been unable to get to her feet after using the toilet one night and had been obliged to call Vivian Harrower to help lift her. She said to Vivian that she felt as if the muscles in her legs were "no use". Though Margaret's milky skin showed no signs of bed sores, the nurses on the team were worried. Fran Sowton brought some lotion for back rubs and resurrected the natural fleece Jay MacGillivray had given Margaret in the hospital.

"She had forgotten about the fleece," Fran wrote in the log, "so now this is on the sofa and giving her much comfort. Sheepskins were used in England and now elsewhere to prevent pressure sores. They were also used by cavalry to prevent saddle-sores on long rides."

When Kathy Johns, a member of the collective that staffed the Margaret Frazer House, was preparing breakfast, Margaret asked her to strain the black-currant jam. She explained she found the seeds hard to swallow. For the same reason, Sheila Mackenzie was crushing millet for Margaret's breakfast porridge in a coffee grinder. A day or so later Fran Sowton wrote, "Margaret is not particularly uncomfortable, but is weak and uninterested in food."

Others reported that Margaret occasionally was cranky. She snapped at Helen Gough that she should "get a hearing aid", after Helen asked Margaret a few times to repeat herself. To Sheila File, Margaret complained angrily that the Simonton healing groups were not beginning until the end of June.

"I *need* that healing group," she exclaimed. "I want to *get better*. There are things I want to do. It's frustrating that I can't do my own gardening. There are weeds to pull in the rose bed. I've got to shake myself out of this."

Sheila wrote in the log, "It was good to see the strength of those feelings."

Another time, when Margaret was in the garden with Anne

Grasham, Anne noticed that the tulips were past their bloom. She began dead-heading them, clipping them near the ground, as she does her own. Margaret flared at her. "Not *the leaves*, Anne!" Anne then cut them the way Margaret wanted them, closer to the head, and noted with amusement that Margaret was contrite about her outburst. Though she didn't apologize, she made a show of asking Anne's advice about gardening and sweetly admired everything Anne had to say, contradicting nothing.

A few days later Margaret again raged against her increasing frailty and the discomfort she was experiencing in places that hadn't hurt before. Glenys McMullen wrote in the log, "I agree with Sheila – better for Margaret to vent her anger than keep it within."

"Margaret's a lot weaker than when you left," Liz warned me. "When she stands up now she reminds me of an old dog I once had who used to make three tries before he could get to his feet."

Heather Sutherland dropped in to see Margaret one day when she happened to be in town taking a break from thesis-writing. Margaret was looking comfortable in the green chair where she had her Codetron treatments, contentedly reading. After a pleasant visit Heather rose to go. Almost as an afterthought she said, "By the way, you'll be interested to know that Jim and I have made a decision. I won't be joining the order after all. He's leaving so we can be married."

Margaret said, quietly, calmly, and with strong emphasis, "Very good."

Kathy Johns was the only staff person from the Margaret Frazer House who joined the team. The others, newer to the house, had not had much contact with Margaret and didn't feel they knew her well enough. I talked to Kathy one October evening in the comfortable, shabby office of Margaret Frazer House, both of us lounging on cast-off furniture and sipping tea. A candid, resolute woman with short brown hair and huge blue eyes, she was dressed in army fatigue pants and a flannel shirt.

179

"I first saw Margaret at a board meeting late in 1983 after I was hired here," Kathy explained. "I was curious about her, because the house was named for her, and I saw that she was a really neat woman. That spring and summer of 1984 she came to the house about once a week. She took three of the residents, one at a time, to Centre Island and taught them to canoe. One of them, with a frightful history of being treated violently, was a person who was hard to reach, but she adored Margaret. She said, 'Margaret knows where it's at.'"

Kathy heard at a board meeting that Margaret had cancer. She saw her the next day and made some reference to it. Margaret said casually, "Well, it's going to be fine. Don't worry about it."

Kathy said, "I want you to know that whatever happens, I'll be thinking about you."

"Thanks," Margaret said, giving her a level look.

Kathy felt a connection was made in that exchange. When later she heard about the team, she notified Joyce that she wanted to be on it. She attended the second team meeting in Holy Trinity and was impressed. She was struck by the soul-searching about respecting Margaret and consulting with her about the care she wanted. Kathy's mother had died six years before of cancer. "When Fran Sowton remarked at that meeting that it was important not to let Margaret be someone else in our lives, that we should see Margaret as herself and not someone else we know who has died, that struck home with me."

Kathy's second shift was an overnight that she says she will remember all her life. She and Margaret had a conversation that began with Margaret asking her, "Do you live alone?"

"No, I live with a woman who works at Nellie's. She's an Anglican minister."

Margaret drew out of Kathy the story of her leaving her husband, "a fine man", and two children for the woman she loved. Kathy spoke of the pain of that decision and her struggles with guilt. She said, gratefully, "Margaret gave me support for the choices I've made. She understood how I was feeling. When we talked about the future she told me lovingly that she knew I would make the right choices when the time came, that I would know the right thing to do."

Margaret's kindness lifted a burden from Kathy. Kathy had often wondered what her mother's reaction would have been if she had lived to see the changes Kathy made in her life. It seemed to her that Margaret represented her mother not only because Margaret was of her mother's generation but also because the two had been classmates at Hamilton Central Collegiate. Indeed, as Kathy learned, Margaret was connected to a number of people in Kathy's family. She had been a student of Kathy's grandfather at McMaster University, and Kathy's father, a physics professor, knew Margaret through his involvement in CAMMAC. When Margaret gave Kathy her blessing, Kathy was moved to hope that her mother would have done the same.

"It felt such a gift that I was glowing for days," Kathy told me. "Margaret's message to me was that I was a fine person and that I should feel good about myself."

Some people arrived to visit Margaret, putting an end to the intimacy, and Kathy left. She and Margaret said goodbye. Kathy had a sense, which proved true, that she would never see Margaret again. "Her farewell gift was that conversation. There was an eye-to-eye exchange of incredible warmth, and I felt the love between us as we hugged."

Kathy cleared her throat as she described the scene. Then she added, "Some days I feel better about myself and who I am than other days. But I have Margaret's tremendous acceptance of me, her lesson that life isn't without challenges. When I can hold on to that, it's very helpful to me."

Nancy and Bill Whitla returned from Greece, and on Sunday, June 2, visited Margaret to bring her Holy Communion. Margaret was overjoyed to see them and so was Glenys McMullen, who had been spraying the roses with a leaky hose. Bill Whitla, the team's reliable Mr. Fixit, promised to make the repair.

I went to visit the Whitlas one August afternoon when the summer sky was black with an impending storm. They live in

Toronto's west end in a serene home filled with reflections of their cultivated tastes. The living-room is furnished with books, a grand piano, and fine stereo equipment, and the walls glow with Nancy's paintings, some of them passionate oils and others misty watercolours. "My style changes so much it makes it difficult when I have a show," she remarked with a grin.

Nancy Whitla is a small, centred woman with cropped grey hair and a quiet, shy manner. Besides painting professionally, she's the volunteer co-ordinator at the Toronto Catholic Children's Aid Society and made an impressive showing in her first attempt to be elected a trustee on the Toronto Board of Education. Bill Whitla had a parish in New Brunswick soon after he was ordained, but he usually combines the theological with the academic. After a few years as chaplain at the University of New Brunswick, he moved to Toronto's York University in the English department and now is head of humanities.

He's a burly, friendly, kind man, with an absence of pretension well suited to the easy style of Holy Trinity. The Whitlas joined in 1973, and their first impression of Margaret Frazer was that she seemed to be everywhere. The church was deep in negotiations with Eaton's and the developer, Cadillac Fairview, builders of the Eaton Centre, and Margaret was on most of the committees that fought about space, light, access, housing, and compensation.

"She had just decided to retire from teaching," Nancy recalled, "and she was bursting with things she wanted to do, stuff she wanted to learn."

Margaret wasn't always easy to get along with, according to Bill. "She could be bristly, and she had firmly held opinions that she would defend against all comers. There are lots like Margaret at Holy Trinity."

What touched the Whitlas was Margaret's appreciation of their children, 'Becca (for Rebecca), nineteen, and Michael, seventeen. "It wasn't the usual interest in someone else's children," Nancy said. "It was much more. I remember how delighted Margaret was when I told her that I sat beside 'Becca while she practised piano to keep her company. She told me she remembered feeling lonely when she practised piano as a child. And she was pleased when Michael decided to learn the flute and very encouraging when he brought it to Holy Trinity to play at a service."

I dropped in to visit Margaret on Tuesday, June 4, and found Patti Welsh sweeping the front walk. Patti is a young, slender woman with the face of an angel and a manner of such ethereal delicacy that she seems as fragile as mist; but she's a tough-minded, efficient person who is active on Nellie's board of directors and serves on the fund-raising committees of both Nellie's and Jessie's.

Margaret was in a testy mood, Patti told me, keeping her voice low, and was at that moment having a Codetron treatment. I found Margaret attached to the electronic octopus, the mohair blanket wrapped around her despite the warm day.

She seemed to have shrunk in the week since I had seen her last. Her face had the simian cast of a very wise, very old, very ill monkey.

"I'm getting along fine," she assured me. "The pump is doing a good job on my legs, and I've had two bowel movements today. It's just that I'm so *weak*. I can't understand it. Last week Vivian had to help me off the toilet, and lately I spend most of the day sleeping." That day she had eaten two bites of Shreddies at breakfast and tried one nibble of toast, "but it wasn't worth the effort."

Something in the petulant tone reminded me of my children who, when they were small and kept in bed with spots or fevers, would cavil about boredom and missed birthday parties.

I said, "You look like a child of five, tucked in that way under the blanket."

"I'm going backwards, I think," she agreed, catching my drift.

I changed the subject. "Were you happy as a child of five?"

She closed her eyes and shook her head impatiently, "Too big a question."

Holy Trinity members of the team had gathered two days previously after the Sunday service. Some were concerned that Margaret had not made her will, others that the memorial service wasn't decided, others that Margaret wasn't facing the reality of her death, others that her diet was replete with lemon snows and maple syrup over ice cream, others that the Simonton healing team wasn't available. Linda's advice, relayed through Hilda Powicke, was that the team should let Margaret decide how she wanted to handle her illness. This was all very well as an overall philosophy, some team members were saying, but it wasn't meeting the practicalities.

Hilda circulated the word. We would all meet on Sunday, June 9, at Holy Trinity.

Joyce Brown made up the schedules for the month of June and left a note in the log that she was going to western Canada for a while, so Buffy Carruthers would be preparing the July schedule. She made it sound easy, but in truth problems were developing. A few regulars were leaving for vacations or summer courses, but a few others who became suddenly unavailable were, she suspected, avoiding Margaret because the end was approaching.

One of these, a music friend of Margaret's, confessed to Joyce that she couldn't bear to watch Margaret die. "I'm thinking that I never want to be friends with an older woman again," she told Joyce tearfully, 'because they might die too. I can't go through another loss."

"It pissed me off," Joyce told me angrily. "I thought, 'For Christ's sake, get it together.' Margaret used to ask about that woman. She really missed her and wondered why she didn't come around any more."

Some of those approached by Joyce to join the team were willing but genuinely too busy. A few refused in a tone that suggested they were affronted that Joyce had even asked. Others felt Margaret would be better off in hospital and flinched from taking part in so personal and amateur a service.

Joyce told me over lunch one rainy day in late August that she had lived in fear of someone cancelling a shift at the last minute when she might be stuck at Nellie's and unable to rush to Margaret's to fill the gap. This never happened, though twice because of misunderstanding or memory lapse people simply did not show up. Both times occurred early in Margaret's decline, at a time she could manage by herself, but they worried Joyce, who took responsibility for the smoothness of the network.

"Considering there were more than forty people involved, all of them with busy lives, the system worked remarkably well," Joyce reflected as we waited for our salads. "People came through." She added, "And I was very impressed by the men who were around. Ian Sowton was exceptional."

Diane Savard was one of the handful who went once and then quit. I was surprised at that. Diane is one of the most generous, giving people I know. Two months after Margaret died, we went to Centre Island on a beautiful day in August and rented a paddle-boat so that we could talk about it undisturbed. Our knees pumping in comic unison, we explored a lagoon while she explained.

"I went to Margaret's for only one night," she said, "and I was glad that I had that one night. But afterwards whenever Joyce called I told her I was busy. Instead of telling Joyce that there was *no way* I would go back, I made excuses. It wasn't just that Margaret was dying. I think I could handle that. It was all the pain. No one told me there would be pain."

Diane Savard, twenty-nine, is a tall, raw-boned, wary woman with light blue eyes and arms that are tattooed and scarred from some terrible years when she was in and out of jails. She gives her whole heart to anyone or anything helpless, but is especially tender if the creature in need is a homeless cat, a wounded bird, a lame squirrel, a one-eyed rabbit, or a baby anything. Once a policeman shot her in the stomach and when she recovered I asked if she planned to sue. She was incredulous, "What! Sue a man whose name is *Michael Thrush?*"

She has attended school intermittently, trying to make up for lost years, but at the time of Margaret's illness had found a job at All Saints' Anglican church in Toronto's tenderloin area, where a group of homeless women derisively known in the media as "bag ladies" had found permanent shelter. Diane, who is rough tongued, observant, independent, reliable, careful about personal dignity, intelligent, fiery in the defence of what she protects, instinctively kind, and possessed of street savvy, was exactly what All Saints' needed.

Diane was one of the earliest residents of Nellie's. She came to the hostel the first summer we were open, a likeable, rebellious, stormy teenager. After that Nellie's was never out of touch with her; Elizabeth Greaves all but adopted her, and there was a period when Diane worked on the staff.

"I saw Margaret Frazer around Nellie's and took her for a prim and proper old lady. I thought that I'd better be on my best behaviour or I'd get a kick in the head," Diane recalled, adding apologetically, "I wasn't big on the human race in those days. Then you had that party for Nellie's at your place one afternoon, remember?" I did, but vaguely. "Margaret got a little bit tipsy, and we sat at the piano in your living-room and sang. I decided she wasn't prim and proper at all. I fell in love with her."

Diane spotted a dead crow on the bank of the lagoon and insisted that we steer in that direction so she could bury it. While I complained that what she was doing was ridiculous, she dug a place in the soft earth and tenderly covered the bird over.

When Diane heard that a team was being organized to help Margaret stay in her home, she was positive it would never work. "I predicted that people would get bored and drop out," she said as we resumed pumping the paddle-boat. "I told Joyce that I knew the others wouldn't follow through, but she could count on me. For one thing, I wanted to show interest in Margaret's cat, Cleo. When you spend eight years with a cat, as Margaret had with Cleo, a bond develops. How would Margaret feel if no one showed any concern for her cat?"

Diane arrived for her first shift just as Nancy Dodington, a former Nellie's staff person who now works at Jessie's, was preparing to leave. Nancy lingered for a cup of tea and then said her farewells. About forty-five minutes later, Margaret had a stabbing pain.

Diane was aghast. Margaret tried to assure her that it was nothing, just pressure on a nerve, but the younger woman was distraught. Margaret thought she might be sick to her stomach. She refused Diane's offer to help her upstairs and was in the bathroom quite a time. She returned to the couch slowly and laboriously, her face still twisted by pain.

186

Diane went into the kitchen, where Margaret couldn't see her, and cried.

"I rattle on a good bit, as you know," Diane told me, steering us toward some mallard ducks for a closer look, "and I was really unsettled by Margaret's pain, so maybe I talked even more than usual. Twice she said to me in a sweet voice, 'Diane, it's time to shut up.' I understood her need for privacy, so once or twice I went upstairs to her little office and sat there so she could be alone."

After a while, when the overnight person was almost due to arrive, Diane asked Margaret, "Do you want me to leave now?"

Margaret gave her a gentle smile and answered, "Yes."

When Joyce called to arrange another shift, Diane made an excuse. "I thought, what the hell, there's not much anyone can do and there are plenty of people around. And it didn't help Margaret that I had to leave the room to cry. So that's how I justified not going."

The family of ducks glided around a corner and we paused, reluctant to pursue and frighten them. "There was no way I would say no if they were really stuck. I'm a firm believer that people should die in their own setting. But I kept saying, no, I was busy."

We turned to head back to the paddle-boat marina. Diane said, her face wistful, "I was wrong about the team when I said it wouldn't work, because it did. I just wish everyone could have people like that to care for them."

The log-book for the week of June 3 is full of references to Margaret's pain and weakness. Some extracts:

MONDAY, JUNE 3, 5 to 9. Margaret seemed relaxed but fatigued when I arrived, resting on her sofa with Cleo and without the usual music. A bit of talk, but mostly companionable silence.... Although experiencing only minor pain, I found Margaret very different tonight – perhaps fatigue. Liz Greaves.

MONDAY, JUNE 3, OVERNIGHT. Margaret was exhausted last night and needed some help getting up the stairs.... I rubbed her feet

187

before bed with some lotion. Vivian Harrower.

TUESDAY, JUNE 4, 10 TO 4. Margaret was resting when I arrived. She wanted to sleep and did until 11:55.... Patti Welsh.

TUESDAY, JUNE 4, OVERNIGHT. Margaret was tired when I arrived. We did the Codetron and went to bed soon after. Massaged her feet and noticed that some of the toes are getting a bit purplish. Should keep an eye on this I think. Both of us had a good sleep. New schedules here for everyone. Thanks for being such a great team. I'm off to the west on Saturday. See you in July. Joyce Brown. P.S. If someone is here with cables, could you try and jump-start Margaret's car?

WEDNESDAY, JUNE 5, 10 TO 4. Margaret slept for close to two hours.... We had a late lunch listening to Mary O'Hara, a very spiritually moving songstress.... Love you, Margaret. Wendy Farquhar.

WEDNESDAY, JUNE 5, 4 TO 9. Margaret has been quiet and has rested listening to music.... When she was exercising after the sock [the Jobst boot] was taken off, she had quite a lot of internal pain, which came quite suddenly.... She is weaker than she was last Wednesday.... I'm glad Linda is back. Helen Cram.

WEDNESDAY, JUNE 5, OVERNIGHT. Margaret's pain was considerable for a while but eased with the help of Vivaldi and Tylenol No. 3. Then we plugged into the Codetron and got into quite a talk about music and her emotional and spiritual needs. Some talk of her grief for her sister, parents. Much reminiscing and musing on various topics. Anyway, we rattled on for two solid hours. Then massaged her and tucked her in. Jay MacGillivray.

THURSDAY MORNING, JUNE 6. Emergency visit from Dr. Linda Rapson, who wrote: Margaret is weaker.... She had quite a lot of pain.... Her abdomen is quite firm, and her bowel sounds are high-pitched and tinkling, which happens with some obstructions. It is not complete, of course, because things are still moving, but it may mean she won't feel much like eating, and I wouldn't push it. M's colour is not so good either, but she can be comfortable if she doesn't make sudden moves. Please start recording times she takes Tylenol in case we have to put her on a regular regimen every four hours. I'll start a page for that. Margaret had a good talk with Jay last night. I shall be available at all times and will come here as often as necessary. Don't hesitate to call. It's good to be back. Love to all.

THURSDAY, JUNE 6, 10 TO 6. When I arrived Margaret was asleep on the sofa. Jay said she'd had a bad morning, didn't want breakfast, and she's called Linda (see above).... Not long after Linda left, we had lunch. Margaret had carrot soup and tea. After lunch we went for a walk in the garden.... About 3:30 M had a pain in her left leg that she described as throbbing and almost like electrical shock. She said she'd had this once before but not nearly so severe. Ginny Peacock.

THURSDAY, JUNE 6, 6 TO 9. Margaret described the pain in her left thigh as a "nerve". Massage did not help, and she refused Tylenol. She also mentioned that everything was "strange" and said she's been "an ENSURE woman" for a while. Elizabeth Greaves.

FRIDAY, JUNE 7, 10 TO 4. Margaret sat up for quite a while at lunch, reading and eating.... Margaret wanted to go outside and weed and then sleep, and not have Codetron before visitor at 3:00 p.m. Says she needs sleep more. (She didn't sleep, either, and Eileen Swinton was here when I left.) Merylie Houston.

FRIDAY, JUNE 7, 5 TO 9. Margaret was sitting up reading Roy Bonisteel's book *Man Alive*. She was tired, seemed thinner in the jaw. She admired my red suit and remembered it was Friday and wanted to know if I was tired. I told her just a little of my week.... She enjoyed her time in the garden today. Helen Gough.

SATURDAY, JUNE 8, 8 TO 11. When I arrived Margaret was resting. She seemed very tired and told me just to talk to her. So I started to tell about our trip to Europe and she fell asleep. Slept until about 11:30. She seemed to be in pain whenever she

189

moved but did not want medicine. Carmen Bourbonnais.

SATURDAY, JUNE 8, 11 TO 5. Margaret seems to be in a lot more pain than when I last saw her (May 18) – less energy and thinner as well. Ate small bowl of soup and apple sauce for lunch. I managed to get her car going, but it should be run 10-15 minutes every 2-3 days for a week and then once a week after that. Sat out in the backyard for close to an hour. Now, sleeping. Gail Flintoff.

SATURDAY, JUNE 8, 5 TO 9. I have not seen Margaret for five weeks as I've been in England. I was taken aback by her poor colour when I first saw her and how much thinner her face is. She could not seem to remember my name as she introduced Gail and me (apologized for this later). She asked me to just talk to her…. She asked if her face looked thinner. I brought in roses and was instructed as to their careful placement for maximum viewing appreciation from the couch. After a while Margaret suggested that the vase with the red roses was too tall perhaps. Was there another? … At two different points during the evening she said, "Ruth, I want to get better and I'm not. I want to get *well*." She has been burping a lot but making light of it. "I sound like a sheep." She commented as Sheila was doing the Codetron that her legs seem bigger than ever. Ruth McKeown.

SATURDAY, JUNE 8, OVERNIGHT. Margaret wanted to go straight upstairs after the Codetron but had to sit down for a while. The stairs were very difficult – my heart ached for her by the time we reached the top. It's as though she's lifting a hundred pounds of lead with each step…. Massaged legs and feet and hands and arms, talking very little. She did ask me if I had done an overnight before and seemed relieved that she didn't need to instruct me on what to do. Suddenly she had a severe sharp pain in her upper left leg. It continued, and she agreed she would take a Tylenol No. 3 (it was about 11:00 p.m.). The pain was so severe she could not get herself into a position where she could drink water to swallow the pill. I got her to put the pill back in her mouth, and I poured the water into her mouth a little at a time. After 5-10 minutes, the pain left, as she said "… of its own accord.

It's much too soon for the pain-killer to be working". Then she snuggled under the covers…. In the midst of it all she suddenly shrieked, "Damn this pain!!" My sentiments exactly. Sheila File.

SUNDAY, JUNE 9, 10 TO 4. Sheila has left and Margaret is snoozing. She will take Communion at 12:30 and then lunch, etc. No trips to the gardens of north Toronto as I'd hoped. Is it time for milkshakes? Smooth milk and yoghurt drinks with yeast and eggs hidden away in them…. A windy and wonderful sit outside. Cheers. Buffy Carruthers.

SUNDAY, JUNE 9, 4 TO 9. Margaret slept and seemed in quite a bit of discomfort. A visitor came with flowers, and Margaret didn't recognize her and felt upset about her memory failing. Margaret is more lethargic than previously, and yet we had a good time looking through a series of photographs of birds, on which she is very knowledgeable and interested. We played some jazz and some Mozart and talked less than usual. I enjoyed giving and Margaret enjoyed receiving a foot massage. Nigel Turner.

Letter from Margaret published March 2, 1948, in the *Globe and Mail*.

The comments of Dr. Wallace on Chancellor Hutchins' recent address to the Secondary School Teachers' Federation both interested and puzzled me. I still find it difficult to reconcile two sentences in Dr. Wallace's letter. Men, he says, "engage in a futile search for happiness in excitement and power, whereas real happiness can be found only in a love of beauty, a delight in thought, and a desire to contribute to the well-being of the community." Yet, "the great majority of men will continue to find their education and their happiness chiefly in their daily tasks rather than in the more intellectual and aesthetic pursuits."

I am loath to admit that the fundamental truth of the first statement is not practicable. Certainly the higher reaches of man's thoughts are not for all. Professor Wallace mentioned particularly the large numbers of unfit in our universities. But as a secondary-school teacher I cannot accept the implication of the reference to the great masses of men as "those whom Providence has doomed to live on trust".

If much of our secondary education may be termed vocational, all of it is not. We are trying to teach children to think, not just how to earn a living. We are far from doing all that we might to hold before our students "the habitual vision of greatness" ... but I cannot forget the expressions on the faces of children who were listening to great music, though it was only on records in a classroom. I have watched great literature provoke to thought and stir the imagination of young people who are certainly unfit for college. I believe that great books and great art are powerful to give meaning to the daily tasks and human associations of the masses of men, provided that this greatness is made availbable to them and that they are introduced to it as simply and directly as the little child first explores the world around him. It is this faith I teach.

Margaret Frazer

Letter from a parent, dated June 3, 1966:

Dear Miss Frazer:
For some time now I have thought how much you give of your time and efforts to the students at Bloor. As the mother of one of those boys who have been helped by your kindness, may I express my thanks and appreciation at this time. Your interest and faith in Donald have given him something which he needs badly: faith in himself. From childhood onward he has always needed faith and commendation from others to bring out his best efforts and this you have done by asking him to write essays and teach the class. It has not been easy for him as he must work hard for every little achievement, but the very fact that you asked him to partici-

pate in these different activities has been a wonderful blessing. I thank you sincerely for all that you have done. E.C.

Report of a meeting of Grade 13 students at the home of their teacher, Margaret Frazer, October 10, 1967:

The students wanted to know why their ideas on the teaching of English in Grade 13 were being sought. Then they plunged into a free and at times chaotic discussion. I guided it as little as possible not to interfere with their intense involvement in the subject. Flashes of humour lit the depth of their seriousness. Wryly, they caught themselves in contradictions, glimpsing mysteries of learning they could only guess at.

Vexed questions soon emerged. Why must we have Shakespeare every year? ... They are hungry for modern books to study.... They are acutely aware of the poverty of their reading background. They wished they had not missed George Eliot and Conrad and had had more of Shaw....

Underlying much of their talk was the paradox they recognized: learning is natural; why do so many of us resist it? ... Boredom is one reason the desire to learn fades.... The plea for variety underlies many of the suggestions they made. But more intense was the cry for involvement.

Margaret, once so reticent about her personal life, spent the last weeks of her life talking about herself, particularly her past as a child and young woman. People who feel their mortality seem to do that; their roots tug at them. Margaret was taking what seemed to be a nostalgic, backward look tinged with a number of regrets. She never mentioned her successes as a scholarship student, as a beloved and respected teacher, as a thirty-nine-year-old pulling off the amazing feat of getting Grade 10 in piano at the Conservatory of Music, as someone for whom an important and valuable facility had been named, as one of the saviours of Nellie's, as a bulwark of her church, as a woman approaching her seventieth birthday who had learned to play the flute creditably. What was on her mind instead was the Baptist crucible that had formed her nature and how much she had yielded most of her life to the expectations of others.

With me she talked about the severity of the rules and prohibitions she absorbed from her family and society, and how long she lived with fear of disapproval. "I should have broken out much sooner," she mourned one day. She told Fran Sowton about a teacher for whom she formed a romantic yearning. Their relationship was never more than a warm friendship, but her feelings for him were stronger than he knew. He moved away, but they corresponded affectionately and continued to confide in one another. One day he wrote that he was about to be married. Margaret was surprised how much that hurt.

The long talk with Jay MacGillivray began with Margaret in a sad mood, discussing her relationship with her sisters. She grew up thinking she was the dud in the family, she said, and trying to impress her parents with her worth. The struggle had never stopped, even though the two people whose approval Margaret sought were dead. "I've been so *driven*," she said to Jay. "It was stupid of me to try to live up to the ideal my parents had for me, but I couldn't get beyond that need to prove to them that I wasn't a failure."

Margaret also talked about the women she had loved. She told Jay, who is a lesbian, that she wished she could have lived her life openly as Jay does. "If I had it to do over again," she said sorrowfully, "I would be straightforward about my relationships. But in my generation people didn't do that. How silly we were."

Then she wept for her dead sister, Lynn, and for her parents. She said through tears, "I guess I'm crying for myself, too."

Jay said approvingly, kindly, "You're really letting go, aren't you?"

Margaret squeezed Jay's hands without speaking.

Another time Margaret wanted to know what I knew about sibling rivalry. "Not much," I told her. The next day I looked through the research on my book about emotions but could find little there.

"Preposterous," Margaret snapped when I told her. "Sibling rivalry is *very* interesting."

Though the log-book records Margaret's diminishing strength, her occasional disorientation, and the bouts of sharp pain, the notes are a reflection of the team's dismay at these changes and do not give the whole picture of what was still a functioning, appreciative, alert, assertive human being. Margaret continued her lifelong habit of reading one or two books every week; she walked in the garden most days and sat for an hour or more admiring her flowers; she talked with Gwen and Jenny Hiseler, the children next door, about what mattered to them: worms, swimming, a birthday party. When Eileen Swinton came to call, Margaret wanted to know about ticket sales for the Nellie's benefit. She chose the music she wanted to hear and listened to it intently, kept busy with loading and changing tapes on her machine so that the house was rarely without glorious sounds. She was concerned about her car's battery, the collapsing Tory government in Ontario, and the weeds among her roses. On Thursdays someone had to bring her a *Globe and Mail* so she could read my column, and on Saturdays she wanted the *Toronto Star* so she could read Doris Anderson.

Jay's recollection of the overnight shift when Margaret talked intimately about herself provides a glimpse of the essential Margaret. With only weeks left to live, she was still a spunky, independent person very much in charge of her household. Jay recalled that when it was time for bed, Margaret could almost not climb the stairs. It was an ordeal of will power over weakness that took fifteen minutes, with Margaret pausing for a long time on each step and longest of all on the landing. "My legs are so heavy," she sighed.

None the less, once at the top she insisted to Jay that she could manage by herself in the bathroom. She went in and shut the door firmly. As Jay hovered outside, Margaret called out reprovingly, "I'm all right. *Thank you.*" From the sounds, Jay guessed that Margaret was washing herself. Then the door opened and Margaret called, "Okay now."

Jay helped her undress, noting sadly the distended belly and huge legs, and the body that otherwise was only bones and loose skin. Margaret instructed her to put the clothes she had removed in the hamper. She asked sharply who was doing the laundry the next day. Jay didn't know and Margaret gave a "hmph" of annoyance. Under Margaret's close supervision, Jay found her a clean nightie, prepared the bed, fluffed the pillows, massaged her feet and legs, brought the sleeping pills and the water – "not too cold, please, room temperature" – and turned out the lights.

Twice in the night Margaret needed help to turn over, but the next morning she astonished Jay by preparing to dress for the day as if nothing was the matter. Seeing how Margaret had laboured to climb the stairs the night before, Jay had been positive that she had reached the stage where she would stay in her bed. She was wrong. Margaret washed herself behind a closed bathroom door, applied her deodorant, brushed her hair, dressed in a fresh jogging suit, and slowly descended the stairs to take up her usual position on the living-room couch.

Margaret made no reference to the revelations and tears of the night before, and Jay understood. "You don't cook, do you, Jay?" Margaret said sweetly as Jay spread the green mohair blanket over her. "Then I'll have Shreddies and tea for my breakfast."

Bill Whitla talked to Margaret on the telephone shortly after he arrived home from Europe, and she expressed anxiety to see him. Nancy Whitla thinks that Margaret's seeming disinterest in her will and the funeral stemmed from her decision to have Bill handle those matters. She had been awaiting his return. Bill said he would drop in on Tuesday, June 4, with some books about Greece that might interest her.

At the back of his mind was a plan to raise those sensitive issues with her if he could find an opportunity, but when he saw Margaret he decided the discussion could not be delayed. He would have to plunge in.

He suggested that Margaret go into the garden with him where they could look at the books. Margaret's faith in Bill's tact and wise judgement was justified; what followed could not have been more considerate. When they were settled in a shady place, he said he had some matters to raise with her before they looked at the books.

"I have three things on my agenda that I want to get straight," he explained gravely. "You can talk about them or not. Maybe you don't want to talk about them at all, and that's fine, or maybe you'd rather talk about them with someone else, and that's fine too."

"Go ahead," Margaret said, very composed.

"One is about family," he began. Jane Davidson of Holy Trinity and Bill had tried to find Lynn, Margaret's missing sister. Jane had instigated a search through the Canadian Embassy, and also used a *Globe and Mail* tracking device, hunted through motor-vehicle registry lists, and asked for help from the professional organization to which Lynn's husband supposedly belonged. When Jane heard a rumour that the couple might be living in Grenada, she asked a member of Parliament to check. Every effort failed; Lynn was not to be found. So Bill was concentrating on the remaining sister, Phyllis Cockram, who lived in retirement in Florida.

"Have you been talking to Phyllis about your illness?" he asked. "Does she know your real condition?"

Margaret assured him that Phyllis knew. "She's coming to visit me in August," she said airily.

Bill drew a breath. "Don't you think she should come sooner?" he suggested. "You are weaker, Margaret, and you've lost weight, and you're eating less. Don't you think Phyllis should know what's happening with you?"

Margaret agreed that Phyllis should be told. She promised she would mention her poor condition the next time Phyllis telephoned.

As it happened, Bill answered the telephone later that afternoon and the call was from Phyllis. Before putting Margaret on the line, he introduced himself and suggested that Phyllis might think about coming at once instead of waiting until August.

"I don't think Margaret has much time," he said.

Phyllis said she would think it over and call back. That night, at the urging of her daughter, Barbara, Phyllis called Margaret to say she would arrive in a few days.

Bill's second item during the talk in the garden was the will. "This is a more difficult matter than the first," he warned Margaret. "It concerns your will. You had me look for the old one but, as you remember, I couldn't find it. I think in any case you need to think about a new one, unless that old one reflects your views now."

Margaret said it was fifteen years old and out of date. One of the main beneficiaries in it was her nephew, Ronald Cockram, Phyllis's adopted son, who had committed suicide some years ago.

"Well, I don't want to be part of any discussion of your will," Bill continued, "but you should be in touch with your lawyer. Who is your lawyer?"

Margaret said, "Laura Legge. I used to rent the top floor of a house where she and her husband lived. But she's very busy. She's the treasurer of the Law Society of Upper Canada. I don't like to bother her."

"But Margaret," Bill protested. "She's a friend. She sent flowers. I'm sure she would be happy to come. Do you want me to phone her?"

Margaret said decisively, "No. I'll do it."

"Well, let's set a time limit, shall we? How about if we agree that you'll call Laura Legge before next Tuesday?"

When Margaret nodded, Bill moved cautiously to the third matter.

"This is the most difficult," he said, picking his words with great care. "Have you given any thought to your funeral? I don't want to be morbid, but I know you have definite ideas, and it might relieve your mind to make those arrangements and then you would be free to get on with the rest of your life. People who love you would be very happy if you would involve yourself in planning it."

"I *have* been thinking about it," Margaret said in a faint voice. "I'm a member of the Toronto Memorial Society."

"I'm happy to hear that," Bill said. "Do you want a funeral service at Holy Trinity?"

Margaret recoiled. "No, definitely not." She made a disdainful gesture indicating her body. "I don't care what happens to this."

"Would you like a simple memorial service at HT then?" Margaret said that would be fine. "What about the hymns, the music, the readings?"

Margaret said at once, "There will have to be Bach." Then her eyes filled.

"We could talk about the music now," Bill said gently, "but perhaps it is too much to burden you with today. Do you want to put it off?"

Margaret gratefully agreed to postpone the discussion for a week. Then she grinned. "Well, if those are your three things, Bill," she said cheerfully, "that's not so bad."

They looked at the books together for a few minutes, and then Margaret said she was tired. Bill helped her into the house, where she lay down on the couch and fell asleep.

Once when Linda Rapson was applying the Jobst boot treatment, Margaret said suddenly, "You have beautiful hands."

Linda was almost too taken aback to speak. Her hands are important to her and she was startled at Margaret's perception.

I arrived at Holy Trinity on Sunday, June 9, just as the service had ended and the congregation was drifting toward the lunch table, where Elaine Hall and a few others were busily setting out plates. Elaine, Sheila File, Fran Sowton, and I gathered at the coffee urn and talked about Margaret.

"I have a friend who used to believe that people loved her only because she did a lot for others," Fran was saying. "Then when she was dying, people flocked around to help, and she was surprised. Margaret has made the same comments as my friend did, that she didn't know so many people truly cared about her."

199

"She's so appreciative," said Sheila File. Sheila is a loose-jointed, enthusiastic, open person employed by the Ontario government, who has a degree in political science, and had worked for three years as a volunteer in Toronto's Distress Centre, dealing with calls from suicidal people. Fifteen years ago her husband, a clergyman, left her and their five children, the youngest of them only three years old, but she has managed. Holy Trinity means a lot to her, and she is a passionate Anglican who once took a course to fit her to assist hospital chaplains. She was much drawn to Margaret for her kindness and was delighted to be included in Margaret's traditional Christmas-carol songfests, one of forty people packed into Margaret's living-room and dining-room and singing lustily out of the *Oxford Book of Carols*.

"I'm so touched by the way she notices everything people cook for her," Sheila was saying.

"I think Margaret's sense of taste is gone," Fran remarked slowly. "I suspect she's just being polite when she says something is delicious. It seems that something like a lemon flavour comes through, which is why she loves those lemon snows that Liz Greaves brings. Maybe we should avoid bland food now."

"She ate a great breakfast this morning," said Sheila. "Juice, Shreddies with honey, tea and three small glasses of ENSURE."

We marvelled. We are all mothers, and the habits run deep: *eat*, my child, and stay well.

Fran Sowton chaired the meeting that Sunday, June 9, in Holy Trinity. We heard that Linda might not come because she'd had a severe attack of flu during the night, but she was right on time, pale but beaming. "I filled myself with ginger ale," she explained. "I'll be all right. I think."

The first topic was Margaret's stabbing pain in the left thigh. It had occurred three days in a row. Consulting with Larry Librach, Linda had concluded that Margaret's tumours probably were pressing on a nerve. Not much could be done about it, she said, except to help her try different positions. Sometimes the pain went away abruptly when she stood up.

Linda was concerned about bed sores, since Margaret lay in

the same cramped position all day on the couch. Vivian Harrower, who had helped Margaret dress that week, reported that the skin of her back was unbroken. Margaret's legs, however, were so swollen that the elastic cuffs of her jogging pants bit deeply into the pulpy flesh. Fran Sowton said she would remove the elastics and replace them with drawstrings.

"The fluid in her legs could be her heart giving out or some imbalance in her system," Linda told us. "I can't be sure. You don't run a lot of tests on dying people to see what causes these changes. There's no point in adding to their discomfort. Margaret could slip away very suddenly."

We all had stories about Margaret's struggles to climb the stairs. Linda said she expected Margaret eventually would be staying in her bed, but in the meantime we might consider placing a portable toilet, a commode, in the living-room. The notion of a toilet in Margaret's living-room wasn't aesthetically appealing, so we talked of arranging a screen around it. Would Margaret use such a thing? someone asked. On reflection we thought not.

We considered alternatives. It would be easier all round, some-one sighed, if Margaret would stay in bed. One woman was indig-nant at the suggestion. "Margaret is valiantly trying to live as normally as she can," she said, looking distressed, "and she's quite unready to stay in bed!"

A gloomy silence fell, then someone had an idea. What if Margaret got dressed, as she insisted on doing, but spent the day on a chaise we could place in her upstairs study? Others were doubtful. They pointed out that Margaret felt more in charge of her fate when she was downstairs on the couch. Tucked away upstairs, her courage and pride would suffer.

Still, it was an inviting compromise to meet what would soon be an insurmountable mobility problem. Nigel and Wendy offered to take Margaret a catalogue that afternoon in case she wanted to make her own selection of the chaise or cot.

There were other details. Someone knew of rented equipment that could be installed on Margaret's toilet to provide a raised seat with supporting bars on either side, to make it easier for her to stand after using it. We decided it was needed at once.

Next, we spoke of the elastic straps that held the rubber electrodes of the Codetron in place. Because Margaret's legs were
grotesquely swollen, the straps weren't long enough to go comfortably around. Nigel offered to get longer ones. We bemoaned the
coldness of Margaret's feet, despite the fleecy booties, and decided
to get her outsized wool socks to wear under the booties.

"Be careful when you help her stand," Linda warned. "There's
a right and a wrong way to support someone. I don't want a lot
of bad backs out of this."

Merylie Houston started to describe how to help Margaret
stand. "Sit beside her and let her put her weight on you as she
rises," she said. "Don't bend over her and lift." We wanted a
demonstration, and Merylie leaped to her feet to oblige. She
knows a lot about backs. A few years earlier two discs in her
spine ruptured, resulting in six weeks of paralysis, a year in bed,
and three years of pain. We watched attentively as she stood in
the centre of our circle of chairs and mimed the movements.

"Make sure you're well braced, with your weight evenly on
both feet, before you begin to help Margaret walk," she said. "Let
her hold on to you, rather than you hold on to her. When she's
going upstairs, brace your arm with your hand under her forearm,
so she can lean on you, and place your other hand on the small
of her back."

We talked about food, but it no longer was a contentious issue.
No one objected when Linda said, "Don't worry about it. The
less in, the less out. The wonder is that Margaret doesn't vomit.
Judging from the sounds of her bowel, there's an obstruction
there. It must come and go, which accounts for the vagaries of
her appetite."

Bill Whitla, amid cheers of congratulation, described the conversation about Margaret's will and her funeral. He had learned
that Laura Legge had telephoned Margaret to inquire if she wanted
to work on a new will, but Margaret had put her off.

"I've given Margaret a week to call her lawyer back," he told us.

"That's too long," Linda said, her expression sombre. "Her

mind gets hazy at times. We have to do it while she's still clear or it isn't legal."

Bill nodded slowly. "All right. I'll see what I can do right away."

When the meeting broke up a few minutes later, I was edging through the crowd toward the door when Sheila File drew me aside. "I think we should make this experience available to other people who want to do palliative care," she said earnestly. "We're learning a lot that would be useful. What do you think of you and me and Fran and some others getting together to prepare a sort of manual?"

I thought it was a great idea. Sheila explained, "Palliative care has been on my mind a lot since last winter. There was a woman in our office who got cancer, and it was dreadful. She was well enough to be out of hospital, but there was no one at home to look after her. Eventually she went to Scotland to stay with a sister, but I felt that we all had failed her. I didn't know how to help her in the way we're helping Margaret. I didn't have the brains to just barge in and say I'll help. I'm really keen now on learning all I can about palliative care. I've signed up for a course in it. Next time someone I know is in that situation, I'll be ready."

Later I learned what a harrowing night Sheila had just experienced with Margaret. Sheila had been dreading at every shift that Margaret would have pain that couldn't be eased, and her worst fears were realized toward dawn when Margaret began to scream. "I can't move, I can't move!" she shrieked. With difficulty, as she recorded in the log-book, Sheila got the pain pill down Margaret's throat as Margaret continued to scream. "I'm a tactile person," Sheila later told me. "I didn't know what else I could do, so I just stroked her. In five minutes, the pain went away. I marvelled at myself. I hadn't fallen apart as I had thought I would."

On Tuesday I went to a committee meeting at Jessie's and found Liz Greaves hunting through a stack of paper on her desk. Her expression was grave. "Margaret is weaker," she said. "Yesterday it took an hour and a half for her to finish half a cup of soup. And she's jaundiced."

Fran Sowton mentioned the downstairs commode to Margaret. "It will save you the trouble of going up to the bathroom during the day," she said. Margaret didn't like the idea at all. Peering at Fran over her reading glasses, she said, "I need the exercise."

Later, Margaret asked Fran to start her car to see if the battery was working. Fran tried, but the motor wouldn't turn over. Margaret was upset. Fran tried to calm her, pointing out that there was no immediate need for the car. Margaret burst out, "But I like everything to be in order!"

Fran left a note in the log to say she would be away for the next two weeks. She would be in London, Ontario, attending a course in embroidery conducted by the noted American fabric artist, Barbara Smith, under the auspices of the Canadian Embroiderers' Guild. Her place on the team would be filled by her husband, Ian. In case Margaret needed some service during Ian's shift that was better provided by a woman, Mary Hiseler, the next-door neighbour, was ready to come at a moment's notice.

Fran worried at first that it was an imposition to ask Ian, who was ready for a rest after a full academic year of teaching at York University, to fill in her shifts. She thought of asking someone else but changed her mind, telling herself, No, he's going to get out of it what I am getting out of it. I wouldn't have missed this experience for the world, the energy and dynamic of all this caring. Not only is Ian needed for his strength because Margaret is fading, but he will appreciate experiencing the group's energy and love, the instant rapport between strangers.

She reasoned correctly. Ian was touched that the almost entirely female team accepted him without hesitation. "That was very moving," he said. "The team was primarily a women's collective. It was very important to me that I felt I belonged."

The feeling for Ian Sowton went beyond mere acceptance. He is a steady, sensitive, kind, funny, and unselfconscious man who won us all. One night, only a few days before Margaret died and after a day punctuated with some terrible moments during which Ian had been a bulwark, I turned to him as I was preparing to leave. I said fervently, "Ian, if ever you are single and I am single,

I want to be first in line to marry you."

"No you don't," grinned Vivian Harrower. "I'm first in that line."

Linda made a house call on Monday and noted the jaundice, a sign that cancer had spread to Margaret's liver. The hard part had arrived for Margaret and the team. Linda wrote in the log: "The leg pain is clearly related to position and can be relieved by moving. *So don't panic* if she gets it. You can help get rid of it. Otherwise things are much the same. You're all great."

The next morning, when Linda made her regular phone call, Margaret responded, "I'm very sleepy and slow, but here I am."

When Elizabeth Greaves came that evening, Margaret asked her to try to start her car and was vexed that the battery still didn't respond. "I want it in working condition for when I get better," she complained. Later, as twilight gathered in the living-room, Liz sat in the small rocking chair by Margaret's feet and they talked peacefully about the early days at Nellie's. Margaret drifted into sleep.

The next morning, Tuesday, June 11, Patti Welsh arrived to find Vivian Harrower waiting and Margaret seated at the dining-room table, eating breakfast. When she finished, Margaret settled herself on the couch to sort through her mail and read the paper.

As Patti dusted, Margaret talked about her dream the night before. In it she was shopping for groceries for Nellie's in the neighbourhood to which the Hiselers were moving. The dream brought together the conversation with Liz about the time when Nellie's was short of food and Margaret's sadness about the imminent departure of the Hiselers from the house next door. Patti marvelled that the dream was so innocent, but all Margaret's dreams, or at least the ones she told us about, were free of the horror of her dying. When Linda asked what she dreamed about, Margaret replied lazily, "Food mostly. Last night it was lasagna."

The novelist Joy Kogawa came for a visit that Tuesday afternoon, and Bill Whitla was there for the evening shift. He made some mushroom soup, adding mushrooms chopped fine, but Margaret choked and couldn't swallow the pieces. Ian Sowton dropped in with laundry, and Mary Hiseler came with lemon squares, a great favourite with Margaret. Anne van Egmond slept the overnight shift, noting in the log that Margaret "was distraught at needing help to get up from the couch and the toilet" and had a restless night.

The next day Margaret was grouchy with Wendy Farquhar, complaining that there were "too many people around". When Linda made her Wednesday house call, Margaret demanded an explanation for feeling so weak.

"Does it mean I won't get better?"

Linda looked at her. "I don't think it is likely that you will," she said quietly. "Your chances are very slim."

Margaret was shocked, which surprised Linda. It was clear that Margaret had believed that she could postpone her death for months. Margaret protested hotly, "But I *want* to get better! I'm trying to get better! I really thought that I was improving."

They ate lunch together, talked idly of flowers and birds, and listened to music. Though Margaret seemed calm, Linda was worried and reluctant to leave. She offered to brush Margaret's hair, and Margaret instructed her where the brush could be found upstairs in her bedroom. Linda had fetched it and was trying to subdue Margaret's stiff white hair when someone knocked at the front door and entered the house, calling, "Yoo hoo." It was Laura Legge.

Linda sets the scene by describing Laura Legge, a distinguished lawyer whose immaculate grooming is reminiscent of Margaret Thatcher, as "looking like she had come from a meeting of REAL women". Linda happened to be dressed in old jeans, soiled running shoes, and a faded, turquoise-blue sweatshirt that asked the burning question, "HAVE YOU HUGGED YOUR HORSE TODAY?" When Linda, hairbrush in hand, introduced herself as Margaret's doctor, Laura Legge was dumbfounded.

"I know I don't look it right now," Linda grinned at her.

Laura Legge said helplessly, "If I am interrupting anything.... "

"Oh no," Linda assured her. "It's all right. I'm just brushing Margaret's hair."

When she finished, she and Wendy withdrew to the garden to give the lawyer and her client privacy.

Laura Legge told Margaret that she "just happened to be in the neighbourhood", but in truth she was responding to a call from Bill Whitla to say that time was running out for Margaret. Taking in Margaret's withered appearance and yellowed skin and the huge legs elevated on a bank of pillows, the lawyer saw at once that Bill had not exaggerated. While Linda and Wendy chatted out of earshot in the garden, Margaret discussed what she wanted in her will. She named Laura Legge and Bill Whitla as executors and said she wanted a large sum to go to her niece, Barbara Weddle, and a smaller sum to her sister, Phyllis Cockram. She wanted Fran and Ian Sowton to distribute her personal possessions as they saw fit. Proceeds from the rest of her estate, consisting mostly of her mortgage-free house, were to be divided evenly among Nellie's, Holy Trinity Church, Amnesty International, the Toronto Rape Crisis Centre, Jessie's Centre for Teenagers, Margaret Frazer House, and Interval House. The last is a home for battered women and their children.

When the estate was settled at the end of the year, each of the designated charities received $14,000.

Linda came indoors to answer the telephone as Laura Legge was leaving. When Margaret was alone with Linda and Wendy, she beamed at them. "I've just done a new will," she said with satisfaction. "It's good to have it off my mind." She sketched the decisions she had made and then stopped, startled. She had thought of an addition, and asked Wendy to telephone Laura with new instructions.

At that point, Fran Sowton arrived with the raised toilet seat. She installed it and Margaret, after the first use that night, when she hated it, came to be fond of it and dubbed it, "the throne". We all loved it, a bright blue toilet insert, with a comfy padded seat high enough to make standing up easy after use. On either side of the seat were strong chrome bars to give hand-grip support.

Wendy wrote in the log as she left that afternoon, "I am glad I have been here today, and it has been very difficult seeing M's realization (acceptance) of the meaning of wills, etc., for she is very saddened by all of this. My heart is with her and all of you at this time."

Fran Sowton, doing her last shift before leaving for London, observed in the log-book, "M very relieved that the will was finished with. We reminisced about Nellie's and about her childhood. Peaceful and seems to be coming to terms with a poor prognosis."

Laura Legge went to extraordinary trouble to help her dying friend. She had copies of the will ready that night and brought them to Margaret. She was accompanied by her son, John, to witness the signing, and explained blithely that they were going to a wedding reception nearby. "I though we might as well get this settled, since you're on our way," she said. If Margaret thought it was unusual for a will to be dictated, typed, witnessed, and signed in six hours, she made no comment.

That night I was moderator of a panel discussion about AIDS — acquired immune deficiency syndrome. The event was sponsored by the AIDS Committee of Toronto and was attended by a number of people who knew men who had died, or were dying, of AIDS. I spoke of the palliative care that Margaret was receiving, though I did not name her, and mentioned that we were considering a how-to pamphlet to help others. The response was so positive that I told Linda about it the next morning.

She called back later. She had passed the information along to Bill Whitla, and he had suggested that I speak to Margaret about it. He thought she might be interested in participating, or maybe she would want to leave some of her estate for such a purpose.

I said, "I'll be seeing Margaret tomorrow when I do my Thursday shift. I'll mention it to her."

"Good," Linda said. Then she added impulsively, "I wish Margaret hadn't decided to sell the house. It would be nice if she had left it to Nellie's or someone like that. Then we could go there every spring and see Margaret's jack-in-the-pulpit at the foot of the garden."

Thursday, June 13

Elaine Hall called in the morning to ask if I could replace her an hour earlier than usual. She wanted to attend a session on naturotherapy, a system of healing without chemicals, at the Alternative Health Clinic where she is a colon therapist. As I arrived on a lovely summery afternoon, she was helping Margaret down the stairs, going very slowly. Together we helped Margaret lower herself laboriously to lie on the couch. Margaret's face was gaunt and her eyeballs yellow with the jaundice; her skin hung loosely on her stick-like arms, but her lower body was bloated into obesity. We fixed pillows on the arm of the couch and gently lifted her heavy legs on to them. I replaced a down-filled bootie that had fallen off one of her puffy feet.

Elaine and I made no comment as Margaret let out a groan, but our eyes met in despair.

Fran Sowton had commented about "the instant rapport" that members of the team felt for one another, and it was true. We were a disparate lot, as Jay MacGillivray had noticed with alarm at the first meeting of the team, and half of us did not know the other half, but we never met as strangers. Anyone encountered at a shift change – whether man or woman, old or young, articulate or taciturn, lesbian or straight, dressed in flowered print or army-surplus fatigues – could be assumed to be sensible, interesting, principled, and free of humbug. The continuity that ran through the team outweighed the differences.

Their range of occupations included oil trader, university professor, clergyman (and woman), social worker, nurse, artist, psychologist, civil servant, writer, publicist, teacher, counsellor, and graduate student. As someone observed at Margaret's wake, the team was made up in good part of people involved in caring professions. Undoubtedly an element that contributed to the team's effectiveness was that most members were care givers by nature and by training. When the network intersected in Margaret's living-room, it was unified and made whole by the small woman curled up on the couch.

In my theology, the human race expresses its divinity when people are kind to one another. The Margaret team was a confirmation of that faith; Margaret's home was a cathedral, and every minute there was for me a religious experience.

Reflecting on the closeness the team felt, Helen Gough described it as continuity: "a strand that ran all through those people." The summer after Margaret died, Helen and I talked about the team in her office overlooking a school playground. She added, "Margaret pulled that strand and brought us together tightly. We learned a lot about one another in ways we had sensed but never experienced. Sheila Mackenzie, Grace Ross, and others – I saw them in a new way, on a whole new level. We hug one another a lot in Holy Trinity and we do express our affection, but there's a sense that it happens once a week. This was more. Much more."

Kathy Johns said, "The team said something about what a community can be. There is lots of talk about that in churches, but you don't often see it happen."

Many on the team made lasting friendships with someone met for the first time at Margaret's or with someone whose worth emerged during those months. For instance, Elaine Hall of Holy Trinity fit uncommonly well with the Nellie's people and after Margaret's death worked with them on a committee to establish a hospice in Toronto. Elaine is a shy woman with fine-grained skin and a warm smile. A nurse, she is happily married and the mother of two children. Ten years earlier she was one of a group of people ejected from a congregation because they wanted "to allow our children to take Holy Communion before they were confirmed, and that sort of thing – all the things we do at Holy Trinity ".

She wasn't aware of Margaret Frazer much when her family switched to Holy Trinity because she was too occupied with child raising to join the committees, but her children were impressed with Margaret because she remembered their names. Margaret was HT's plant woman, Elaine said. Margaret went to service every Sunday with a watering can, scissors for pruning, and a sprayer, and Elaine fell into the habit of helping her tend the potted flora.

"I liked Margaret because she talked to me," Elaine told me one afternoon in August. We had met outside a downtown drop-in centre on Church Street where Elaine is a member of the board of directors. "Margaret always remembered what you told her. Some people don't do that, but you could rely on her."

Elaine was startled in March when Margaret, preparing to go to hospital, asked if she would be the "next-of-kin". Margaret had been asked by the hospital to name someone who, in her words, "would pick up my valuables if I die". Nothing in their relationship had suggested to Elaine the closeness that the request implied, but she agreed without hesitation.

Margaret's choice of Elaine to stand at her back isn't difficult to understand. Elaine is one of those true, dependable people on whom, like the centre-pole of a tent, a hundred can lean.

Elaine's undertaking to organize the Holy Trinity network for Margaret's care was a natural extension, as she saw it, of the commitment she made when she accepted being Margaret's "next-of-kin". Her quiet and effective role in Friends of Margaret didn't mean, however, that she and Margaret became intimates. Both women continued to be reserved with one another and were never entirely comfortable together. Elaine's shifts had none of the long and intimate conversations that others knew. Instead she cleaned the house and worked diligently in the garden, pausing only to share pleasantries over lunch or a cup of tea.

Once Elaine found a tarragon plant in Margaret's compost. She was puzzled, wondering how the plant had been mistaken for a weed, and went inside to ask Margaret. Margaret, hooked up to the Codetron and reading, made an impatient gesture and said rudely, "Don't bother me now. I'm trying to get better."

Elaine was hurt and withdrew. Later she reasoned that Margaret had acted out of embarrassment, realizing she was the one who in a moment of confusion had asked to have the tarragon pulled. Elaine forgave the slight. As she was leaving, she looked long at Margaret and said softly, "I love you."

When we were drinking tea on the patio of the drop-in centre, weeks after Margaret's death, Elaine reflected on that farewell. "I had never said that before, but it seemed very appropriate. I admired her very much as she was dying. She had things so in hand. Margaret's attitude, plucky and optimistic, got her through a lot of things in her life, so she used it for dying."

Elaine surprised herself in those three months of caring for Margaret. As a hospital nurse, she had avoided dying patients as much as she could. She sympathized therefore with people at Holy Trinity who told her they were ashamed they couldn't help Margaret but didn't think they could bear to be close to someone dying. One woman whose marriage was breaking up told Elaine that she couldn't volunteer for a shift because she didn't think she could take any more stress.

Elaine comforted them, saying she understood, and wondered how she herself would manage. But when Margaret died Elaine realized that she had overcome her own avoidance of death. "I've done some reading lately about death, and I've got some insight now that I didn't have before. Margaret helped me in that way. She helped us all, in fact. The people at Holy Trinity are closer now than we've ever been."

On the Thursday before Margaret died, Elaine did nurse-like bed care for her that was beyond the expertise of most of the team. She brought lemon and glycerine mouth swabs to stimulate the flow of saliva in Margaret's dry mouth and expertly administered a back-rub. When she left, Margaret gave her a weak grin of gratitude and said, "You're so good to me, Elaine. Thank you for everything."

"I love you," Elaine replied.

"Love you, too," Margaret whispered.

That evening Margaret for the first time allowed me to spoon feed her. Her dinner consisted of a few mouthfuls of mushroom soup, without the mushrooms, and some ice cream mixed to a puddle with maple syrup. With long rests between, I put tiny amounts in her mouth with the smallest silver spoon I could find to spare her the effort of opening her mouth wide.

Margaret seemed distracted and distant. I pushed the coffee table out of the way and pulled up the rocking chair so I could sit beside her and hold both her hands in mine. She said, "Linda thinks that I will ... that there's more of a chance that I will die than get well. What do you think?"

I said carefully, "It doesn't look good, but who knows?"

Margaret received this with an indifferent nod, as confirmation of old news. Then she lay back on the pillows and looked out of the bay window at sunlight sifting through her maple trees. Suddenly she turned to me, eyes blazing, and cried out, "I'm not going to die!"

I said, "Yes you are. But no one knows when."

She closed her eyes. I held her hands tightly and watched her slow, exhausted breathing. I began to cry. Tears rolled down my cheeks and my nose dripped. I didn't want her to hear me sniffle and I didn't have a hand free to get a tissue out of my pocket. As I was struggling for control, she sensed what was happening. She opened her eyes and looked at me with a fathomless gaze.

"I don't want you to die," I explained helplessly.

There was nothing to say. She simply closed her eyes again and, after a moment, I let go one of her hands and wiped my nose and my wet face.

When I had cleared and washed our dishes, we arranged ourselves for a social chat, our expressions back to normal. I told her about the proposed manual for the palliative care of people dying of AIDS. "Is there something you'd like to include in it? Something from your experience of being an extremely sick person?"

Margaret said at once, "People shouldn't wave their arms so much when they talk. It's very tiring."

Dry and economical as her suggestion was, it opened a door for me. I remembered suddenly how our daughter, recuperating from terrible injuries after a traffic accident, had created a womb-like environment of gentleness around her. *Pace* matters greatly to the very ill, I realized. Perhaps on the psychological level there is a sense of slowing the world down in order to be longer in it,

213

but the reality is that disturbed sleep, pain, and fear are a mixture that rubs nerves raw. Sick people need to be cushioned in every sense. For their well-being, everyone around them must speak in low voices, move softly, avoid rattling dishes or equipment, and keep gestures small and sparse.

Guiltily, I thought of the many times Margaret had said to me, a woman who habitually dashes everywhere, "Please, *don't hurry!*" when I would leap to my feet to fetch her a pillow or a cup of tea. I thought she was being considerate, but in truth she was trying to protect herself against the abrasion of hustle and clatter.

We listened to Mozart and then talked about Bloor Collegiate. "It is ten years this month since I last stood in a classroom," she mused. "I missed the students, especially at first, but I had to give up teaching as soon as I qualified for the full pension. There was so much I wanted to do with my life. I had to leave so I could do the things I had been postponing all those years."

"Remember when you first retired," I said. "You said you were going to read everything by and about Virginia Woolf."

"A big project," she said, with a wan smile. "I never did get around to it."

Linda came at about eight that night, bringing her gusto, confidence, and good humour. She picked up the hairbrush from the mantel of the living-room fireplace and began to smooth Margaret's stiff white hair.

"You've got wonderful hair, Margaret," she crooned. "So thick."

"It needs a wash," Margaret replied, lulled by Linda's tone. "Maria is coming on Tuesday to give me a shampoo."

Linda looked at me. I raised my eyebrows in a question, and she shrugged *who knows?* At Linda's suggestion, Margaret changed her position. She sat erect with pillows behind her back and Linda sat next to her with one hand in hers and her other arm snug around Margaret. Margaret drooped her head against Linda's sturdy shoulder with a look of perfect peace on her face. We listened in companionable silence to the Mary O'Hara tape.

We agreed we liked "Bridge Over Troubled Water" best, but Margaret was also fond of the sprightly "Lord of the Dance", which Mary O'Hara sings at the conclusion of side two of the tape.

"We sing 'Lord of the Dance' at Holy Trinity," she told us in a fuzzy voice. "If we feel like it, we get up and dance around the pews right in the middle of the service. Once when Helen Gough was here and we were playing Mary O'Hara, we both joined her in singing 'Lord of the Dance'. And Pat Capponi was here that day and she knew all the words too. I said to Pat, 'You're a Muslim, how come you know "Lord of the Dance"?' and Pat said, 'Everyone knows "Lord of the Dance".'"

We laughed and Margaret, leaning tiredly against Linda, said, "There was a drunk who used to come to Holy Trinity services and he would insist on leading the choir. I found him a trial because he was always half a beat off. Then he stopped drinking, and someone told me that Holy Trinity had something to do with his rehabilitation. But he still leads the choir, and he's still half a beat off."

That night Linda began to keep a private journal about Margaret to augment the notes I was making. In her first entry she wrote: "I arrived around eight after work. June was there dressed in her Jessie's sweatshirt, looking upset and moved by the turn of events. That night we established ourselves as a team who would see Margaret through the last week of her life with compassion and humour and help each other bear the pain of her death."

I don't remember that we put the pact into words. I don't think we had to.

Sheila Mackenzie arrived, looking dishevelled and indomitable, and sat quietly with us in the darkening room. I said an emotional goodbye to Margaret, kissing her tenderly, and told her I would be back Monday.

"Will you be here?" I asked her pleasantly.

She grinned like Margaret of old, and nodded.

Linda sat in the dining-room, writing in the log-book by the light of an overhead fixture, while Margaret and Sheila listened to baroque flute music. After a moment, Sheila rose from the rocking chair and sat where Linda had been on the couch beside Margaret, with her arm around Margaret's shoulders.

Friday, June 14

Margaret woke Sheila around four-thirty that morning, groaning and crying out in pain. She took a Tylenol, which she had great difficulty swallowing, but half an hour later it was clear to Sheila that the pill wasn't strong enough. At five-thirty she called Linda, who recommended that Margaret take Leritine, the drug the hospital doctor had prescribed. Despite this reinforcement, however, Margaret couldn't get back to sleep.

Sheila put the Mary O'Hara tape in the machine and placed it next to the bed. Margaret had said when she wakened that "Bridge Over Troubled Water" had been running soothingly through her head. "I think the tape helped M a little as the pain ebbed," Sheila wrote in the log-book. "It sure helped me." Sheila stretched out on the floor beside Margaret's bed as Margaret dozed fitfully, little cries escaping from her. From time to time Sheila would hold her in her arms. Margaret gasped weakly that this was the longest-lasting pain she had yet experienced.

Margaret was in the bathroom when Linda arrived around eight-thirty that morning. Sheila, whispering in the guest bedroom, was describing the torment of the night when she was interrupted by Margaret's voice calling from the bathroom. "I'm going to take a shower now," she trilled.

Linda, astonished, opened the bathroom door "to see a skeleton covered with skin standing at the sink, trembling with weakness". Linda suggested that Margaret should wait until Fran brought a bath seat promised that day and Margaret agreed. "I've already washed myself anyway," she said, "so now I just have to get dry."

Linda and Sheila rubbed Margaret with towels. As Margaret turned to go back to her bedroom, she bent almost double. Linda leaped to hold her from behind and called to Sheila to get in front as they moved in a sort of lurching frog-march into the bedroom. Margaret collapsed in a sitting position on the edge of her bed and directed the two women to find her deodorant, her underwear, and the pink jogging suit. "When we'd hoisted her up to pull up her panties and sweatpants," Linda wrote, "she sat down on the bed with another thud."

216

"Where now, Margaret?" Linda asked, knowing full well what the reply would be.

"Why I'm going downstairs, of course," Margaret replied sunnily.

With Sheila on one side and Linda on the other, she staggered to her feet. They waited until her dizziness cleared and then helped her to the top of the stairs. Linda gripped her on one side and Sheila stood on the step below, poised to catch her if she fell. Margaret grasped the handrail and said with a lilt, "Away we go!"

When they got her safely to the couch, pillows under her head, the swollen legs elevated on more pillows, and the mohair blanket spread over her, Linda asked, "How do you feel?"

Margaret beamed lovingly. "I feel protected by you two," she said. Then she announced she'd like some porridge. "So *gutsy*," Sheila thought, tears in her eyes as she stirred the mixture in a pot.

In the living-room Linda asked Margaret casually, "What does Sheila do?"

Margaret replied with a satisfied smile, "She be's an interesting person."

Then she belched noisily and looked at Linda inquiringly. "Do you want it in another key?" she asked.

When Margaret had eaten half a bowl of cereal, she ordered Sheila upstairs to get some sleep. "You had a terrible night," she told her in a motherly way. "You need to get some rest."

Linda went to her office, leaving instructions in the log that Margaret was to be given a Tylenol No. 3 every four hours, even if she had no pain, in order to forestall an onslaught like the one of the past night. She promised to telephone hourly through the day and return as soon as she could. She called me to report on the episode.

"I'm sure Margaret will live until two o'clock this afternoon," Linda told me, "because Jack Adam, the new minister of Holy Trinity church, is coming to introduce himself, and Margaret will want to look him over. But I doubt that she'll get up those stairs again."

She asked me to telephone Bill Whitla to advise him that the end was close. She said I could say that it wouldn't matter if people wanted to drop in instead of waiting for their regular shifts. Margaret was becoming vague and probably wouldn't notice. Bill's voice was heavy and slow. "I'm not surprised at the bad news," he said, "but still it's hard to take. You'll be interested to know that Margaret and I have talked further about her memorial service. She is definite that she doesn't want too much talk. Instead she'd like some Bach, maybe by her friends at CAMMAC, and perhaps some violin. What do you think about asking her flute teacher to play?"

"Good idea," I said, admiring his devotion to Margaret and his thoughtfulness.

"And what happens about her obituary?" he asked. "We don't really know much about her life history, though we could get it from her sister Phyllis."

I said I had been keeping notes for a column about Margaret that I planned to write for the *Globe and Mail*. I thought I had enough biographical material to put together an obit if we couldn't reach Phyllis.

Sheila was asleep upstairs in the guest room that morning when Merylie Houston let herself in the front door. Margaret was so disoriented that she thought for a moment that Merylie was Jack Adam. When Merylie suggested that she should have her session in the Jobst pressure boot, Margaret assured her that she'd already had two treatments and wouldn't require another. Checking in the log, Merylie saw that Margaret was mistaken but made no comment. The boot could wait.

Around noon Margaret agreed that it was time for her Codetron treatment. With difficulty Merylie helped her into a sitting position on the couch and prepared to assist her across the room to the chair next to the Codetron equipment. Margaret tried to heave herself to her feet but couldn't move. She tried again and again to stand, without success, and Merylie was unable to lift her unaided because of the fragile state of her injured spine.

Margaret's solution was to drop to her knees and crawl across the room. When she reached the chair, she couldn't lift herself to sit in it. Merylie ran upstairs to get Sheila, and between them they managed to get Margaret, who was a dead weight, into the chair. "She had absolutely no strength in her arms and legs," Merylie wrote in the log-book. "It was very scary for her, because it happened so suddenly."

Merylie called Linda, who advised her to leave Margaret in the Codetron chair until she could get there after office hours. "She's going to have to stay on the couch or in her bed very soon," Linda said. "She can't go up and down those stairs. We'll have to carry her."

Linda called me and explained what had happened. Sheila had to leave, and Linda didn't want Merylie to be alone in case Margaret needed to be lifted. Would I be able to go to Margaret's at once? Of course.

I was still at the stage of putting faces on the Holy Trinity people I met as names in the log-book, but I knew which one was Merylie Houston. When Merylie gave her name during the first meeting of the Friends of Margaret in the church, Linda Rapson had said, "You're not Merylie to me. To me, you're Mary." I was baffled until it was explained that Merylie plays the role of the Virgin in Holy Trinity's famous Christmas pageant. The casting is easy to understand. Merylie is a small, tousle-haired woman whose face reflects extraordinary sweetness and the strong look of a focused life.

Linda's indirect compliment was gratifying. Jim Houston leaned toward his wife and whispered, "You see, you *are* appreciated." Months later, in a crowded cafeteria one bleak November day, Merylie reflected on the nature of volunteerism. "Much of what I do is in the women's world of unpaid work," she said. "You burn yourself out in ten years and another woman comes along and replaces you. You don't exist any more. You really wonder what your life has been about. That was very nice, very unexpected, Linda knowing that I play Mary."

Merylie and I drew up chairs on either side of Margaret, who was seated in the Codetron chair, pillows behind her, her legs supported on pillows on the footstool, and the green mohair blanket tucked around her.

"I can't understand why I'm so confused," Margaret said faintly.

219

"I've never been like this in my life. I can't remember even simple things."

"Maybe you're sick," I said, stroking her hair. "Or you're tired because you had a bad night."

"It's more than that," she sighed.

She withdrew into her thoughts, and sometimes seemed to be asleep. Merylie felt that Margaret was recouping, taking a breather, so we talked in low voices over Margaret's dozing form while she rested. Merylie and I did not know each other except for the times we attended Friends of Margaret meetings so I wasn't aware that she is considered by the Toronto Board of Education to be the most formidable parent-activist in the city. During a heated time between the board and parents, Merylie chaired a parents' convention that was a rousing success.

We happened on the topic of education and I was dazzled. Merylie was wonderfully informed. She knew which separate-school systems were being sensitive about teaching jobs that would be lost in the public schools by the Ontario government's decision to extend funding and which ones were behaving badly. She described some strategies that were in the planning stages and some sensitive programs already in place. It was all new to me.

"How do you know so much about schools?" I asked.

"I've been involved in the politics of education for twelve years," she explained.

She had good news she had shared with Margaret, who appreciated what it meant more than I would. Merylie had just been accepted for graduate study in the modern languages centre of the Ontario Institute for Studies in Education. Margaret, who knew how difficult it is to get into OISE's high-powered courses, was thrilled for her.

Margaret began to rouse. She had some coherent and alert comments to make about streaming young people in different schools. "We had all the religions at Bloor Collegiate," she told us. "I was in the guidance department there for years, though I hated the word 'guidance', and we dealt with a good many problems arising from the different faiths in the school. But that's the way young people learn to overcome bigotry."

She had a sudden thought and fixed me with a fierce look. "This isn't your regular time," she said sharply. "Shouldn't you be at home working on your book?"

I said, "It's all right. I started the chapter on guilt this morning. It's all about Baptists."

That amused her, as I had hoped. "Of course," she said approvingly.

Merylie checked her watch. Margaret's revival was right on time. The minister was due to arrive any minute.

Jack Adam, Holy Trinity's new minister, was a little late, held up by a funeral service that went longer than he had anticipated. A vigorous, cheerful, greying man with the outline of a beard on his jawline and an ingratiating grin, he appeared flustered and a bit hearty. He introduced himself to Margaret, not in the least put off by Margaret's dreadfully ill appearance, and she lifted her hand to him as regally as a queen. Merylie and I served him tea and cakes, placing the tray on the piano bench near his chair, our own manner a bit hearty as well. Then Merylie went to the pharmacy to replenish the Tylenol supply and I went to Margaret's study upstairs, where I browsed among the books.

Margaret's shelves extended to the ceiling on all four walls, with the books arranged according to alphabet and category. One section dealt with organic gardening, another with women and Christianity, another with birds, another with books on feminism. The novels included Doris Lessing, Virginia Woolf, and a lesser-known Margaret Laurence work, *The Tomorrow Tamer*. The poetry collection, with lots of Keats and Shelley, covered an entire shelf. Near a pull-out typewriter table were her reference books and a hefty edition of the *Shorter Oxford English Dictionary*. In another place were travel books, books on yoga, a report on the proposed Mackenzie pipeline by Tom Berger, and poverty reports.

Merylie returned from the drugstore and joined me in the study. We could hear Margaret's voice, strong and well, going on and on downstairs, punctuated occasionally by short interjections from the minister. Half an hour went by and I grew concerned. It seemed to me that Margaret was using strength she didn't have, and the penalty would be great. Merylie shared my distress, so we drifted downstairs as a hint to the clergyman.

Margaret saw our design and rejected it. "I'm fine," she called. "We're having a *wonderful* talk."

We went into the garden and in ten minutes returned. We could hear Jack telling Margaret that he should go, he didn't want to tire her. "I'm enjoying this," she said insistently. "Please stay." Merylie and I meekly returned to the garden.

After auditioning the new minister for almost an hour, Margaret put her stamp of approval on him. When he left, she was excited and happy. "He's just a wonderful choice for Holy Trinity," she told us, her sunken eyes dancing in the yellowed face. "I told him things about myself that I've never told anyone in my life. He's nifty."

Linda had decreed that the team would double up on shifts. "Margaret is going to need two people to lift her," she explained. "And, besides, she should never be left alone for even a minute. People shouldn't die alone."

Vivian Harrower, the parish secretary of Holy Trinity, took to the telephone in a scramble to rewrite the schedule that Joyce Brown had left. I knew Vivian only slightly. She did Monday night shifts, taking over from Liz Greaves or me and never a minute late. She is a tall, slender, dark woman with a stillness about her like someone in grief. She is separated from her children and husband, a clergyman. Looking for a parish, she somehow happened upon Holy Trinity.

"I wasn't in very good shape when I came to the church," she told me when we talked one October day in the church office, "but people took me in. They accepted me and didn't ask a lot of questions."

She encountered Margaret Frazer almost immediately. "She reminded me of a high-school Latin teacher I had, the brusque type we all feared and loved. I didn't see much of her because I avoided the politics of the place. I just didn't have the energy for that, but I could see she was a very intelligent and questioning kind of person."

Vivian has a memory of Margaret in the pulpit one Sunday. Two policemen had raped a young woman who had been living at Nellie's, and Margaret, furious, told the congregation about it.

Beyond those impressionistic fragments, there was nothing personal between the two women. Vivian was working on a master's degree in theology, which kept her busy, and Margaret was on a half-dozen committees. Once Margaret invited Vivian to the Christmas carol sing at her home, but Vivian had another engagement that night and couldn't go.

Because Vivian lived around the corner from Wellesley Hospital, she visited Margaret in hospital more than she might otherwise have done and "got to know her". They were never alone together on those occasions because Margaret had so many visitors, but Vivian saw Margaret at her feisty best, her blue eyes snapping with indignation at reports that in her absence committees were being slothful or errant. Vivan discovered she was very fond of Margaret and, when the idea of the team was broached, signed up for Monday nights.

The relationship between them those nights was warm, but they kept their privacy. Vivian is constitutionally incapable of violating another's space, and when Vivian was with her Margaret was content to just be. "We didn't talk about her death, but I felt she was so open, so vulnerable. I wondered if her fight to get well wasn't somehow her feeling that we were there to prevent her death and she would be letting us down if she died."

Vivian's mother had died a year earlier in a hospital in Florida after a long deterioration on kidney dialysis. As Vivian helped Margaret undress on the last few Monday nights of her life, seeing on the distorted body how rapidly Margaret's disease was advancing, she was aware that she was providing for Margaret the kind of tender care that distance had prevented her from giving to her mother.

Vivian's revised schedule was being communicated by telephone, but she promised to bring a copy the next night. Merylie and I were told to expect Helen Gough, but around five-thirty it was Linda who bounced through the front door. Merylie made her farewells, lingering over Margaret, and when she was gone Linda asked, "What is there to eat? I'm starving."

"Cat food," I replied. "Also custards."

"Sounds delicious," Linda said. She was studying Margaret, who was beaming at her. She didn't like Margaret's thin arms resting on the wooden arms of the Codetron chair, so she folded two pillows and tenderly placed Margaret's arms on them. Margaret, the tension gone from her face, looked blissful as Linda fussed over her.

We discussed Margaret's lack of mobility. She hadn't required that we take her upstairs to the bathroom all day, a sign that her kidneys were failing and the bowel was again obstructed, but if Margaret had needed the toilet it would have been almost impossible for me and Merylie to have carried her upstairs. Seated on either side of Margaret, Linda and I munched on some stale peanuts that I had found in the fridge and talked about the limited range of possibilities.

"Margaret," I said, "I'm really good with pillows. I am, in fact, bloody marvellous with pillows. I can fix a nest of pillows in your bed upstairs that will be heavenly. We'll tuck you in.... "

Margaret glared at me. "On what assumption are you operating?" she asked me coldly.

Linda intervened. "We are operating on the assumption that you can't even get to that couch over there, much less up and down the stairs all day."

Margaret was not at all sure of that. She said she wanted to move to the couch. We made preparations accordingly, moving the footstool out of the way and shifting the coffee table. I picked up the clutter of tapes and books stacked on the floor beside the couch and Linda fluffed up the pillows on the couch and laid the green mohair blanket ready. Then we braced ourselves, one on each side of Margaret, and lifted her, swaying and tipsy, to her feet.

When she was steady she sang out, "Away we go!" We had taken only a few steps when Margaret stiffened. "Look," she said in an offended tone, "the feet of the couch aren't on the rug."

Linda and I were incredulous. The small light sofa had been pushed closer to the bay windows than usual, so that its wooden legs were on the hardwood floor. Margaret apparently liked to position the front legs on the rug. Linda began to laugh helplessly that this frail, emaciated, dying woman was standing in the middle of her living-room worrying about the placement of her couch.

"Have you got a good grip on her?" I asked.

"Got her," grinned Linda.

I lifted the couch so the front legs were on the rug by a few inches.

"Has she got it straight?" Linda asked. "Is it straight enough?"

Margaret, her face twitching in amusement, said it was fine.

Linda thinks that was the moment when we fell into what she called "our routine" of kidding Margaret. At some deep level, I'm sure, there is a swarm of psychological explanations for the mood of good humour that descended on us. I'm not equipped to understand that, but I know that laughter made it possible for us both to bear the pain of watching Margaret die.

Some were shocked. One team member said to me in gentle reproof, "I don't think this is a time for levity." Perhaps not. Probably not. I'm still not sure. But Linda Rapson and I spent a lot of time with Margaret over the last week of her life, and most of it was merry.

I found some weeks-old lasagna in the freezing compartment of Margaret's fridge, and Linda and I ate it at the dining-room table with an ameliorating glass of wine. We used Margaret's delicate stemmed wine glasses from her china cabinet and set the table prettily, but it was a strange meal. In the dining-room were two healthy women talking trivia and in the living-room, of which the dining-room was an extension, Margaret lay listening contentedly to our chatter, and dying.

I left when Helen Gough arrived. Helen is a member of Holy Trinity, an angular woman with a sharp, narrow face, a wealth of snow-white hair twisted in a loose bun, a loose-jointed gait, and impressive clarity of mind. She's fifty-five, a teacher with a degree in theology and another in political science, who works

225

as a community-relations officer in a low-income area of the Toronto Board of Education.

Helen later referred to that night as, "The beginning of the send-off."

Margaret lay peacefully braced against five or six pillows, her legs on two more, as Helen and Linda talked idly in the living-room. Linda said she was waiting for the overnight person, Pat Capponi, and Sheila Mackenzie was also expected. It was news to Margaret that two people would be staying overnight, and she protested. Linda reminded her that she was finding it difficult to move, but Margaret was adamant that Pat Capponi alone would be sufficient. She also vetoed being wakened every four hours to take a Tylenol. "That won't be necessary," she said firmly.

Sheila Mackenzie telephoned. She agreed to stay home but remain on standby in case Pat Capponi needed help in the night.

Margaret, speaking like a plaintive child, asked Linda to sit beside her. Linda moved the coffee table out of the way and drew up the small rocking chair in its place, taking hold of Margaret's hand.

"When I hear you talking to other people, like June, I wonder if there's a problem," Margaret said.

"Do you think we talk about you behind your back?" Linda asked.

"It isn't that," Margaret said. "It's that you all seem so concerned about the stairs."

Then she added thoughtfully, "Maybe I should try the stairs."

Linda asked if she needed to use the toilet and Margaret said she didn't.

"You mean you want to *practise!*" Linda asked, in amazement.

Margaret nodded.

Linda laughed. "No, absolutely *no*. You have to conserve your strength."

Five or ten minutes passed and then Margaret said, "Maybe if I went up and sat on the throne I could do something."

Linda and Helen helped her to her feet and she shuffled to the foot of the stairs. The elastic in her jogging pants, loosened to

226

avoid pressure on her swollen abdomen, wasn't sufficient to hold up her pants, so while Linda held Margaret's body in her strong arms Helen Gough followed behind holding up the pants.

Margaret was in the bathroom when Nancy and Bill Whitla arrived. Helen Gough, thinking the whole affair rather a hoot, went to the kitchen to make tea. The moment Margaret saw Bill she exclaimed excitedly, "Guess what! Laura Legge came, and I signed the will."

The thespian in Bill rose to the occasion, and he pretended that this was news to him. He helped Linda bring Margaret downstairs. At the foot of the stairs, Margaret said she thought she could walk unassisted to the couch, and did. Then they all drank tea.

Pat Capponi came soon after the Whitlas and Helen Gough left. Linda sized Pat up at a glance and knew she had nothing to fear in leaving Margaret alone in her hands.

Linda wrote in the log-book, "Bravo to Margaret: guts she's got.... We are watching a woman of great determination maintain a hold on life. It reminds me of the song 'My Way'. Margaret is doing this *her* way and we have to respect that – we can adapt to anything. Pat is here and at last we meet. I realized immediately she is strong and capable and I leave M in good hands. It's been a long day and I'm tired. Sleep well, Margaret."

Linda called me when she reached home. "Pat Capponi is *wonderful*," she said. "Haven't you met her yet? You'll love her. She's very strong."

Thinking of the lifting that Margaret needed, I asked, "Is she a big woman?"

Linda said, "No, not that kind of strong."

Pat hadn't seen Margaret for two weeks. Someone filled in for a Friday-night shift to allow Pat to attend a feast and prayer service held by the Pakistani Youth Cultural Forum to mark the end of the Muslim fast. Pat was horrified at how greatly Margaret's appearance had deteriorated in the brief interval.

"She looked like she weighed about fifty pounds. I knew, and she certainly knew, that the time was coming. I felt defeated, and she did too, and really angry. She had said, 'I have so much to do. I have all these plans, but when I wake up I feel too tired.'"

Pat sat beside Margaret, holding her hand and hurting. Neither spoke for a long time. Then Margaret patted her arm consolingly. "We'll be all right, Pat," she said gently.

After a while Pat excused herself, saying she needed a cigarette. She stood outside on Margaret's front porch and cried.

Saturday, June 15

Margaret slept peacefully for almost eleven hours Friday night, awakening at close to ten on Saturday morning. Pat Capponi found her confused and disoriented but determined to stick to her routine. When Margaret laboriously had completed the ritual of washing, deodorant, and dressing in a clean jogging suit, the stairs were almost more than she could manage. With Pat supporting her, they descended slowly, resting after every step. Once settled on the couch, Margaret was ready for the day. She ate a bit of cereal and worried that Cleo was looking ragged, the consequence of worry and irregular feedings. The cat was decidedly thin and developing some white hairs. "Poor Cleo," Margaret mourned.

At Margaret's insistence Pat went to the corner for newspapers. Pat's picture was on the front page of the *Globe and Mail* in conjunction with a story about the deplorable housing conditions for ex-psychiatric patients in the Parkdale area. Margaret, delighted, demanded that Pat read every word of the article to her, though it was a long one.

When Linda arrived around noon she found Pat and Margaret companionably going through the newspapers together. Margaret, her glasses on her nose, was reading Doris Anderson's column in the *Toronto Star* and instructing Pat about which sections of the paper she wanted to read and which should be stacked on the radiator cover in the dining-room. Margaret's appearance, the burned-butter colour of her skin and her skull-like head balanced grotesquely on a neck withered to the size of a stick, was at complete odds with the normalcy of her behaviour. Linda, braced for a death-bed scene, dropped into a chair and laughed.

Pat departed and Linda telephoned me. Something had gone wrong with the shifts, she said. The day person hadn't turned up, and she was alone at Margaret's. I had planned to go in mid-afternoon but said I would be right over.

Margaret's house was filled with the roar of a vacuum cleaner as I came up the steps. Margaret, even her eyeballs a rich amber colour from jaundice, was stretched out on the couch placidly looking at her mail. Her physician was in the dining-room, stooped under the table, vacuuming cat hairs off the rug.

"Dr. Rapson, did you learn vacuuming in medical school?" I inquired.

"No," she replied sunnily, "actually, my father taught me. He's the fussy one in the family."

When I went into the kitchen to make tea, I noticed that the floor was tacky. Finding a pail and scrub brush, I got on my knees and washed it.

Margaret looked up and observed drily, "This is certainly an impressive cleaning team."

Linda assembled the Jobst pump, and I watched with interest as she slipped the plastic boot over Margaret's bloated foot and leg. As she turned valves and switches, the layers of the boot slowly filled with air, squeezing Margaret's limb with evenly distributed pressure. Checking her watch, Linda waited fifteen minutes and then did the same with the other leg. The intent of the pressure sleeve was to push some of the fluid out of the tissues of Margaret's legs back into her circulation. Margaret's ballooned legs and feet were almost unrecognizable as human, each pale toe standing out from the others like the fingers of a rubber glove filled to bursting with water. To me, the Jobst boot was on the order of King Canute instructing the tides to recede, but Linda could see that it helped to keep Margaret's edema in control.

We paused for lunch, and Margaret allowed me to feed her,

slowly, slowly, one small spoonful at a time, a little custard and maple syrup. While I did it, Linda gave me some news. Margaret's sister and brother-in-law, Phyllis and Ted Cockram, would arrive the next day.

"I thought he has Alzheimer's and can't travel," I said.

"He does," Margaret informed us, "but he's getting better."

I gather this is not generally a course that Alzheimer's takes, because Linda chuckled.

Next we hooked Margaret to the Codetron. She was tiring, retreating from us into sadness.

"Would you like to go out in the garden?" Linda asked impulsively.

Margaret's face lit up. "Oh, yes," she said fervently.

We helped Margaret from the couch to the wheelchair, where we buttressed her with pillows and wrapped a warm wool stadium blanket around her. Amid a din of instructions to one another to "Be careful!" and "Watch out for the flower box!", we carried the wheelchair backward down the stairs of the front porch with Margaret tipped at such an angle that she gazed at tree tops. In a leisurely way, pausing to examine every clump of flowers, we then strolled down the driveway and into the back yard.

A drop of rain hit my face. I suggested that we go inside.

"It looks okay to me," Margaret said, ignoring the drops that sparkled on her blanket.

"You don't want to go inside, do you?" Linda asked understandingly.

Margaret said, almost desperately, "No, not yet."

Linda and I looked at one another. It was daft to have a dying woman outside in the rain, but why not? I ran inside for an umbrella.

The rain held off, however, and Mary Hiseler, spotting us from her kitchen window, came to visit. She brought with her nine-month-old Rob Hiseler, a baby with the disposition of an angel. We served tea and chatted. Margaret took little part, but her eyes were fastened hungrily on the baby and her face glowed. I looked up from hugging the sturdy little boy and saw that Margaret's eyes were shining with tears.

Mary later confessed to Linda that our jolliness in the presence of a dying woman made her uncomfortable, which was why her visit was short. I can only say that response to death is an individual matter. For some, laughter is a rescue from the unbearable pain. For instance, our son Casey Frayne hated yard chores. When we buried his ashes under our apple tree, digging his grave ourselves, my husband paused to get his breath and, leaning on the shovel, said, "One thing sure. If Case were here, he wouldn't be helping."

When Mary and Rob Hiseler left, we pushed Margaret's wheelchair close to the roses so she could enjoy them.

"Look at all the weeds," she commented sadly.

The few I could see were well within the limits of my tolerance for weeds, but to be obliging Linda and I stooped and pulled out a few. Margaret watched us critically and made a sound of protest. Admittedly, our method did tend to leave the roots intact. Margaret informed us pointedly that we could find weeding tools among her gardening supplies. Properly equipped, we set to work in earnest, giving one another a great deal of guidance. Margaret supervised.

"What about this, Margaret?" I said. "It looks like wild violets."

"It *is* violets," Margaret informed me crisply, "Take it out. That bed is only for roses."

"Margaret, this is forget-me-not," Linda said. "Shouldn't I leave it?"

"Absolutely not," Margaret said. "Out."

"Do you mind if I take it home?" Linda asked. "I'd love to have forget-me-nots from your garden."

"Take all you like," Margaret told her with a wave of her thin hand, ignoring the implication.

We laboured on, mesmerized by the rhythm and endlessness of the task. I was finding that there were dozens of weeds, hundreds of weeds, *thousands* of weeds in Margaret's rose bed. Sitting back on my heels and wiping my forehead, I asked Margaret if she thought we had done enough. She looked doubtful.

"The least you could do," I said, returning to the task, "is thank us. I see no sign of gratitude for the wonderful job we are doing."

Margaret said, "Thank you," with a comical lack of sincerity that made all of us laugh.

When the rose bed was almost to her satisfaction, we took Margaret back inside. Once in the house, she stood up from the wheelchair with difficulty, swaying and unable to take a step. We braced her until she recovered. When she was ready, she sang "Away we go!" and we helped her to the couch.

We made her comfortable and sat close to her, talking easily. Margaret rested, her profile seeming to be carved in amber bone and her deep-socketed eyes closed. Occasionally she made a comment on what we were discussing, and sometimes she cried out involuntarily, though she insisted she was not in pain. We listened to Glenn Gould's Bach and then Mary O'Hara singing "Bridge Over Troubled Water". Gail Flintoff arrived, saw at once how it was with Margaret, and dropped seamlessly into the pool of tranquillity in the room.

Linda sat beside the couch, holding Margaret's hands.

"Have you always been this stubborn, Margaret?" she asked fondly.

Margaret didn't respond.

"I mean, this determined?"

Margaret, lifelong enemy of sloppy speech, snapped open her eyes. "They aren't the same thing," she said disapprovingly.

Hunting around in the kitchen cupboard a little later, looking for Cleo's cat food, I happened on Margaret's liquor supply. Most of the bottles, I discovered, contained an inch or two of wine that had turned to vinegar. Consulting with Linda, we decided to heave out everything undrinkable. While the clatter was proceeding, I went back to the living-room to sip some tea. Margaret gave me a frosty look. "I am *not* a teetotaler," she said.

"I can see that," I grinned.

I left reluctantly. Margaret's house felt like a protected place and everywhere else, by contrast, raw and unstable.

Gail Flintoff wrote in the log: "M had half a cup of soup and a glass of ENSURE. Did boot at 5:30 and Codetron at 8:30. Tylenol No. 3 at 6:00 p.m. Had interesting discussion ranging

232

from hijackings to nationalism to spirits (the ethereal kind). Now fairly exhausted, though agreed to do break dancing with me. Take care all. You are wonderful."

At nine, Buffy Carruthers turned up and Gail left. Buffy was aghast at the size of Margaret's legs and wondered how Margaret would have the strength to haul their heavy weight up the stairs. When they tried the ascent, Buffy discovered that Margaret had very little control. She could just barely lift her legs from one step to the next. Buffy thought, "My God, if she falls it will be like holding up a tree."

Around one in the morning, Margaret rang the bell beside her bed. She was in pain, and Buffy gave her a Tylenol and massaged her back. She reflected that the serious nursing had begun; for the team it no longer was a case of just being with Margaret.

At three Margaret woke again, gripped by a dreadful dream that a faceless man had raised and then abandoned her, suspended in space. "We must eat," she told Buffy in an agitated voice, not fully awake.

Buffy held her until Margaret's daze lifted. She said she wanted to go to the bathroom, but when Buffy tried to help, Margaret couldn't move her legs at all. She said it didn't really matter. Buffy gave her a sleeping pill. Twice more in the night Buffy helped Margaret move; her legs were so heavy she couldn't roll from one side to another without assistance. Each time, Buffy gently rubbed Margaret's back, legs, and feet to help her relax into agitated sleep.

At seven in the morning Margaret wakened, her mind clear but with no memory of the events of the busy night. She rang, and when Buffy came sleepily into the room Margaret was flat on her back, an injured expression on her face. In the tone of a petulant child, she glared at Buffy and complained, "No one is supposed to sleep in the same position all night."

Margaret was exhausted. "She kept zizzing off," as Buffy put it. Buffy watched her in despair. She thought it entirely possible that Margaret would simply stop breathing. In one of the moments Margaret was dimly awake and making a motion to throw back the covers and stand, Buffy suggested that she should stay in bed a while and sleep. "It might be difficult for us to get you up the stairs today, since you're so tired."

Margaret wanted to see the schedule. Glenys McMullen was coming, and Wendy Farquhar and Nigel Turner, and Arlene Parks from Nellie's, and Sheila Mackenzie. "They're strong people," Margaret observed.

"Yes, they can get you downstairs all right," Buffy agreed, "but I don't know about coming back up if you need the toilet."

Margaret sank back and slept again. "The idea of getting up was just too huge," Buffy said. "She just let that go."

A few minutes later Margaret wanted her dentures. Buffy tried to place the teeth properly, but Margaret's jaw was loose and the teeth seemed to float, at one point slipping to the back of her throat where they gagged her. Buffy snatched them out, saving Margaret from choking, and eventually got them into Margaret's mouth approximately where they belonged.

The next time Margaret wakened, Buffy helped her into clean flannel pyjamas, a not-inconsiderable task. She made a note in the log-book that Margaret would need flannel nightgowns, which would be easier to put on her than pyjamas. When Buffy placed clean pillowslips on Margaret's pillows, Margaret gave her a grateful look and slipped into what appeared to be a coma.

Sunday, June 16

Margaret was waxen when I came into the bedroom around noon, her jaundice in mysterious retreat. She was breathing deeply, her lips cracked and dry. She opened her eyes and gave me a wan smile of greeting as I sat, stricken, on a chair I pulled up to her bedside. I stroked her hair and asked if she was comfortable. She closed her eyes and grunted in the affirmative. Glenys McMullen, a Holy Trinity person with a practical, unflappable, no-nonsense demeanour, left me to watch over Margaret and went downstairs to finish some chores in the kitchen.

Margaret began to squirm, her face twitching. She made pluck-ing gestures in the region of her mouth. "Is it your dentures?" I asked, a guess. Without opening her eyes, she made a sound like a wail and nodded. I opened her mouth and pulled tentatively on her lower teeth. They didn't budge.

"Glenys," I called. "Do you know anything about dentures? I don't know how to get them out." Glenys was as inexperienced as I, but she was willing to try. She attempted to lift out the same lower teeth that I had tugged, but with the same lack of success.

"I'll wet my hands with warm water," she said. "Maybe that will help."

She pulled on Margaret's lower teeth again, exerting a good bit of strength, but the denture didn't move. Margaret was making crying sounds that we took for acute discomfort, so Glenys con-tinued to try, still without success. Margaret didn't open her eyes, but her expression was one of profound annoyance. Since there was nothing we could do, Glenys went back to the kitchen and I took Margaret's hand.

I heard a small commotion downstairs and Bill Whitla came into the room. He and Nancy had brought their children, 'Becca and Michael, to join in Holy Communion with Margaret. Here was the team's Mr. Fixit, and I seized gratefully on the opportunity to solve the problem of Margaret's dentures. I told him that Margaret wanted the denture out but Glenys and I couldn't get a grip on it.

Bill reached in Margaret's mouth and effortlessly lifted out her bottom denture. Glenys and I had been pulling on the only two teeth in Margaret's lower jaw that were her own.

Bill bent over Margaret, who opened her eyes with her whole heart in them. "I've brought you Communion," he said to her. "Nancy and 'Becca and Michael are with me. Would it be all right if I brought them up?"

Margaret nodded, her pinched face full of gratitude.

"I'll be right back," he promised. "June, you can have Commun-ion with us, if you like."

I was aghast. The ceremonial trappings of religious ritual depress me. I have a fairly good understanding of why this has happened, but the reasons don't matter. So long as I stay out of churches I can avoid addressing the emotional turmoil that rites, particularly Catholic rites, provoke. I waited unhappily for the Whitlas to return, moving out of the chair by Margaret's bed and taking up a position with my back against the bedroom wall.

Margaret had not said one coherent word in the hour since my arrival, but now she opened her eyes and gave me a look of benediction. "You don't have to stay," she said in a clear, normal voice.

"I want to," I said immediately, stung to tears that she could remember my peculiarity at such a time and extend herself to look after me.

The Whitlas crowded into the tiny room whose space was taken up almost entirely by Margaret's double bed and two sizable chests of drawers. The teenagers politely concealed their shock at Margaret's appearance, but their eyes were full of suffering. I had almost forgotten that Bill was a priest, but now he was every inch a pious man of the cloth. He performed the service with great dignity and feeling. Though her voice was weak, Margaret joined in the prayers and the singing, her voice husky on "Hosanna in the highest," and she swallowed the communal wafer and wine.

After this Bill conducted what he called a laying-on of hands, a last-rites ceremony. The four Whitlas reached out and touched Margaret as he commended her spirit to whatever awaited.

I would not partake in the Communion or recite the prayers, but I put an uncertain hand on Margaret's brow when the others did.

"'Becca would like to play for you, Margaret," Bill said gently when it was over, "if you would like her to."

Margaret turned to 'Becca with a radiant smile and said in a faint voice that she would like that very much.

We waited what seemed a long time after 'Becca went downstairs and seated herself at Margaret's piano. 'Becca, it turned out, was waiting for a signal to begin. After a few minutes, she started, and the house filled with exquisitely played, liquid Chopin. Margaret sighed, clasped her hands over her heart, and wriggled with pleasure.

Linda Rapson arrived as 'Becca was playing and came quietly up the stairs, stretching out on the bed beside Margaret and taking Margaret's hand. When the Whitlas were ready to leave, Linda and Bill and I went into Margaret's den to confer. Phyllis and Ted Cockram, Margaret's sister and brother-in-law, were expected late that night and were planning to stay in Margaret's house. However, double shifts were now in place on an overnight basis, requiring the team to use both spare bedrooms. In addition, the normal obligations of hospitality – cooking and caring for the Cockrams – would be difficult for the team in this time of crisis.

Not far from Margaret's were several inexpensive apartment hotels. Bill agreed to explain the situation to Phyllis and make arrangements to house the couple there.

As the Whitlas were leaving, Michael Whitla bent over to kiss Margaret and said, "I wish I could have played for you."

Looking up at the tall youth with love in her eyes, she replied, "I wish I could have played for *you*."

The service had drained Margaret, and she slipped into a comatose state. "I'm worried about bed sores," Linda said. "She's so inert that her skin could break down." Together we turned Margaret on her side, bracing her with a row of pillows behind her back. She made mewling sounds of protest, but didn't open her eyes.

Linda lay down again on the bed beside Margaret, and I sat in the chair at her bedside, where I could stroke her arm. Margaret seemed utterly at peace, breathing evenly and lightly like a child. She was going to die in her beloved home after all, as she had wished, with almost no pain, with her friends around her, with her roses freshly weeded. I looked at Linda and said, "Well done, Dr. Rapson."

"Not bad," Linda said, her voice catching in her throat.

Jack Adam, Holy Trinity's in-coming priest, arrived fresh from conducting the Sunday service in the parish he was leaving. Margaret responded distantly to his presence, murmuring some words of greeting and rallying to thank him politely for a bouquet of yellow flowers he brought. He left a few minutes later, and I found a tall vase and put the flowers on the window-sill so Margaret could see them without turning her head. She lay still, with closed eyes. When I asked her if she was feeling all right, she grunted in affirmation.

Glenys made tea. For a while I helped her in the kitchen, cleaning out the freezer compartment, removing the hopeful leftovers, sprays of herbs, balls of suet, and unidentifiables that are found in most freezers. We set a few things, some sausages and pieces of fowl, to thaw in order to assess them later on the basis of odour. Then we tackled Margaret's spice cupboard, where we found dozens of bottles of spices whose flavour had vanished, all of them faded to the same indistinct shade of dingy grey. These we dumped.

We were inordinately cheerful on the superficial level as we cleaned out the hoardings. We felt a sense of naughtiness as we made arbitrary decisions about Margaret's belongings much the way little girls feel when trying on clothes from their mothers' closets. If Margaret had suddenly appeared in the doorway, we would have been devastated with embarrassment.

We also felt the pain of our own mortality, realizing that some day other women will clean out the dulled spices and frosty hamburg in our kitchens, and they too will chuckle over such eccentricities as an over-abundance of tarragon or six jars of artichoke hearts. A woman's kitchen is a private place, more illustrative of her nature than any other room in the house. We discovered that Margaret had a filing system for her groceries, each category of food on its own pull-out shelf, and that she was passionately frugal, reluctant to throw away elastic bands or jam jars. As we opened her cupboard doors and exposed her nature, her idiosyncrasies of home management, her dedication to rational order, we were fully aware that we were participating in a kind of funeral.

The house was full of music, a lot of it Bach. Linda noted that we all had an air of vigil. Margaret slept on. At one point Linda bent over her to rearrange the pillows. **"Is your head too low?"** she inquired. Margaret didn't open her eyes. "For what?" she asked.

Linda chuckled and then tried another question. "Are you dreaming?"

"Oh yes," Margaret said.

"What's it like fighting a disease?" Linda asked. "Is it like a war?"

There was no reply. Linda concluded that Margaret thought the question too dumb to merit a response.

Wendy Farquhar arrived for her usual Sunday shift, sparkling with goodwill, and found Linda, Glenys, and me in the kitchen still cleaning out the fridge. Wendy is a vibrant woman, the kind of enthusiastic, giving person who makes fifty-five – *fifty-five* – gingerbread houses to give away at Christmas. She perched on the side of Margaret's bed across from me and proceeded to tell us about an amazing formal wedding she had attended the day before at Holy Trinity.

I didn't know the participants, but Linda did and was vastly amused that they had decided to marry after living together for seven years and parenting two children. None the less the bride wore white, complete with virginal veil and a gown with a very long train. I was entertained by Wendy's account of the four-year-old son of the bride and groom who acted as train bearer and from time to time wiped his nose with the satin hem of his mother's gown.

Wendy is a witty and funny woman; her description was hilarious, and we laughed a lot, Linda holding one of Margaret's hands and I the other. Margaret didn't move or smile, but the sounds of her friends' voices must have penetrated. She looked relaxed and contented.

I went home but Linda remained. Wendy's husband, Nigel Turner, arrived and the three ate some food that Wendy had brought. Margaret roused and took some sips of juice. Sheila Mackenzie turned up just as Margaret became aware that she was in her bed.

"I want to go downstairs," she told Linda indignantly.

239

"It's too difficult," Linda explained. "We want to be able to turn you, which we can't do when you're on the couch. Besides, you're tired. You haven't the strength to get up."

Margaret glared at her, her fists clenched, and said bitterly, "Well, I suppose I might just as well die right now."

Linda grinned. "Margaret, if I know you, you'll die when you're good and ready."

Margaret liked that but wasn't reconciled. Nigel and Wendy had just left. Sheila ran down the street after them for a conference. If Margaret was to be moved, Nigel would have to help carry her. The team dithered over the decision. Sheila felt strongly that Margaret should have her wish. She thought that being downstairs was Margaret's life force: it represented getting well. However she was out-voted. Darkness was falling, and the others decided that it was best to leave Margaret upstairs in her bed for the night.

Margaret seemed to have given up the fight to be moved. She submitted quietly in her bed as Linda administered treatments with the Codetron machine and the Jobst boot. Looking wistful, she said she wished she could read. Linda found the biography of Mozart Margaret had been reading, her place in it marked with a piece of paper, and began to read it aloud to her. Margaret paid close attention, her face full of concentration, and when Linda closed the book she asked, "What age was it again that Mozart died?"

Linda replied, "Thirty-five."

Margaret sighed with regret, "Such genius."

Linda had been keeping track of the amount of pain medication Margaret had been taking, and it was astoundingly low. Before the use of the Codetron machine, Margaret had taken six Leritine pills, the strong drug prescribed by her surgeon; after the Codetron, she had needed Leritine only once. Her total count of Tylenol No. 3, taken on an as-needed basis, was fifty-six pills in eighty-two days. Considering that pancreas cancer can be one of the most painful ways to die, Margaret's comparative comfort was something of a medical miracle.

240

Linda gave much of the credit to the Codetron machine. "I've had one hundred per cent success treating cancer patients with Codetron," she would say deadpan, adding only when necessary that she was speaking of one patient, Margaret Frazer. Linda took some slide pictures of Margaret using the Codetron and uses them now to illustrate her acupuncture lectures. They make a persuasive argument for the method. In them, Margaret is sitting in her chair with the electrodes attached to her body and afterwards lying on her couch. It is clear in the slides that she is a seriously ill person, her pallor and emaciated body plain to see, but what shines in all of them is her beatific beam of contentment.

However, two other factors certainly influenced the good outcome of the Codetron. One was Margaret's own stoical nature and her aversion to taking a pain pill, which she seemed to regard as a sign of weak character. Everyone on the team was acutely aware that she tolerated much more pain than she let us know. Many times she would grimace or groan, but she always insisted that she was really fine.

"Would you like a pill?" she would be asked.

"No, no, no," she would say assuringly. "It's a passing thing." Maybe it was.

The other element in what seemed an almost pain-free illness was the cushion of good feelings – no, *love* – that enveloped her. Some sixty alert and caring people surrounded her with a wall of tenderness. Margaret was shielded from irritation, tedium, pettiness, and stress to the best of the team's ability. She was spared the mundane daily chores and decisions for which everyone, but women especially, feel a nagging responsibility.

Margaret had nothing unpleasant to face except death; many dying people are not so fortunate. The final three months of her life were spent in warmth and tranquillity. Her wishes were respected to the letter; she was the centre around which everything in the house revolved. She was stroked, kissed, hugged, and surrounded with music and attention. Because kindness didn't make her uneasy and gifts didn't distress her, she released in the team a capacity for benevolence that grew with the giving. Accordingly the three months in Margaret's house were strangely full of happiness. The sustained radiance and peace of the place *must* have been a factor in Margaret's almost miraculous freedom from pain.

Linda wrote in the log-book that night, "We're all sad, but we have to be happy too. We've given Margaret a wonderful gift. She's been in her own home, surrounded by people who care for her, her cat, her garden, her music. She's had a quality of life in the past twelve weeks that few people achieve under these circumstances. And we all did it – everyone has been so giving and creatively helpful. It's been an experience I shall never stop learning from."

Although Margaret had not taken any pain medication for twenty hours, Linda was concerned about the agony that might lie ahead. She drove to her office where she had some liquid morphine left over from a supply ordered the previous summer for her dying friend, Joan Partridge. Linda set up the simple equipment and the drug, instructing the overnight person, Arlene Parks, a woman who works at Nellie's, on its use. Linda was pleased to discover that Arlene, a no-nonsense woman with a notable ability to keep calm in a crisis, was a nurse.

Listening to the doctor's instructions, Arlene's training flooded back.

"What is her blood pressure?" she asked professionally.

"Damned if I know," Linda replied. "I haven't taken it for weeks. I didn't want to bug her."

Sheila Mackenzie, the second overnight person, turned up. She sat in the chair by Margaret, her blonde hair lit by the bedside lamp, and held Margaret's hands. Margaret smiled at her drowsily and then slept.

Linda went home quite convinced that Margaret would die in the night. Expecting to hear the telephone ring, she slept little.

Margaret's sleep was also broken. Once she wakened gasping with pain and asked for a pill. Arlene prepared to administer the morphine but Margaret dropped back into a semi-coma before the dose was ready. Another time Margaret wakened and gave specific instructions where she wanted her legs moved and how to rub her feet. While Arlene and Sheila were doing this, Margaret suddenly demanded, "Why are there two of you here?"

Sheila replied, "So one of us can sleep."

"That makes sense, I guess," Margaret grunted, and dropped off again.

Sheila noticed that Cleo was curled up on a chair beside Margaret's bed, something no one had ever seen the cat do before. Once when Margaret wakened, she noticed the cat with an appreciative smile. Twice she commented on the bouquets of white peonies in the room, remembering who had brought them. She always called Arlene and Sheila by name, never mixing them up.

She said wistfully, "I wish I could pee."

Sheila said, "Well, do you want to pee?"

Margaret retorted, "No, I wish I wanted to pee."

The women divided their shift, Arlene sleeping for three hours after midnight, with one break when she prepared to give the morphine, and Sheila going to bed between four-thirty and seven. While they sat at the bedside, with the light very low, they fortified themselves with herbal tea and tarts that Wendy had brought.

Several times Margaret wakened, wanting to be turned or to have her legs moved. Sheila discovered how hard it is to put into language how you want your body arranged because people are accustomed to making such adjustments without thinking about it.

In the middle of the night, as Sheila sat beside her, Margaret said suddenly, "Let's pretend."

"All right," Sheila replied readily, but Margaret was asleep again.

Sheila Mackenzie is an enigma to many people, though she takes fewer pains to conceal her opinions than almost anyone I have ever met. She's fifty-seven, a woman with a comfortable body and a wardrobe that seems to be made up entirely of costumes and beads. Indeed there is much about her that resembles a grumpy, warm-hearted, and clairvoyant gipsy. A flat-out proponent of truth in relationships, she bristles at the folly of self-deceit and often disconcerts the comfortably armoured. She's also a witty woman whose insights are phrased in pungent language that has the zing of first-rate literature. Some fear her tongue and candour, but most are drawn by her originality and intelligence.

Sheila is a long-time member of Holy Trinity; she joined about the time that her marriage broke up, leaving her to raise four children in a handsome but run-down Rosedale mansion. Sheila met Margaret soon after the latter joined Holy Trinity and admired her for what Sheila describes as Margaret's "clarity and brightness". Sheila also liked Margaret's firmness on matters of principle.

"She never wavered, but she wasn't a fanatic," Sheila told me one chilly November day when we sat in her kitchen drinking tea and talking about Margaret. "She was never cowed by the dangers and threats involved in taking a position, but she didn't go beyond the political realities either."

Sheila came to respect Margaret's judgement of people. If Margaret gave a little shake of her head at the mention of a name, or made a certain grimace of distaste with her mouth, "you knew exactly what she thought. There were lots of people Margaret thought were not too solid."

On the Monday night before Margaret went into hospital for the futile exploratory operation, Sheila valiantly waded through a blizzard to get to Margaret to keep her company for a while.

"It was to be our first conversation, in a sense," Sheila explained, lighting a cigarette. "It was to be about her, who she was. Our relationship from then on would only be about the important things. To be known, to be comfortable, to be perceived, that was what was important for her."

Margaret spoke frankly to Sheila. "I want you to know me," she said, and proceeded to confide details of her life and her loves. Sheila left sooner than she would have wished – she had another commitment, and the night was so foul that it had taken two hours to make the trip; but a bond was formed. Without having to say so, they both knew that Sheila would be by Margaret's side to the end.

As with so many of the women on Margaret's team, Sheila

was reliving in Margaret some part of her own mother's death from cancer of the pancreas. "A lot was involved for me in Margaret dying of that disease," she reflected, "especially toward the end when Margaret began to look more and more like my mother."

Sheila's style is the Jungian and Socratic know-thyself school, so she was annoyed that Margaret did not share her view that diseases are clues, and that Margaret could fight her cancer best if she saw it as an opportunity to explore herself. In the beginning she thought that this might be Margaret's direction. In the hospital Margaret faced the fact of her dying unflinchingly and they cried together, Sheila grateful for the emotional release of the shared tears. They talked about Margaret's belongings – what would happen to her books, to her piano. "She wanted to solve the piano problem at Holy Trinity by making the church a gift of her piano," Sheila recalled. "She gave me highly technical reasons why this would work with Holy Trinity's acoustics or whatever."

A month passed without contact because Sheila was out of town. When she returned and signed up for Thursday nights on the team, she found Margaret was no longer interested in admitting that she was dying. Instead she seemed closed against intimacies and was behaving, as Sheila put it, "like an imperious child". Sheila didn't take gently Margaret's tendency to give instructions about how her tea was to be served and which spoon she wanted for her porridge.

"Margaret trained us all how to make her comfortable," Sheila observed, "and that part was all right. But her attitude fed into the rebellious child in me. I felt I was the downstairs maid."

It was a frustrating time for them both. Sheila has a constitutional aversion to order, but she was being required to submit to Margaret's compulsive rituals. Furthermore, Sheila's views on nutrition are deeply and vigorously held, and it was shocking for her to watch Margaret dining almost exclusively on desserts. To make it worse for Sheila, when she appealed to Linda Rapson to address the problem of Margaret's diet, she met what she saw as indifference.

In the forced intimacy of the situation, Sheila and Margaret, both strong-minded women, were confronted by their disparities. The signals of collision certainly had occurred in the past, but they had not mattered because the women saw little of one another. Sheila recalled that when she and many at Holy Trinity were enthusiastic about the potential of primal therapy, Margaret had dismissed it as nonsense.

"None of those differences helped the way Margaret and I were getting along," Sheila confessed. "I was unhappy about her good-child act. It worked for her, but it kept us all at a distance in some feeling way. And I didn't find out for a long time that she had been in bed for almost a year as a child. No wonder she was resistant to being told what was good for her. I felt that was a terribly important thing, that she had been an invalid child, but we never dealt with it. All in all, I was finding it difficult to leave on Thursdays to go to Margaret's. I was getting there later and later."

"I know," I said.

"Oh, of course you do," Sheila said. "You or Liz Greaves would be waiting for me."

The tension between them was only part of the load that Sheila was carrying. Apprehensive over the eerie resemblance of Margaret's illness and appearance to her mother's, Sheila was finding herself in great need of the therapist she saw every Friday morning immediately following her shift at Margaret's.

Sheila's mixed feelings about being at Margaret's were plain to see. One evening when I was there, she came in the door without speaking to either of us, went upstairs to the bathroom and then into the kitchen and, finally, equipped with a cup of tea, joined us. On another evening she came in the door and, wanting to rest quietly for a while, sank into a chair without speaking. Margaret interpreted Sheila's behaviour, correctly, as reluctance to be there. She was hurt and furious. On another occasion when Sheila was pressing Margaret to improve her diet, Margaret snapped at her, "I can't take any more," and went upstairs to bed. Sheila, tossing restlessly that night, knew from the sounds in the next room that Margaret also was sleepless.

"After that," Sheila said in a flat voice, "I backed off."

The truce was total on both sides. They returned to the smooth ground on which they had started the journey. For the final weeks of Margaret's life, she and Sheila had no prickly moments. Their relationship was layered with so much texture that an almost conspiratorial mood developed between them, like adults sharing a secret the children don't know. Margaret had extracted from Sheila the high price of her compliance and surrender, and Sheila had freely given her that gift.

On Thursday nights I observed Margaret listening for Sheila with a glow of expectation on her face. When Sheila came in, going straight to Margaret for an embrace, Margaret's face would melt with tenderness and pleasure.

Monday, June 17

Margaret's house was full of the smell of frying sausage when I returned shortly after noon on Monday. In a place that for many weeks had known only the purity of custard and almond tea, the aroma fell on the senses like violence. I discovered two strangers in the kitchen amid an uproar of food preparation.

"I'm Phyllis," said the woman. "Margaret's sister. And this is my husband, Ted Cockram. We're just fixing some lunch."

Phyllis is a taller, stronger-looking woman than Margaret, with a military bearing that owes something to her years in the Canadian army during the Second World War and her subsequent job in the personnel department of the Cincinnati police force. Her face is full of echoes of Margaret's face, as happens with siblings, but the proportions are different. Her husband, tall and white-thatched, is a pleasant, quiet man.

The stove was covered with pots, all of them simmering, splattering, or boiling hard.

"What's all this food?" I asked in consternation.

"We're having sandwiches," Phyllis explained. "That stuff on the stove is Sheila's."

I went upstairs to inquire. Sheila Mackenzie was sprawled on the bed beside Margaret, who gave me a woozy smile of greeting, Ian Sowton was seated beside the bed, stroking Margaret's forehead, and Nancy Whitla was at the foot of the bed gently rubbing Margaret's puffy feet. "She gets cramps in this leg," Nancy explained. "Sometimes it helps to massage the muscles." The food on the stove, Sheila said, was the thawed-out debris of the fridge-cleaning Glenys and I had performed the day before. Sheila was cooking all the bits of meat before they spoiled.

While I was receiving this information, Margaret looked around at the four of us, exasperated, and cried, "Let me rest!"

Three of us cleared out, leaving Ian on guard.

"I want to talk to you," Sheila said.

We strolled up and down the sidewalk in front of Margaret's house for half an hour, so deep in conversation that we hardly noticed the glorious summer day or people passing us. Sheila was upset by the decision to leave Margaret upstairs. "It's important to Margaret to be downstairs," she said vehemently. "That's where she feels *strong*."

I agreed, but I wanted to talk about what had happened the day before, when Margaret felt my distress at staying for the Communion and roused herself from near-unconsciousness to give me permission to leave.

Sheila was impressed. "She's in a state where she's something of a child, with the strong psychic powers of a child," she said thoughtfully.

When we returned to the house, I asked Phyllis about Margaret's early life. We sat in the dining-room, sharing tea and the lemon squares that Mary Hiseler had baked in anticipation of the Cockrams' visit, and Phyllis talked while I took notes. Their father, A.C. (Archie) Frazer, had been born in England, and had arrived in Canada penniless in a era when many companies hung out signs saying, "No English Need Apply". Despite the prejudice, he found work at the Steel Company of Canada and by retirement had for some time been its much-respected personnel director. He died in 1973 at the age of eighty-seven. I remembered Jay

MacGillivray telling me something about Margaret's father. In his last few years, he lived, sick at heart, in a nursing home. Margaret, visiting him one day toward the end of his life, insisted that he leave his room and come with her to the piano in the common room, where she urged him to sing to her accompaniment. At first he wouldn't, and then he couldn't, but in the end he managed a few songs in his lovely, true tenor and was deeply moved to hear his voice again.

His wife, Phoebe Emerson, was the daughter of a Baptist minister and a reader in the Burlington Baptist church where the family worshipped. As Margaret often had told me, the family observed the Sabbath with Baptist severity, prohibiting not only such activities as card-playing but even the reading of newspapers.

Margaret's illness, which Phyllis remembered as "something rheumatoid", occurred when she was ten or eleven and kept her in bed for a year. "That's when Margaret became a great reader. In our family album, Margaret is holding a book in most of the pictures of her."

The music came from their parents. Their mother played the church organ and their father was tenor soloist in the choir. Margaret studied piano at the Hamilton Conservatory of Music and then the oboe and flute. Margaret and Lynn, the youngest sister, were the two keenest about music. They used to compete in guessing the name of the piece or the composer of music they heard on the family radio.

"The family was very happy," Phyllis told me. "We were very close."

"What about Lynn's disappearance?" I asked. "Margaret thinks she's dead."

"No," Phyllis scoffed. "That's just like Lynn, not bothering to write. I don't think she's dead."

We were all bumbling around, Nancy Whitla, Sheila Mackenzie, Phyllis, Ted Cockram, and me, when Linda Rapson came at four o'clock. She found Ian and me upstairs with Margaret trying to ease the cramps in her calf muscles. Margaret had not urinated since Sunday morning, so Linda thought some of her abdominal pain might come from the pressure of her full bladder. We decided to see if Margaret could empty her bladder. Ian withdrew, and I slipped a bedpan under Margaret, urging her to "let go". She clenched her face with effort, but nothing came.

Eyes shut tight, she began to make crying sounds. Linda bent over her and asked, "Do you have pain?"

Without opening her eyes, Margaret fairly bellowed, "No!"

"What's the problem then?"

Eyes still shut, she said, "It's just that I think it would be better if ... "

"You mean," said Linda, "you want to go downstairs."

"Yes," Margaret said, opening her eyes and letting out a long sigh.

Linda said, "Okay, Margaret, you're going downstairs."

We had to get the couch ready, replacing the stiff cushions with the futon, piling pillows on both arms – three pillows to support Margaret's head and shoulders and another to cushion her legs – and preparing the green mohair blanket to cover her. Linda and I wrestled flannel pyjama bottoms over Margaret's water-swollen legs. Then we stood around her bed trying to figure out how to transport her.

I suggested the fireman's carry, but there wasn't room on the stairway for two people to descend with Margaret seated between them. That left the option of carrying her as one would a child. Ian isn't a big man, but his body is compact and strong. He said he was sure he could do it. He and Linda gently lifted Margaret's shoulders to allow him to slide one arm under her upper back. Then Linda lifted Margaret's knees, and Ian put his other arm under them. He lifted Margaret's frail body in his arms and, with Linda taking some of the weight of the heavy legs, they brought her downstairs and lowered her to the couch.

I fussed with the pillows behind her head.

"What are you doing!" Margaret demanded crossly.

"I'm trying to make you comfortable, you twit," I told her.

Phyllis, hovering nearby, misunderstood the exchange. She said, "See Margaret, you can push me around, but you can't push your friends around."

Phyllis took the silence that fell for sympathy and added, in an aside to me, "With Margaret you're wrong if you do and wrong if you don't."

"I haven't found that," I said coldly.

Eventually I came to understand Phyllis's mood. She bears the intolerable pain of the probable suicide of her twenty-two-year-old son, Ron, seven years ago, and the bad luck that when each of her parents died she had been living too far away to be with them. Family deaths therefore were an emotional crisis for Phyllis that went beyond the usual sorrowing and put her on edge. As her daughter, Barbara, had recognized, it was important for Phyllis to see Margaret before she died, but heightened emotions of the situation were roiling old hurts and unresolved family conflicts.

The sisters were not close. Margaret once wrote in a diary after Phyllis ended Margaret's Christmas visits to her, "I've been a difficult guest for her. There's so little we share beyond music and family memories."

In the painful circumstances of Margaret's dying, Phyllis appeared torn. Part of her was a child who couldn't put aside her resentment of an officious older sister. "It would be gawdawful to be Margaret Frazer's younger sister," Sheila Mackenzie once observed understandingly. Another part was in agony at having to face the reality of another family death. And there was also the loving Phyllis who was unpractised in showing her affection and expressing grief.

Margaret, soft and open, was in a different frame of mind. Nancy Whitla was present when Margaret first greeted her sister. She said that Margaret was inarticulate but deeply moved. Her eyes filled, and she took Phyllis's hand and said weakly, over and over, "Phyllis, Phyllis, Phyllis."

We covered Margaret with her beloved green blanket and Linda brushed her hair, while the rest of us transferred her bouquets of flowers from her bedroom to the living-room. The heavy, heavenly scent of peonies filled the house as we played some Vivaldi and then the Mary O'Hara tape. Margaret wore an expression of perfect peace.

Sheila and Ian prepared to leave. Sheila said to Linda, referring

251

to the move downstairs, "I'm glad I lived to see this." Then her eyes lit with glee and she added, "I love adventures, and *this* is an adventure."

Bill Whitla drove Phyllis and Ted to their apartment hotel and then returned to join Nancy, Linda, and me for a cup of Emperor's Choice herbal tea, Linda's favourite. Margaret slipped into a deep, calm sleep as we talked in low voices, drinking in the tea, the music, the peonies, and a curious sense of completion.

When the Whitlas left, Linda and I were alone with Margaret. Ian telephoned, offering to bring dinner, but I assured him we had enough. We set the dining-room table with Margaret's best silver and stemmed glasses and dined on boil-in-a-bag dinners and white wine. Linda and I toasted one another for various virtues we perceived, invented, or exaggerated, expressed our mutual gratitude for the support we each had received from the other, and praised Margaret, who slept on against the background music of Bach. A sudden summer rain began, bringing a smell of wet earth.

Margaret's breathing was becoming irregular. Sometimes it was shallow, then it stopped, then she would take a long breath, then some quick panting ones. Linda and I, intensely conscious of every change, continued to chat idly.

Margaret drew a noisy ragged breath, followed by silence.

"Is that person still breathing?" I inquired.

She gave Margaret's sleeping form what she pretended was a lazy inspection. "The blanket's moving up and down, so I think so," she reported.

Around seven Margaret stirred from what had been a three-hour sleep. We changed her position carefully to ease her sore body. Linda applied the Jobst boot and the Codetron treatment, but after the latter Margaret began to groan and squirm. Her legs were hurting, she said.

"Do you want some pain medicine?" Linda asked.

"Yes," Margaret gasped.

"I have something new," Linda told her. "You'll like it because it's sweet. And I know you love sweet things."

Margaret rewarded her with a thin grin. I sat rigid as Linda went into the kitchen to get the liquid morphine. She had managed for three months to avoid giving the narcotic, knowing it would hasten Margaret's death, but now the time had come when the drug was needed. For the past two days, Margaret had swallowed only two or three ounces of fluid. She had not urinated for thirty-six hours. Most of Sunday she had been comatose, and she was now too profoundly weak to move herself. Putting those observations together, Linda realized that Margaret's vital organs were shutting down. The best she could do was to make Margaret comfortable and hope she wouldn't last too much longer.

Linda's face was controlled and intent as she measured the dose in a syringe like an eye-dropper. We were playing the Mary O'Hara tape again, and the song was "Bridge Over Troubled Water". As Linda carefully dripped morphine on Margaret's dry tongue, Mary O'Hara was singing, "Sail on silver girl,/ Sail on by./ Your time has come to shine./ All your dreams are on their way./ See how they shine."

"We'll start giving her morphine around the clock now, every four hours," Linda said quietly. "I don't want her to suffer."

Anne van Egmond entered, shutting the screen door gently behind her. She's sixty, a squarely built woman with pure white hair cut short like a cap and the slight accent of her native Netherlands. Anne is a CAMMAC friend of Margaret's. They were together at the summer musical camps for many years and also saw one another when CAMMAC would stage cantata readings once a month in Holy Trinity church, something Margaret arranged for the group. Anne was string convener, taking responsibility for the violins and violas, and she remembers that on those occasions Margaret would bustle around making coffee and tea for the musicians.

A mental-health nurse with the city of Toronto's department of public health, Anne worked in the Parkdale area and, in that capacity, had another connection with Margaret. She was a city representative on the Supportive Housing Coalition that Margaret tenaciously encouraged. In the winter before Margaret's illness,

253

the two women grew closer. Going home together after a meeting one evening, they decided to play four-handed piano at Margaret's house and, on another occasion, tried piano and violin duets.

"It wasn't a personal friendship," Anne told me one October afternoon after Margaret's death as we drank grapefruit juice in the Toronto City Hall cafeteria. "It was mainly around the activity of music making."

Still, when she heard about the Friends of Margaret team she called Joyce Brown to volunteer. Despite the potential for intimacy of the new relationship, the friendship between Anne and Margaret continued to be pleasant and practical, almost impersonal. The only time Margaret confessed weakness or fear was one evening when she needed help to stand.

"It's not going too well," she said quietly. Anne made no comment.

"As a nurse it surprised me that Margaret was able to be so independent until the last week," Anne observed. "It showed her determination, her desire to be in control."

On the last Tuesday night of Margaret's life, Anne had volunteered to be one of the overnight double shift. She joined Linda and me in a kitchen consultation, where we agreed there was no point in trying to get Margaret upstairs to bed. We would leave her where she wanted to be, on the couch. The issue of bed sores was no longer relevant, and the need for a toilet was over: neither her bowel or kidneys appeared to be functioning. When Wendy Farquhar, her face grave, arrived to be the other overnight shift person, I got wearily to my feet to leave. We all hugged, needing no words. I kissed Margaret's hot face and left.

Linda phoned minutes after I got home. "There's no end to this woman," she told me admiringly. "Margaret's just had a bowel movement!"

An involuntary movement, it had happened shortly after Linda left. Wendy and Anne became aware of it because of the odour. They cleaned Margaret's body gently, and Wendy went into the basement to wash the fleece that had been under Margaret's bottom. During the clean-up, Margaret was detached and unembarrassed, viewing the event as something quite removed from her personally.

Anne was gratified to employ her bedside nursing skills again after many years as a community nurse, away from active treatment. She cleaned Margaret's dry mouth, washed her face, and put cream on her lips. Margaret looked at her with cloudy eyes full of longing. "Oh, Anne," she whispered, "how I wish you had brought your violin."

Anne sat with her in the dimly lit living-room as Margaret slept that night, uttering occasional groans. When Anne was administering morphine at midnight, giving her little sips from a syringe, Margaret suddenly said, "It's the Americans, isn't it?"

Tuesday, June 18

Wendy and Anne took turns sitting beside Margaret through the night. A few hours after dawn, around eight in the morning, Margaret roused and asked desperately for a bedpan. By the time the bedpan was ready, it was too late. Anne wrote in the log-book, "She had a good b.m., so we took the opportunity to wash her and give her a rub. There is a bruise on the left hip. She liked the treatment and does co-operate fully as long as she knows what you are going to do with her.... The fact she did not express any pain when we turned her is encouraging."

Margaret drank a few spoonfuls of apricot nectar and asked to have lotion rubbed on her face.

When Linda called for the morning report, Anne told her about Margaret asking for the violin. "Why don't you get it and play for her?" Linda suggested.

Anne fetched her violin. She decided on a favourite piece, Bach's "*Vist dir Mier*" ("Stay With Me, O Lord"). For some reason, it had been in her head for a week. While she played, her eyes were on her fingering, and when she finished and looked up, Margaret was asleep.

255

Wendy wrote in the log, "I am leaving for out West tomorrow morning. Glad I had the chance to be here overnight. I feel this is probably my goodbye, as I won't return until late Sunday night. And yet, knowing Margaret ... "

Margaret's neighbour on the other side, Marian Ross, came to offer help and left with the soiled bedding.

Vivian Harrower had missed her regular Monday overnight shift because she had tickets to the musical *Cats*, so she signed herself in to share Tuesday morning with Patti Welsh. Both women were nervous, alarmed that Margaret would have a crisis they couldn't handle. "Also, I wasn't sure that I could cope with something like a bowel movement," Vivian confessed. In response to their appeal for reinforcement, Heather Sutherland came around noon, and it was Heather who gave Margaret her morphine.

Heather was stricken by the change in Margaret's condition. She had missed one Tuesday shift because she was in Chicago attending a convention of the Association of Humanistic Psychology. In the two-week interval since she had last seen Margaret, the deterioration was drastic.

Margaret spent the morning in a groggy sleep, though she would open her eyes when she heard the front door open and responded with grunts to questions about her needs. She seemed dimly interested in everything around her but too weak to participate.

When I got to Margaret's that morning, Heather and Patti had triumphant expressions. Margaret had just had another bowel movement, which they thought something of a medical marvel under the conditions, and this time the bedpan had been in place. Afterwards, Heather gave her a wash, and she and Patti slipped a blue plastic incontinent pad under Margaret's flaccid hips. Margaret fell gratefully to sleep to the sound of Mozart.

She wakened when I came into the living-room and gave me a lovely smile, lifting her arms for a hug. I noted that her eyes were clearer than they had been the previous day, and that her skin was not as yellow; her jaundice was almost gone.

256

A few minutes later Phyllis and Ted Cockram appeared. Margaret's expressive face lit up, and she said to Phyllis, "I'm so glad you came."

I withdrew to the kitchen, where Patti and Heather were making tea. Phyllis joined us there, looking distressed. "She held one of my hands," she told us, "but she's holding *both* of Ted's."

Margaret was alone when I returned to the living-room. I sat beside her, feeling too much despair to speak. She pulled some strength from her secret supply, glared at me and said fiercely, "I am going to live."

"I guess you are," I replied with a smile.

Linda Rapson said she laughed all the way to work that morning, thinking of Anne van Egmond playing her violin for Margaret. She reflected that the morphine was slowing Margaret's breathing but hadn't touched her love for music. Margaret's failure to urinate worried her, however, because it was a potential source of pain. She called Elizabeth Greaves to pick up a catheter set at a medical-supplies store.

Heather Sutherland was in the living-room with Margaret when Linda arrived that evening, shortly after I left to attend a board of directors meeting at Jessie's Centre for Teenagers. Linda felt Margaret's abdomen and noted that the bladder was more distended than the previous day, but Margaret insisted she felt comfortable. Then Linda looked at Margaret's legs and was astonished: they had shrunk to almost normal size.

She got on the telephone at once to Dr. Larry Librach, her cousin-in-law and consultant: "Where did the fluid go? What's happening here?"

He said that the fluid had gone into Margaret's system, absorbed by her dehydration. As Linda told me later, chuckling, Margaret had organized her own intravenous.

Larry also advised against catheterization. "If Margaret is comfortable," he said, "just leave her alone."

Margaret revived with Linda's presence and had what Heather described as "one of her moments of sparkle". It was time for Heather to leave, but she reflected that she would never see

257

Margaret again and couldn't face the farewell. She was "watering the flowers and fiddling around", as she put it, when Linda asked, "How is your thesis going?"

Heather replied, "I'm in the last stage of writing it."

Margaret said from the couch, her voice composed, "And I'm in the last stage of my life. I want to thank you, all of you, for looking after me so well."

Heather was astonished. She had never heard Margaret acknowledge her dying; almost none of us had. She was grateful for the opening it gave her to speak from her heart. She knelt by Margaret's side and held her. "You have lived a noble life, Margaret, full of accomplishment," she said. "You have so much to be proud of. You have helped many people, and you've been especially supportive and helpful to women. We've always felt your encouragement of what we try to do. You helped me a lot. I'm not sure Jim and I could have worked out our decision about marriage without my sense of your concern for me. Holy Trinity wouldn't be as it is today without you. And maybe your greatest gift to your friends has been to allow us to look after you. That's a priceless gift."

They said their goodbyes with tears, and Linda was left alone with Margaret. She sat beside her, holding her hand. Margaret drifted into a restful sleep, her chest heaving gently and evenly.

She roused and said weakly, "Oh, Linda, such a short time to know you ... " She slept for a few minutes and then wakened and tried to lift her arm. Linda realized that Margaret wanted to hug, so she got on her knees and put her arms around Margaret, who said, "Oh, Linda, Linda."

"I love you, Margaret," Linda said gently.

"I love you too," Margaret said, and slipped into sleep again. Linda, holding her, thought that Margaret might die in her arms, but Margaret's breathing didn't falter. After a while Linda pulled the rocking chair over and sat in it, holding Margaret's hand. She was first puzzled and then worried that Jackie White-Hampton, who was due for the evening shift at five o'clock, had not arrived. She looked for Jackie's telephone number but couldn't find it. She felt vulnerable and frightened, though she admonished herself: "Big-shot doctor. You're supposed to be competent to handle any emergency."

She telephoned Jessie's and left a message for me to call her. When I got it a minute later, I was certain that Margaret had died. I called in a panic and Linda had to reassure me. She said Jackie hadn't arrived and there was no food in the house. I said, "Order a pizza. I'll be right over."

Jackie arrived around seven, bringing carrot soup. It had been two weeks since she had done a shift and she was unaware of the change in Margaret's condition. I followed a few minutes later, in time to share the pizza and soup.

Margaret was sparkling again. She held out her arms to Jackie and said, "I'm so glad you're here."

Linda and Jackie were in the kitchen, and I sat beside Margaret, who was feeling conversational. "You're so beautiful," she told me. "You have such a beautiful face, Jackie."

"You twit," I told her fondly, "I'm June."

She blinked and gave a small grin. Her eyes closed and I held her hand tightly. From where her mind was wandering she suddenly said, quite loudly, "I'm amazed."

Linda lifted the blanket and proudly showed me Margaret's legs. "Isn't it wonderful?" she said.

"How did this happen?" I asked. "And how come she isn't jaundiced any more?"

Linda shrugged. "Don't ask me such questions. I don't know what's going on."

"Fine doctor you are," I muttered.

I asked Margaret if she wanted something to eat, and she amazed us by asking for ice cream and maple syrup. I stirred the mixture together until it was soft and had lost its chill and then spooned a little into her mouth, maybe ten small sips.

"You're in our arms," I said to Margaret, and she nodded.

Linda, lazing in an armchair across the room, observed, "I think we all learn a lot from Margaret."

It was time for me to leave. As I said goodbye, kissing her, I

259

explained, "I'm June."

"I know," Margaret said. Her mouth twitched and she added, "*Now.*"

It was almost dark as I went down the familiar sidewalk to my car, parked conveniently next to a hydrant. Margaret's neighbour, Bob Ross, a big, quiet man, was watering his lawn. He asked, "How is she?" I said she wasn't expected to last much longer. He shook his head admiringly. "I'm surprised she's still at home. We thought she'd be going back to the hospital. She's a tough woman."

The overnight shift was shared by Marjorie Perkins, a school psychologist, and Pat Capponi. Linda waited for their arrival and thought they made an odd couple, Marjorie the picture of femininity in a pretty dress and Pat in blue jeans secured with a wide leather belt, a man's shirt and vest, a black leather jacket, and a black fedora. Linda briefed them on how to care for Margaret through the night, and Marjorie decided she would need to wear something more practical. While she was gone to change into jeans, Eileen Swinton called to ask if she could visit Margaret, and Linda assured her she was welcome.

Margaret, however, was becoming feisty. At one point she yelled at Pat, "Come over here and move me!" and at another she said to Eileen, giving her a severe look, "What are you doing here? You're not part of the team."

Between the bursts of crossness, she wanted to know how tickets for the Nellie's theatre benefit, *Trafford Tanzi*, were selling. Eileen confessed that sales were disappointing. Many people who support Nellie's are feminists, and it looked as though most of them already had seen the play during its first run. Margaret, fully herself, made some practical suggestions. Eileen sighed that most of the standard emergency measures had been tried.

Linda came into the room from time to time to keep an eye on her patient. Margaret seemed increasingly uncomfortable. Linda, Pat, and Marjorie tried to arrange her on her side, but it didn't seem to help. Linda asked, "Do you want to sit up?"

"Yes, please."

260

A massive change was made in the pillows to prop Margaret upright, the first time in forty-eight hours that she had sat up. A look of contentment spread on her face. She instructed the women – Linda, Jackie, Pat and Eileen – to sit in a circle around her and have some tea. She even managed to hold her cup herself, though shakily, and take a few sips unaided.

They talked about religion, marvelling at the different directions their spirituality had taken them. Eileen is a Buddhist, Pat a Muslim, Linda what she calls "a heretic", and Margaret a Holy Trinity brand of Anglican. Margaret said reflectively, "Islam is appropriate for you, Pat. It's a religion where you're supposed to fight back."

Linda asked curiously, "What religion is appropriate for me?" but Margaret had "fluffed out among the pillows", as Pat put it, and didn't answer.

Marjorie returned, and Linda supervised as Marjorie and Pat moved Margaret into a lying-down position. Then, confident of the two women's skills, Linda went home for another troubled sleep. Pat and Marjorie decided they would sleep in two-hour shifts through the night. Margaret slept between midnight and four, occasionally squirming with pain or uttering a groan, but toward dawn her pain grew worse. Pat sat beside her, holding her hand and feeling desolate that she was helpless. Marjorie came downstairs and gently massaged Margaret's back, which seemed to help her. Pat wrote in the log-book, "She earned a place in heaven and in Margaret's heart." As Marjorie rubbed her back, Margaret said, "Thank you, God." What came into Pat's mind was the Jesuit martyrs, tortured by the Hurons.

Both women stayed up, neither willing to leave Margaret. It's true that everything hurts more at night; for people who are very ill or injured badly the dark is the hardest time. As the sun rose, Margaret was still in agony. Linda telephoned around seven and Pat told her what was happening. Linda drove to Margaret's at once.

Wednesday, June 19

"I think it might be a good idea if I use a catheter to help drain your bladder," Linda told Margaret. "You haven't urinated in more than three days, and I think some of this pain is caused by your bladder being so full."

Margaret said, "If you think it will help, go ahead."

Linda worked as gently and carefully as she could, but the catheter would not go in. She hadn't done a catheterization for years, but the problem appeared to be a blockage in Margaret's urethra rather than Linda's lack of practice. As Linda struggled to insert the catheter Margaret gasped, "It *hurts*. Is it all right if I yell?"

"Sure," said Linda. "Yell your head off."

Margaret put her head back and yelled as Linda made a final attempt, but she again was unsuccessful. The doctor was almost overcome with remorse. She wondered if a smaller catheter would have worked, or if she should have tried catheterization at all. For the only time in the three months she had been caring for Margaret, she had caused her patient pain. Months later, she was still regretting the attempt. She wrote in the log that day, "I really don't think anyone could catheterize her easily without it hurting. I don't really blame the fact I'm rusty."

Marjorie Perkins had left for work, and Pat Capponi was watching the clock, already late for her job. Linda studied the schedule fretfully, worried that another gap had developed. The photocopied schedule of "Margaret's Friends" was becoming unreadable, a filigree of deletions and additions in pencil and several shades of ink laid over the original calendar. It appeared that Anne Grasham was due at ten and Sheila Mackenzie at one o'clock, but Linda thought extra help was needed for the morning. She telephoned Merylie Houston, who came at once. Merylie later said that the peremptory summons in that situation was a "ratification of me, it made me feel special".

262

Anne, Merylie, and Linda wrestled with the problem of helping Margaret find the least uncomfortable position possible. Margaret was exceedingly restless no matter what position was found for her. She suggested that she be moved to sit in the chair where she used to have her Codetron treatments. Linda was very worried about Merylie's back but, between the three of them, the women managed to half-carry Margaret across the room. Once enthroned among the pillows in the chair, Margaret changed her mind. She wanted to be back on the couch.

Finally they placed Margaret upright on the couch, pillows crushed behind her back to brace her, and Linda seated beside her with her arms around Margaret's upper body for support. Margaret's head drooped on Linda's shoulder, and she slept in that position for an hour, the first rest she had known since the pain began in the night.

Linda was sure that Margaret's enlarged bladder was part of the problem. Twice that morning Merylie slipped a bedpan under Margaret, keeping her fingers against the rim as a cushion for Margaret's thin bottom, but no urine came. "You can't get much closer to a person than that," Merylie later reflected. "What I was thinking while I was holding her was that it was a privilege."

Linda wondered if Margaret simply was resisting the bedpan, a not uncommon aversion. Anne was dispatched to rent a commode, a portable toilet, which was place in a handy position next to the couch. Margaret's bladder still would not function, though there was more seepage from her bowel. Twice Merylie and Anne helped her into clean pyjamas, and the third time they left Margaret's bottom bare for the sake of convenience. Margaret didn't seem to notice.

Linda observed that Margaret's legs had begun to swell again. Palpating Margaret's abdomen, she found that she could percuss the bladder halfway to the umbilicus. The grossly swollen organ was pressing on Margaret's bowel, which accounted for the frequent stools. Since the bladder could not or would not empty, Linda's only way of combating the pain was to increase the morphine dosage to 10 mg. This still was a small dose for someone in Margaret's advanced state of pancreatic cancer, but it was fifty per cent more than the earlier doses.

Linda administered the first new dosage at noon. She asked Margaret if she wanted something else, a medicine that would relax her. Margaret answered "Yes," in a very decisive voice, so Linda gave her Ativan, a sedative, as well.

Margaret's appearance was devastating. Despite emaciation and the dreadful colour of her skin, she had managed until this day to look herself, an intelligent, interested, interesting woman. But overnight a subtle change had occurred. She had become almost corpse-like, the grey skin of her face so stretched over bone that it wore no expression except anguish. From time to time Margaret made a choking sound, but she would swallow noisily and the spasm would pass. When she cried out, the pain usually was from acute cramps in her calf muscles, particularly the right leg. To relieve it, we would stretch the muscle by slowly pushing her foot to a position at a right angle with her leg while gently kneading the hard muscle.

Linda brushed Margaret's thick white hair, now the only part of her unchanged by the cancer, and marvelled at its health and vitality. She believed that Margaret could live only hours longer, but when she took Margaret's pulse it was strong and steady.

"She looks so awful," she mourned to Sheila Mackenzie in the kitchen. "I really think it is time she died."

Sheila said gravely, "I give you permission."

Linda understood her and shook her head negatively. They embraced silently.

The medication hadn't yet taken effect. Linda sat on the floor beside Margaret and put her head next to Margaret's on the pillows. With her arm around Margaret, they both slept. Anne Grasham observed later, "They looked so sweet together."

In an hour, Margaret was snoring. Linda wearily climbed to her feet and gathered up her briefcase and bag. She wrote out instructions for the increased morphine dosage every four hours and ordered that Ativan be added if required "for persistent distress".

She wrote in the log, "Last evening she had a period of peace and tranquillity during which she said a poignant goodbye to Heather and Heather said wonderful things to Margaret. When I was alone with her she told me she loved me and I told her I loved her. I really thought she was going to go off in a state of tranquillity, but no such luck. It's not easy."

On her way home in her car Linda played the Mary O'Hara tape of "Bridge Over Troubled Water" and cried. She noted with surprise that she was exhausted. There was ample reason for even her extraordinary reserves of energy to be depleted. That particular "house call" at Margaret's had lasted seven and a half hours. The previous day Linda had been with Margaret for almost six hours, and the day before that, Monday, she was in the house for seven hours. Sunday had been the longest visit, close to nine hours.

When I got to Margaret's an hour after Linda left, Ian Sowton was there, stroking Margaret's forehead. The portable toilet, an uncompromisingly frank object, was an eyesore in the middle of the living-room, so I carried it to the back porch. Phyllis and Ted Cockram were moving through the house. As executor, Bill Whitla had asked Phyllis to select what articles of Margaret's she wanted for herself. She pointed out to me some plates that had belonged to her mother, a lamp in the guest bedroom, and the bronze shepherd-boy lamp in the front hall, also a family piece. In the basement was a clock Margaret had discarded that meant something to Phyllis. She was making a small collection of these objects in the front hall. I found some framed family photographs on the wall in Margaret's den, and Phyllis added them to the pile.

Phyllis seemed feverish for distraction. Sitting in the living-room, with Margaret sleeping fitfully on the couch, Phyllis pulled out photographs of her Florida home and showed them to me, pointing out details that I might have missed. She regretted that the picture of her living-room didn't show the Oriental rug, and she lingered over exterior shots of the landscaping. "You'd never guess that it's a mobile home, would you?" she asked with pride. The house in truth is handsome. I admired everything, touched to see in Phyllis's scrupulously maintained home the same devo-

265

tion to order and neatness that marked Margaret's character. But as we chatted over snapshots, with Margaret groaning a few feet away, I had the feeling that I was caught in a Woody Allen skit.

Margaret stirred and opened her eyes. I asked if she would like to try to use the toilet, and she grunted in assent. We brought the toilet from the porch, and Ian lifted Margaret's torso while Phyllis and I looked after her limp legs. The team had solemnly decided that men would not help when Margaret's needs became personal, but the strength of a man was never needed more and none of us felt in the least awkward about Ian's presence, least of all Margaret.

She did try to void, but only about a teaspoon of dark urine was produced. Linda later said it might have helped to pour warm water over her pubis, but none of us knew that trick. We regretfully lifted Margaret from the commode and placed her back on the couch.

At four o'clock Ian administered Margaret's morphine. Since she seemed agitated, we decided to give her the Ativan as well. I crushed the sedative tablet in some maple syrup and fed it to her. Margaret licked the spoon like a grateful child.

Phyllis noticed that the light bulb in the ceiling fixture of the front hall was burned out. We hunted in vain for Margaret's supply of spare bulbs, and then Phyllis sent Ted to find a hardware store. When he returned with the bulb, she was delighted; it was indeed a singular accomplishment for an Alzheimer's sufferer in a strange city.

I had forgotten about Cleo, Margaret's cat; I think we all had. Over the past few days, Cleo had been looking almost as wracked as her mistress. Her fur was coming out in patches, and she seemed to find it impossible to settle down anywhere. Often she would curl up beside Margaret, but if she walked across Margaret's abdomen her weight seemed so painful that we would lift her away. I was admiring Ted's light bulb in the hall when I discovered that Cleo had deposited a huge poop on the rug.

"Cleo's going to pieces," I told Phyllis. "Look at this." While I stood there, hoping the mess would vanish by itself, the redoubtable Phyllis found tissues, cleaned the stool, and sponged the rug clean.

Bill Whitla arrived to confer with Phyllis about Margaret's belongings. She would be returning to Toronto in two months, she said, and would pick them up then. At around six, Phyllis and Ted left. Their plane to Florida was departing early in the morning and they had packing to do and other arrangements to make. Phyllis bent over Margaret, who grasped both her hands. "I'm so glad you came," Margaret said fervently. "I'm so happy. Thank you for coming, thank you so much." Phyllis murmured something in return, kissed Margaret's cheek, and sturdily went out the door, followed by Ted.

Vivian Harrower came a few minutes later, announcing that the double shifts were settled for the rest of the week and there would be no more gaps. I hated to leave. In the past few days Margaret had become the core of my life; everything I did away from her felt remote and desiccated. But I had other obligations. I took a long time parting from her, and when I kissed her dry lips, she smiled sadly with her heart in her eyes. She drew a ragged breath and let it out slowly to say, "Dear."

Bill Whitla, Vivian, and Ian dined on "a gourmet feast", according to Vivian's report. Ian Sowton, it turned out, is a superb cook. Then they sat in the living-room with Margaret, whose breathing was rattling and unsteady, and listened to Bach and some Mozart. Occasionally Margaret would make a choking noise, coughing to clear her throat, but didn't waken.

Linda called me that evening. "I think I'm about at the end of my rope," she said wearily. "Tell me something funny."

I thought carefully. "Tell you what, if Margaret doesn't die tomorrow, we'll go over there and kill her."

Well, it worked. Linda laughed and laughed.

The overnight shift turned up promptly, Janice Hatch, from Nellie's board of directors, and Cathy Goring of Holy Trinity. "There was a lot going on," Jan Hatch recalled. "Bill, Ian, and Vivian were there, Margaret was on the couch, Cathy and I were getting instructions about the morphine and what to do about leg cramps. A lot going on."

Cathy, a nurse, and Jan, had not met before but, towards midnight, they found themselves alone with Margaret. They decided to split the night in half, Jan sleeping the first three and a half hours and Cathy the next. That settled, Jan went up to bed.

Thursday, June 20

Margaret slept soundly after the morphine at midnight, her breathing steady and strong. Cathy woke Jan Hatch around three-thirty and told her sleepily that everything was fine. "Margaret hasn't even moved," she said. Jan was relieved. She had been feeling close to panic to think that Margaret would need something from her that she would be too unskilled to give. Jan made herself comfortable in the softly lit living-room and watched Margaret breathe.

Jan Hatch is thirty-one, a woman of fragile beauty with a shy voice and blonde hair that curls around her delicate face. She looks breakable, but she's Nellie's most articulate and best-informed director, the one the board chooses when it sends a representative to the United Way, for instance. Jan felt "out of my league" when she first joined the Nellie's board in 1982, awed by the array of women lawyers and managers who are drawn to the famous hostel. Margaret Frazer, she decided, was more her speed, an approachable kind of person who was far less intimidating than the others.

Jan was job hunting unsuccessfully in 1983, which gave her time to help with preparations for opening the Margaret Frazer House. She started to see more of Margaret, who was also active in committee work and the hiring process. Margaret asked Jan to assist with the guest list for Nellie's tenth anniversary reception in the summer of 1984, to be hosted by Ontario's then lieutenant-governor, John Black Aird, in his Queen's Park suite. The younger woman was enchanted by the element of surprise in her blossoming acquaintanceship with Margaret. "She wasn't like anyone else I had ever met," Jan recalled one summer evening when we met in a bar for something to eat. "You could never predict what Margaret would think on a given subject."

Jan appealed to Margaret for advice. She was trying to figure out what to do with her life. An accomplished seamstress, she thought she would like to work in a museum restoring costumes. Margaret never could refuse a request from a young person seeking guidance or support. Over the next few weeks she showered Jan with "about five hundred ideas where to go for information about costume restoration".

Sheila Mackenzie once commented on this side of Margaret's nature: "That's what she was good at, helping young women. What she wasn't good at was helping herself. She died with her real self untouched."

Before Margaret could propel Jan into costume restoration, however, Jan got a job with a new two-person organization, the Women's Legal Education and Action Fund, known as LEAF, which was trying to raise a war chest to pay the legal costs of taking test cases involving women's rights to the Supreme Court of Canada. (And LEAF was successful: in the fall of 1985 the Ontario government gave the organization one million dollars.)

After Jan started to work for LEAF, she saw Margaret only at Nellie's monthly board meetings, and it wasn't until the spring of 1985 that she noticed Margaret's weight loss. Margaret was evasive when Jan asked anxiously what was the matter. Even when Jan visited Margaret in hospital after the exploratory surgery, Margaret didn't tell her that she had cancer.

Jan had just separated from her husband and was feeling at a loose end. When she learned of the team she volunteered for the Tuesday overnight shift. She thought overnights would be easiest for her; she wondered uncomfortably what she and Margaret would find to talk about if she did a daytime shift.

At first there wasn't much to do. She helped Margaret to bed and left in the morning, while Margaret was still asleep, in order to attend an early exercise class. She was astonished that Margaret was unselfconscious about undressing and removing her teeth. "My grandmother would never have done that in front of *anyone*," Jan commented to me while we waited for our food order. "I thought it was great that Margaret was so comfortable about it."

After a while it became apparent that Margaret needed assistance to dress and for breakfast, so Jan started to skip the exercise class. She was appreciative that Margaret was precise about what she wanted to eat and how it should be served. "I could then do it exactly as she wanted," Jan said, "which is what I wanted to do. If she hadn't told me, she would have gotten my version of what she wanted."

She reflected, "It was wonderful how Margaret kept her integrity. She never felt she had to take what she got and be grateful. She kept her power and authority."

Jan was unimpressed by Margaret's insistence that she would get well; it never rang true to her. She was intrigued that Margaret persisted in the pretence of fighting her cancer when, in reality, Jan felt, she had accepted that she was dying and was entirely at ease with that knowledge. "There was always a sense of peace about her," she observed.

Mindful of how many people on the Margaret team had been touched by the death of someone close to them, I asked Jan Hatch if she had ever suffered such a loss. She blinked at me behind the huge glasses she wears. "My grandfather died four years ago," she answered. "He was a concert pianist. And my brother committed suicide six years ago. I've never stopped grieving over that."

Jan was out of Toronto for a three-week vacation at the beginning of June. When she parted from Margaret, she wondered if she would see her again. Margaret must have had the same thought. "We had always kissed goodbye and looked into each other's eyes," Jan recalled, "but this was different. Margaret said, 'Goodbye, my darling,' and I knew that she loved me. I was just filled that day, walking down the street, in the subway, thinking that Margaret loved me."

When she returned, Jan switched her overnights to Wednesday

so she could attend her exercise class. What seemed an insignificant adjustment in the schedule put her at Margaret's side when she died.

Margaret started to be restless about half an hour after Cathy Goring had gone to bed, leaving Jan to sit vigil. Margaret opened her eyes and began to flail around in pain. Jan was in a state of terror. Remembering that Bill Whitla was coming at seven, she started watching the clock. She thought, "What will I do if she wants to use the commode? What if she has a bowel movement? Should I be giving her more morphine or more tranquillizer?"

She prayed that Margaret wouldn't need anything. Because Margaret wasn't speaking, she didn't know how she would interpret the sounds if Margaret tried to ask for something.

Jan has a constitutional aversion to noise, and usually can't speak loudly. She says it's because she is too self-conscious. Nevertheless she managed to raise her voice to pierce Margaret's near-coma. She bent over her and asked what was happening. Somehow Margaret made her understand that she had cramps in her leg. Jan massaged the muscle and manipulated Margaret's foot as she had been instructed, but without being able to give relief. By trial and error, she found that she could keep the calf muscle soft by simply holding it in both her hands.

Whether it was a mental distortion caused by fatigue and fright or that she experienced a genuine psychic manifestation Jan will never know, but she had a strong sensation that Margaret was silently asking her for permission to leave. She realized she had been aware of the question from the moment she walked in the house. "There was a clear question I could hear in my head, 'Can I go now?'"

Suddenly Jan felt enormous relief. She realized that Margaret couldn't possibly need anything further from anyone. There would be nothing that she would be asked to do, nothing that she would be unable to do. She was no longer frightened. "And it seemed to me that the minute I stopped being scared, Margaret started to die."

Margaret began to make a terrible noise in her throat and

271

chest. Jan wakened Cathy, who administered some Ativan. When the noise continued Jan began to tremble. Cathy held Jan and asked her if she had ever seen anyone die. Jan shook her head. "That's a death rattle," Cathy explained gently. She telephoned Linda.

Linda was haggard from a difficult night. Around five that morning she had wakened after only a few hours' sleep. She had just finished breakfast at six-thirty when the phone rang. Cathy Goring explained that Margaret was rattling. In reality, the rattle is the noise of pulmonary edema. Margaret's lungs were filling with fluid; she was drowning.

Linda could hear the noise plainly in the background, though the telephone was twenty feet from Margaret's couch. It sounded almost like Margaret yelling. She told Cathy there was nothing she could do but wait. Cathy hung up and put her arms around Jan, who was still shaking. "Even if we were in a hospital," she said, "there is nothing we could do." In a hospital, in fact, something can be done to rescue patients from pulmonary edema, but customarily such heroic measures are not taken when the person is as debilitated as Margaret was.

Jan was rubbing Margaret's leg when the noise stopped. Margaret gasped, breathed twice, quietly, like sighing, and then was utterly still. She lay with her head arched back her eyes wide open, and her mouth agape in what looked like a scream. Cathy took her pulse but found none. She was dead. The two women tried to close Margaret's eyelids and mouth, but her face was rigid.

It was about six-forty, and the summer sun was already high. Margaret's roses were blooming, and the trees were full of singing birds. Cleo was sleeping on the window-sill outside. Everything was in perfect order – except that the figure on the green couch had stopped breathing.

Jan called Linda again to say it was over.

Linda telephoned me, her voice flat. "Margaret just died a few minutes ago," she said.

From habit as much as anything, I said, "I'll be right there."

"I'll see you there," she said.

The telephone rang again as I started to dress. A soft voice I didn't know, Jan Hatch's, said that Margaret had just died. I thanked her for the kindness of remembering to call me. I wasn't feeling anything, just hunting around in my closet for running shoes and something that would be quick to pull on. My husband silently handed me some orange juice, which I drank on the way to the car. The morning rush hour hadn't yet started, so I could make good speed on the cross-town highway. I drove with the top down and noticed it was an exquisite, perfect June morning. Margaret's dead, I said to myself. Margaret's dead. Margaret's dead. I didn't cry until I turned into her street.

As I went up the sidewalk, a woman came out of the house next to Margaret's on the east side, dressed for the office. I had never seen her before, but I realized she must be the neighbour who had been helping with Margaret's laundry. I wanted to tell her what had happened but I couldn't; I was just nicely under control and didn't want to weep again. She gave me a look of wonderful understanding.

Bill Whitla and Ian Sowton were sitting in the living-room with two women I didn't know. The blonde one was Jan Hatch and the dark one Cathy Goring. I sat and stared at Margaret as they briefly sketched the events of the dawn. Margaret was lying under her green mohair blanket, her face reminding me of Picasso's painting of the bombing of Guernica. Her expression was of desperation, like someone straining frantically to get away.

Ian made coffee the campfire way, by boiling water and grounds together, and we drank it, talking desultorily about calling the undertaker as soon as Linda arrived to pronounce Margaret dead, about Cleo who had disappeared, about the roses being in perfect bloom. One of them floated in a glass bowl at Margaret's side.

Linda arrived, looking as though she had been weeping, and I met her at the front door to hug her. I said, giving her an extra squeeze, "You know, you did it right."

Then she stepped into the living-room and stared at Margaret. She thought that Margaret looked tiny, as if death had shrunk her, and to her Margaret's expression looked desperate. She tried to close the protesting eyes, but Margaret's lids still wouldn't move. Then Linda sank to her knees, put her hands over her face and cried. We waited, listening peacefully while she sobbed. She started to fumble with the sheet to lift it over Margaret's face, but it was stuck. She said in a strangled voice, "Should I cover her?"

"Do what you want," Bill Whitla said kindly.

Linda made a helpless gesture and left Margaret as she was. When she stood up, shaking, we all hugged her fiercely.

"I guess I should call the undertaker," she said as she recovered.

"There's no rush," Bill pointed out gently. "Let's have a cup of tea and wait a while."

A long silence fell. I was finding it difficult to draw a breath. I said loudly, "Well, she died the way she wanted to, on that *fucking couch*." It proved a great tension breaker. Everyone burst into laughter, and whatever had been clutching my chest eased off.

Bill Whitla wondered if we should have a wake. Most certainly, we all said. Should it be for all her friends? I suggested that they would be coming to the memorial service at Holy Trinity, but the wake should perhaps be just for the team. Many of us had still not even met, though we had seen one another at the team meetings. We needed time by ourselves. That was agreed. Where should the wake be? Where else, we said, but at Margaret's house. We couldn't be sure of contacting everyone in time to hold it that night, so we settled on the next one, a Friday.

We were feeling composed enough for phone calls. Bill telephoned Phyllis Cockram and caught her just as she and Ted were leaving for the airport. She sounded sad but composed. She had been expecting the call, she said. She wouldn't change their plans and stay for the ceremonies. There was really no point. Then Bill called the undertaker to come for Margaret's body, which would be cremated the same day. Linda telephoned Wendy and Nigel in Jasper to give them the news.

Cathy Goring and Jan Hatch slipped away to go to work and begin the phone-tree that had been arranged previously to notify

274

the team. Before the process could be started, Sheila Mackenzie called, and I gave her the news. She didn't speak. I said, "Why don't you come right over?" She said she was on her way.

Bill and Ian talked about the memorial service and decided to hold a meeting the next day to decide who should participate. It was hoped that some of Margaret's music friends from CAM-MAC and the Concord Singers would take part. "Margaret wanted the *St. Matthew Passion*," Bill told us, "but with the death bits left out." We grinned at that, hearing Margaret's voice giving the instructions.

I brushed Margaret's hair and tried to close her howling mouth, but her jaw was rigid. Mindlessly, I straightened the green blanket over her still chest.

Linda and I went next door to tell Mary Hiseler. She was in her dressing-gown, feeding her children breakfast, and her eyes filled with tears. A few minutes later she dressed and came to visit, sitting beside Margaret with her baby, Rob, on her lap, exactly as she had almost three months earlier when I brought Margaret home from hospital. Mary wondered how she would tell the terrible news to her daughters, Gwen and Jenny, who were larking on the front lawn, excited to be going to Wonderland in a few minutes.

Her voice breaking, she said, "Margaret was always so encouraging of Jenny's athletics, always told her she was doing wonderfully." Looking at the happy children, I saw for the first time that seven-year-old Jen wears a brace on her leg.

We told her about the wake planned for Friday, and she said that the neighbourhood was giving the Hiselers a farewell party that same night. She would drop in, she said, but she couldn't stay. Bill asked if I would write Margaret's obituary for the *Globe and Mail*. I said I would see if the *Globe* would print a small story about her.

"You might say that in lieu of flowers people could send donations to Jessie's and the Margaret Frazer House," he suggested. I wasn't sure the *Globe* would allow that, but said I would try.

The undertaker arrived, a small precise man in striped pants with a professionally doleful expression. He asked if a doctor was present to sign the death certificate. I said yes, and he looked expectantly from Bill to Ian. When Linda, wearing her husband's *famoso advogado* sweatshirt, pink jogging pants, and sneakers, stepped forward to take the document from him, his composure almost slipped.

The undertaker went out and returned with a man carrying a folded stretcher and a dark bag. I went straight to the back porch and waited there while Margaret was placed in the bag and carried away. When I returned to the living-room to find her gone, I cried and was comforted by all.

By silent agreement Linda and I started to straighten the room so it would look the way Margaret liked to see it. We rolled up the futon, replaced the green cushions that belonged on the couch, and carried all Margaret's pillows and bedding upstairs. While Linda tidied the coffee table and tea mugs, I loaded the green blanket and her fleece in my car to take to the cleaners. Together we made a bundle of sheets, towels, and pillowcases that needed to be washed, and I put that, too, in my car. Ian helped me lift the heavy wheelcair into the space behind the bucket seats. The monthly rental was due that very day, so I decided to waste no time returning it.

Sheila Mackenzie arrived and slumped into a chair that faced the empty couch, too desolated to speak. She was thinking, "I'm late again. Once again, I'm too late."

Sheila had seen her mother laid out on a marble slab in the hospital where she died and found it a very satisfying experience. "She was a beautiful sight in her plastic shroud," Sheila told me later. "I took all my children to see her. We need to experience death sensually for it to be real and complete."

Bill announced that he was going to the undertaker's to make some final arrangements and Sheila brightened. She asked if she could go along and left with Bill.

I piled some of the bits and pieces I had brought Margaret into my car: the cordless telephone, the bedpan, some books. I dropped off the wheelchair at the rental place and drove home, feeling

276

drained and listless. For two hours I sat at my computer, trying to write the story of Margaret and the Friends of Margaret team for the *Globe*, but what came out one minute was histrionics and the next a stock report. I showered and changed and went to the *Globe* to ask my editor if she wanted the story.

"Not in my section," she told me crisply.

Joan Danard, an editor on the news side of the paper, felt differently. "I think it will go on the front page," she told me.

I sat down to work in the *Globe* newsroom, so unfamiliar with the terminals there that repeatedly I had to ask for help. But this time something had loosened in me and I found I could work. When I got to the last sentence three hours later, I burst into tears.

I went home to wash Margaret's laundry. After our son was killed, my husband and I went to Kingston to collect his belongings from the house he had shared with three other Queen's students. Because Casey had been writing his final examinations in third-year engineering the week before he died, he had had no time to take his clothes to the laundromat: his hamper accordingly was full of crumpled jeans, shirts, underwear, and socks. Somehow it felt orderly and right, a completion of sorts, that I should bring his clothes home, wash and iron them, and put them away in his room. I had the same illogical compulsion about washing, ironing, and neatly folding Margaret's pyjamas. A final service. A last rite.

Linda called. She was also feeling dislocated. What would we do without Margaret in our lives?

I was wondering the same thing. It was a Thursday evening, and for three months I had spent almost every Thursday in Margaret's living-room sipping Almond Sunset tea with her. I wasn't sure, as I ironed Margaret's tea towels, whether I was mourning for Thursdays and their sweetness, or for my friend Margaret who could sing out "Away we go!" in the last week of her life – or for me.

Linda had a story to cheer me. "Margaret finally peed," she crowed. "After four days, she peed!"

It's really Sheila Mackenzie's story.

When Sheila and Bill Whitla reached the undertaker's, Sheila

277

encountered a curious reluctance to allow her to see Margaret. The man behaved very nervously, saying something about Margaret "not being ready". His resistance aroused Sheila's defiance. "I would not be put off," she later told me. "It was a matter of beating the system again."

The undertaker finally yielded to her insistence and permitted her into the room where Margaret was lying. Sheila was deeply moved to see her friend. She reported at the wake that Margaret's eyes, opaque when I saw her dead, were a clear blue, and her protesting mouth was closed and calm.

"Her face was lovely," Sheila said, transported at the memory, "with a sculptural quality to it, and her gaze was faraway and full of intelligence. Her whole expression was serene and focused and very peaceful."

The undertaker explained his unwillingness. The deceased, he said embarrassedly, had relieved herself of a quantity of urine, and the staff had not yet had time to clean her. He must have been astonished when Sheila and Bill whooped with delight.

The final entry but one in the log-book is Linda's. She wrote, "Margaret and I spoke on the telephone at least once a day, usually twice, sometimes three or four times, over a period of almost twelve weeks. I learned so much from her about living and about dying – about music, birds, and flowers. Mostly tho', how to gracefully let people give from their hearts when they want to help."

That last page in the log-book happened to bear a quotation from George Orwell: "There is also the minority of gifted, wilful people who are determined to live their own lives to the end, and writers belong in this class."

In a handwriting I didn't recognize someone had circled the word "writers" and written below it, "So do *Margarets*."

The Wake

The *Globe and Mail* ran the story about Margaret Frazer on the front page, complete with a huge picture of her face with a glowing smile, under the headline "FRIENDS INDEED – Home-Made Family of 60 Pitched In, Worked Shifts To Let Woman Die At Home".

I had arrived at a guess that sixty had participated by adding the approximate number of people who did shifts – regularly or even once – to the number who brought such special gifts to Margaret as a concert or lemon squares. If all her visitors – flower senders, note writers, and telephone callers – had also been counted, the number of people who touched Margaret's life in its final few months would have totalled twice sixty.

I had been on edge all day. Through lunch with my friend actress Barbara Chilcott I was hyper and prattled feverishly. She tried in vain to calm me by listening with perfect stillness. In the morning I had found it impossible to concentrate on working, and I spent much of the afternoon hanging around the *Globe and Mail* newsroom, grateful for the enfolding hustle and the fact that most exchanges there are breezy because it is impossible to have uninterrupted conversation.

At six I drove into the parking lot behind the medical building where Linda Rapson has her office. I found the good doctor seated on the curb, morosely studying the pavement.

"I've been discombobulated all day," she said as she climbed into the passenger seat. "It's a wonder I didn't kill one of my patients. Thanks for picking me up. I don't think I'm fit to drive, even sober."

"Discontented?" I said. "Adrift?"

"Yeah," she answered. "You got it."

"I sure do," I said.

The key to Margaret's house was at Ian Sowton's, Linda told me. We found the address, only a few blocks from Margaret's, and she ran in to get the key. Ian would be over later, and Fran Sowton was expected back from London in a few hours.

I parked in my usual space by the fire hydrant in front of 47 Deloraine, and we saw Helen Gough waving from the front porch. She helped me carry in Margaret's laundry while Linda and I marvelled at what had happened to Margaret's house. Someone had cleaned it right through to a sparkle, brushed and comforted Cleo, pinned the *Globe and Mail* article on the front door, and placed the *Globe*'s picture of Margaret on the mantel. The place looked and felt ready for a party.

I unpacked some wine and two cakes in the kitchen while Helen pulled out of shopping bags the makings of a great salad. We seemed to be avoiding the empty living-room. We hunted for Margaret's serving bowls, mats, napkins, and platters, working together among her familiar things as comfortably as if we three had been co-hosts a hundred times before, and poured wine all around. Elaine Hall joined us and, worried about protecting the surface of Margaret's table, started to arrange placemats under the serving dishes. None of us found concentration easy. I watched Elaine, normally a disciplined, efficient woman, pile the placemats aimlessly on one another.

Finally we stood in Margaret's living-room and stared at the vacant green couch. Helen strode decisively to it and sat down at the end where Margaret's head had rested. We cheered. Left to my own devices I might have made the couch a shrine to Margaret, but it really was only a piece of undistinguished furniture.

The first guests couldn't stay. They were Maureen and Brian Smith, neighbours from two doors down, who were on their way to the party for the Hiselers but wanted to donate some dip and raw vegetables to Margaret's wake. Behind them came Mary Hiseler bearing the lemon squares Margaret had loved, and after her a dozen people from the Margaret team, each bearing food and drink.

I heard someone say, "So you're Grace."

"Where?" I said. "Which one is Grace?"

"Right here," said a woman with a mop of curls and a great grin. "I'm Grace Ross."

"I know you from the log-book," I said. "It's wonderful to meet you."

A woman from Nellie's joined us. "Did you say you're Grace?" she asked. "I'm Jan."

"Well, I know you," said Grace, "from the log-book."

The small house was filling up. I sat on the radiator in the dining-room talking to a woman I'd never seen before. She told me her name, and I recognized it from the log, but I already had forgotten it. I commented that the team was something of a miracle. Glenys McMullen found it amazing that women had worked together without a moment's friction, but I didn't find that as phenomenal as the fact that strangers whose lifestyles were radically different had blended so smoothly.

"But we're almost all service oriented, aren't we?" the woman pointed out. "We're all nurses or teachers or counsellors or hostel workers, or something like that."

I looked around the room, full of people chattering and laughing, and I could see that she was right.

"I wonder how Margaret would have fared," she went on, "if she had worked for an insurance company and her friendships had been in the business world. For one thing, not many of them would have had the time for the weekday shifts."

"Oh dear," I said. "That's true."

"I wonder, too," she added, "if a man could command this sort of support. A man's emotional tone often is cooler than a woman's. Perhaps it was easier for women to rally around because we were comfortable to be helping a woman."

The exchange depressed me. I don't like to think that what happened for Margaret is unique or can't be replicated. People shouldn't die alone because they are male, or because they have worked in an office. Palliative care shouldn't be reserved for the Margaret Frazers who happen to have spent a solid ten years of their lives helping others. If the human community can't make itself into a tribe to help someone, anyone, in trouble, it isn't worth saving from the bomb.

The image in my mind is the mine disaster in Springhill, Nova

281

Scotia, many years ago, when living people were entombed in shafts that had collapsed. The country wasn't concerned about the social position of any of those trapped men, or what god they worshipped, or whether they were abstemious and thrifty. The rescue attempt didn't consist of teams of social workers to help them adjust to living in a dank mine, or sweet-faced clergy with food hampers and mittens, or psychologists to study the effects of hunger and sensory deprivation. Instead people got the biggest and best machinery that could be found, organized themselves into teams, and dug them out.

It's an approach to social assistance that has great appeal for me.

I was near the front door when Pat Capponi came. I had no idea, since we had never met, what it cost her to be there, but when I heard her name I threw my arms around her. "You were wonderful," I told her. "It meant so much to Margaret that you came."

A small man followed her, looking uneasily around. He told me his name was Dr. Norman Salansky. The name rang no bells. "You're a friend of Margaret's, of course," I said.

"No," he replied. "I never met her. It was my Codetron machine she used."

I hollered an introduction, and everyone cheered.

The three downstairs rooms, kitchen, dining-room and living-room, were so crowded that people were sitting on the floors. I was thinking of slipping away home when Linda called for silence.

"Listen everyone," she yelled, "you've got to hear this story about Margaret."

Kneeling by the fireplace, she began to recount the events of the Friday morning a week before when Margaret had insisted on getting washed and dressed, "and you all know where the Arrid is kept", and first said, "Away we go!" Then she told the story about the Saturday afternoon when she and I weeded the roses. Then she told about Margaret, in reply to the question, "Is your head low enough?" saying, "For what?"

The room rocked with laughter. When Linda started the story about Heather Sutherland's eloquent farewell, we cheered. Linda said the right way to cheer was the way she learned to do it when

she was a medical student. At a graduation party the young doctors
saluted one another by shouting:

> Here's to Linda
> Here's to Linda
> Here's to Linda
> She's a horse's ass

Linda assured us that it was a compliment to be called a horse's
ass. We tried a ragged chorus of,

> Here's to Heather
> Here's to Heather
> Here's to Heather
> She's a horse's ass

The verse isn't as easy as it looks. To make it work, the voices
have to be robust and the cadence has to make two distinct
syllables of "horse's". Our first attempt was uncertain, and the
unison on the last line faltered.

I told the story of Glenys and me trying to pull out Margaret's
real teeth in our attempt to remove her dentures, and we howled,

> Here's to Glenys
> Here's to Glenys
> Here's to Glenys
> She's a horse's ass

It was getting better. We were putting a lot of force into the
chorus. We seemed to be launched on a chronology of Margaret
stories. Grace Ross told us what she had said to Margaret during
that crucial first shift, when she got Margaret to agree to accept
the team. We had a lusty "Here's to Grace". Then Merylie described the Friday morning when Margaret crawled to the Codetron chair. We did a "Here's to Norman", for the Codetron, and
then Linda led us in,

Here's to Margaret
Here's to Margaret
Here's to Margaret
She's a horse's ass

I groaned, "You've gone *too far!*", but they hadn't.

Sheila spoke of what happened Thursday night, followed by "Here's to Sheila". Various people told stories of how imperious Margaret was about how her tea was served, or how bossy she was about the garden. Anne Grasham thought of contributing the story of the time she cut back Margaret's tulips, but she felt shy, and besides she wasn't entirely certain she wanted to be called a horse's ass. Anyway, Bill Whitla was telling about his son Michael kissing Margaret goodbye after her final Communion service, when he said he wished he could play for Margaret and she said she wished she could play for him.

Others recalled how Margaret would focus on them, remembering what they were doing and what troubled them. Jay MacGillivray had a complaint. Her shift was Thursday, she said, and she had news for Margaret she was burning to share. She had just enrolled in viola lessons and she knew Margaret would have been pleased. She felt cheated that Margaret hadn't waited. That got her a "Here's to Jay". Someone remembered how hard Vivian Harrower had worked on revising the schedule for the double shifts. "Here's to Vivian."

I talked about Phyllis. "Here's to Phyllis." Linda described the first dose of morphine, and how it coincided with Mary O'Hara singing "Sail on, silver girl". We gave Mary O'Hara a rousing, "Here's to Mary".

We were playing Margaret's favourite tapes, especially the Mary O'Hara one. It made a sweet background as the final Wednesday-shift people went over the events of that last day. As Jan Hatch began softly to talk about Margaret's last hours, Pat Capponi quietly left. "I can't bear social events," she apologized to me. "It's part of my lingering neurosis." She didn't mind the laughter, she said: "Laughter is like crying." But the truth was that she didn't think she would be able to bear hearing about Margaret's death.

Striding down the darkened street in her black leather jacket and wide black hat, she saw ahead of her a man and woman helping an elderly woman, a small family apparently out to enjoy the summer evening air. As she approached them, the couple pulled the old woman out of Pat's way as though to protect her from something unclean or dangerous. Pat went by them without a word, though she burned with hurt.

"That did the neighbourhood for me," she told me. But the anger helped; being angry, she informed me, is easier than being sad. The next morning when she was sitting on the balcony of her apartment, a butterfly landed on her ankle and stayed a long time. She felt it was a message from Margaret and dissolved into tears.

The wake, meanwhile, had reached its best moment when Jan Hatch finished telling about Margaret's death ("Here's to Jan"). Mary O'Hara was singing "Bridge Over Troubled Water". We stood, swaying with our arms around each other, and sang the chorus. I felt overcome and started to crumple. Someone I didn't know grabbed me and held me tightly while I cried. Then Ian Sowton poured champagne, real French champagne, four bottles of it, and we toasted Margaret:

Here's to Margaret
Here's to Margaret
Here's to Margaret
She's a horse's ass

This time the cadence was powerful and full-throated and sounded exactly right. Sheila Mackenzie told about her visit to Margaret at the undertaker's, and how Margaret had urinated all over the hearse – Margaret triumphing over the system one last time. We roared a chorus of, "Here's to Sheila".

Eileen Swinton told about Margaret's final meeting of the Nellie's fund-raising committee, only hours before her death, and

285

how anxious she was about the ticket sales. "Here's to Eileen."
Gail Flintoff was shamelessly selling tickets to the Nellie's theatre
benefit. "Here's to Gail." Judy Schenkman, Margaret's flute
teacher, told us how determined Margaret had been to learn the
flute despite not having her own teeth. "Here's to Judy." Fran
Sowton arrived, breathless, fresh from the embroidery lectures in
London. "Here's to Fran."

We regretted that Wendy and Nigel were still in Calgary and
had missed the wake. "Here's to Wendy ... Here's to Nigel."
Buffy Carruthers was also regrettably absent. "Here's to Buffy."

Someone had a story from Mary Hiseler. Mary had informed
her children gently the night before that Margaret was dead.
They accepted the news without much comment, but that night,
when four-year-old Gwen was preparing to say her prayers, she
informed her mother that she was going to tell God, "That wasn't
fair."

A number of Nellie's staff had avoided the wake deliberately,
fearing it would be a morbid affair. I sympathized, having the
same concerns, but Margaret's wake had not been morbid. It had
been glorious, even joyous; a release.

We started to clean up the party mess in a mood of contented
fatigue. Diane Savard adopted Cleo. She would care for Margaret's
cat, she said, but she wanted some of us to visit regularly until
the cat "got adjusted".

"You're kidding!" I said. "*Visit a cat?*" Diane was annoyed at
me. "Cats have feelings too, you know," she said. "All right," I
promised weakly.

Morris Manning had arrived to pick up his wife, Linda Rapson.
Linda was gathering up crumpled paper napkins and stuffing them
in a garbage bag held by Ian Sowton, so Morris walked me to my
car. We stood for a moment looking back at the brightly lit house,
the people moving around inside, the music pouring out of the
open windows.

"It's been quite wonderful" I told him. "Your wife has been
having her finest hour."

"She'll have a head tomorrow morning," he predicted glumly.

The Memorial

The Holy Trinity people were impressed with Margaret's timing. Her death occurred just before renovation work on the ceiling that a few days later filled the interior of the church with scaffolding. The Sunday after Margaret died happened to be the last possible day that the church could be used for a memorial service for many weeks.

Bill Whitla and Ian Sowton did most of the planning. They asked if I wanted to do a reading, and I did. Remembering that they're both professors of English, I asked them if a fragment of poetry I remembered, "Death be not proud", was from Dylan Thomas.

"John Donne, I think," Ian told me.

"Handy, knowing you guys," I said gratefully.

Linda and Morris and their daughters, Rachel and Kate, were at the church ahead of me that Sunday evening, June 23, and had saved front-row seats for me and my husband, Trent Frayne, by placing programs on them. The pews had been arranged in rows that faced inward, and a lectern and altar table placed between them. Merylie Houston had brought bouquets for the communion tables. Linda, ever the archivist, had conscripted her twin sister, Lorna, to record the proceedings with a video camera mounted on a tripod.

Strangers were exchanging Margaret memorabilia. A heavy-set man said he had been in Margaret's English class during her second year at Bloor Collegiate, which was then the smallest high school in Toronto. It had no music department, but Margaret found twelve students who could play instruments. She formed a school orchestra, which she sternly led.

"She was very pleased about that," he remembered.

Two women told me they also were in Margaret's English class. One of them, a nurse in a palliative-care unit, said, "I'll never forget her. She was so sure of herself. She was a feminist who was way ahead of the feminist movement."

287

A man informed me that he had been one of Margaret's basement tenants for four years. He was a writer, he said, and she had always been sympathetic about the fact that it was a difficult line of work.

Snatches of music drifted over our heads. Don Gillies, a United Church minister and marriage counsellor, was rehearsing a choir of Margaret's friends from CAMMAC and the Concord Singers. In addition to his other accomplishments, he's a distinguished organist and choir leader and is also a music director at CAMMAC's Lake Rosseau centre in Muskoka.

Wendy Farquhar and Nigel Turner, who had come to the service straight from the airport, rushed in wearing white duck pants and striped jerseys. Wendy burst into tears and was comforted in the church's pantry by Elaine Hall. Michael Creal appeared in a windbreaker and consulted with Bill Whitla, who was wearing a simple white vestment and a stole ornamented in gold embroidery. A dark woman wearing ecclesiastical robes similar to Bill's joined them. She was Virginia (Ginny) Peacock, also an Anglican priest. I had first met her on Margaret's back porch, dressed in jeans, a T-shirt, and a crash helmet, and storing her bicycle. Jack Adams, the incumbent designate of Holy Trinity, was also in white and gold vestments and would take part in the memorial service.

The service began with J.S. Bach's "*Christ lag in Todesbanden*" with John Gartshore at the organ. Bill Whitla, impressively dignified and solemn, gave the opening remarks, speaking of Margaret's "vigorous and enthusiastic" participation in Holy Trinity, and much more.

"Her life is manifested in her wide interests," he said. "In women's issues – and not just in theory but in a very practical way in the work she did with Nellie's and with Jessie's and with the house that is named after her, Margaret Frazer House. But her life is also hidden. It is hidden in the lives of many people whom she touched as a friend and whom she touched as a teacher over many years ... in her causes to do with the environment, and with human justice, and the disadvantaged, and particularly with women.

"She has given us the gift of many smiles and many tears these past few weeks – in fact, these past four months – when so many of us were privileged to spend time with her in her home.... Margaret was a neat and a nifty person, and you recognize that those were two words that she was very fond of ... "

The hymn that followed was Ralph Vaughan Williams' "For All the Saints". Then there were prayers, some led by Ginny Peacock, some silent, and then the congregation sang the words written by Herbert O'Driscoll to Beethoven's "Ode to Joy".

I was next. I knew it violated the egalitarian spirit of Holy Trinity, but I asked the team to rise so "everyone can see how many of us there were". People got up reluctantly from all over the church.

When they were seated again, I began, "We who loved Margaret – and everyone here did – were privileged to be part of the team that tended her these past few months. We have memories that we'll cherish all our lives of her courage, and her grace, and her will, and her intelligence, and her connectedness to us despite the vagaries of her illness. She made us a gift of our giving, which is quite an extraordinary accomplishment. In a sense we are bereft, but we are exalted. We all gained from what we experienced at 47 Deloraine. We had the redemptive experience of being part of a human tribe functioning at its best. We don't have her any more, but we do have our better selves, we have a better sense of the safety of our community. This time the centre held."

I read Dylan Thomas's "Do Not Go Gentle Into That Good Night", after which Alice Chrysler played something lovely on a flute, accompanied by Doris Mary Canter on piano, and Sheila Mackenzie went sturdily to the lectern to read a lesson from Isaiah: "The Spirit of God is upon me because God has anointed me and has sent me to bring good news to the poor; to bind up the hearts that are broken.... " The congregation sang, "O Healing River", with a burly young clergyman Brian Ruttan, on guitar. Heather Sutherland read the Epistle from 1 Corinthians; "Christ was raised to life – the first fruits of the harvest of the dead...."

She was followed by the singing of a Bach hymn, "Sleepers

Wake", and Wendy Farquhar read the Magnificat from the gospel of St. Luke in a quivering voice. Bill Whitla then invited people to come forward, if they wished, to speak about Margaret. The first to accept was Ian Sowton.

"I have two brief things to say," he began. "The first is a friendly word of warning. Look to it, ye choirs of New Jerusalem. Margaret has arrived." Applause and laughter.

"The second is a poem that I just wrote, last night and this morning. It's for Margaret Frazer. You all know she was a teacher, and the poem is about teaching. Those of us who were privileged to be looking after her had to note in a log how our shifts had proceeded, but it seemed to be much more than a medical log. A whole business of us writing up Margaret and being written up by Margaret entered the scene. So that's what this poem is about."

Teacher is right

The foolishness in us
you swallowed not gladly but,
with a pinch of your tart seasoning,
gracefully enough

Lately you were reading feminists:
theology, poetry, psychology
taking it for granted, at sixty-eight,
that you should be teaching,
still, the lesson of yourself,
as-woman to yourself

And then you let us student-teachers
join you in your schoolhouse
for your final term.
"Here," you said
(it wasn't easy) "here is my body:
read me, write me,
learn yourselves in me."

290

You had us all to school.
When death stayed overnight
and did its laundry in your lungs,
we were inscribed deep
in your closing chapter
and you in our continuing stories.
We are *still* learning
for only God She knows how much you taught us.

This was met with appreciative applause, and then Linda Rapson took her turn.

"The *Oxford Universal Dictionary* defines the word 'stubborn' in the following manner," she began. "'Pertinacious or dogged in refusing obedience or compliance. Unyielding, inflexible, obstinate.' The same dictionary states that this word is rarely used in a neutral or good sense. The term 'stubborn' therefore could hardly have been applied to Margaret Frazer. How about determined? Does this mean the same thing? No. This is a positive term defined by Oxford as "resolute, not to be moved from one's purpose, showing determination'. Resolute means 'having a fixed resolve, constant, firm'; resolve implies 'having a firmness or steadfastness of purpose'. *That* describes our Margaret.

"Other words spring to mind: loving, dignified, perceptive, appreciative, valiant. However, if I were asked to sum up Margaret's character in one word I would choose 'unique'. I have never known anyone like her. You might choose the word 'nifty', but alas 'nifty' is not even in the dictionary. I looked.

"The same word can be used to describe the Friends of Margaret team. We seemed to be unique also. Being unique however does not imply that others cannot follow our example and give their support, care, and love to a dying friend. It is my hope that people all across this country will be inspired by the moving tribute to Margaret and the team written by June Callwood in the *Globe and Mail*, and come together to help others as we helped our dying friend.

"It was my privilege as Margaret's palliative-care physician and

291

friend to talk to her every day, for eighty-five days, usually morning and evening, as well as to visit her frequently at home. Our telephone conversations and visits were full of her unique perspective on life and the richness of her language.

"For a dying woman physically restricted by her increasing weakness to describe 'a day full of pleasures' as often as she did, was a source of joy for me. For me to hear her admire Fran's pruning skills or to hear her say, 'It was nifty. Hilda came,' made my day. That should have been enough, but hearing her say she was comfortable was best of all.

"I learned a lot from Margaret, not just about birds, flowers, music, and religion, but about the dignity and wholeness of the person. She remained dignified and whole right to her death on her little green couch. Thank you, Margaret, and thank you, team."

Nigel Turner next: "We're told that how a person dies often tells us a lot about how they felt about life. I came to know Margaret quite well in the last three months of her life, and to me she made a lot of statements about herself and about the world she lived in. The first thing she said to me was a political statement about how a person should die in her own home instead of in a hospital. She showed us that death isn't something that has to be hidden away, but is part of life's process. It's something that the community can care for, rather than have the government do it.

"She also availed herself of medical treatment that is not common in Canada. She wanted to die without drugs. She used her acupuncture machine in order to do away with pain, and she died with very few drugs inside her. This machine was administered by lay people rather than by professional medical people, so she showed that home care can also mean good health care. All of these to me are political statements.

"She also made personal statements about herself and about Christianity. Christianity is about giving, and she showed us in a way that was to me unique how one could give to her in this stage of her life. Caring means coming and being with somebody, talking to them, and just doing jobs around the house. I spent many enjoyable Sunday afternoons and evenings with her, arguing about the rights of the separate-school issue or the new provincial government, or looking at pictures of birds, at which she was an expert, or listening to jazz and classical music.

"Inevitably, as the cancer took its toll, she got thinner and weaker, but her spirit was still full of life and living. My last memory is of a week ago rocking her in her bed upstairs. She was too weak to hold a spoon, but she said defiantly that she wanted to be downstairs on her little green couch in order to be with people. And that's where she was taken.

"She's gone, but with all this in mind her spirit is something that lives on."

Jan Hatch was next, looking ethereal in a pale blue dress.

"I haven't prepared anything," she began. "I was with Margaret when she died. I woke up yesterday morning, and it suddenly occurred to me what Margaret had given all of us while she was living and also in her death. For me, what Margaret gave us was a mirror. She never failed to reflect to every human being she met the complete and absolute faith she had in their goodness, and in their rightness, and in their trueness as human beings. She never failed to remember that she was a good and right and true human being right up until the very end.

"She was not afraid of dying and she was not afraid of living. She really showed every one of us how completely and absolutely wonderful we are by allowing us to see the vision in her face of who she saw, and never failing to remind us of who she saw within us.

"She allowed us to make mistakes, she allowed us to try, to be frightened, to be scared of helping her, or of doing something we'd never done, like weeding her garden or pruning her roses. She never failed to have faith that we would do the best that we could, and if we didn't complete the job adequately, someone else would come along and do it.

"I feel very privileged to have been with Margaret in this life and to be able to see through her eyes the goodness and the humanness of all the people that she came in contact with. And I thank you all for living up to what she knew was inside of you. And I can only say that I will spend the rest of my life trying to remember that inside of me is that good and true human being that Margaret saw."

People were very moved. Many women told me later that they would have spoken about Margaret, but they felt Jan Hatch said everything that was in their hearts.

Glenys McMullen stood up next. She read some verses from the last two chapters in the Bible, Revelation, Chapters 21 and 22. Jan Kudelka, dramatic in flaring boots and a garment that flowed like a cape, strode to the front of the altar and sang, without accompaniment, "For I have been a beggar, and shall be one again", an aria from *The Beggar's Opera* that she had wanted to sing at her mother's funeral but couldn't. "One day I'll walk on flowers, one day I'll walk on stone.... One day I shall be home…"

I had been watching Pat Capponi, who was slouched in the back row against the wall. Before the service Pat showed me a typewritten page, saying it was a poem she had written about Margaret. Did I want it? I urged her to read it, and she said she might. It looked to me as though she wasn't able to summon her nerve. The next person to speak was Deena Rasky, a young music friend of Margaret's who had accompanied her several times to CAMMAC summer camps.

"I'd like to speak for myself," she said, "but I'd also like to speak for someone who isn't here, and that's Hope Hoey. Margaret and I went to St. Sauveur to see Hope, and we had a wonderful time. Hope would bake us bread out of her wood stove and we would pick blueberries together. And we would play music for her and Hope's friend the psychic, and it was wonderful.

"I'd like to speak about Margaret's musical accomplishments. Margaret picked up the flute when she was in her sixties, and she was just getting a new set of teeth. Now that's an accomplishment. Whenever Margaret and I played music together she would always pick the hardest pieces. She would pick a Mendelssohn trio, she would pick Brahms. She wanted a piece to work on that she would get the most out of. I tried. We both tried, three of us tried, four of us tried, and we learned a lot from our trying.

"One time I brought her some music. It was part of Ravel. It was a piece for a dead princess. I told Margaret I couldn't play it because I hadn't experienced any deaths at that time. This was a number of years ago."

She was crying but struggled to finish. "When I found out Margaret had died, I tried to play the piece again. I still couldn't play it, but I tried."

She grinned at that. "I was very lucky to have Margaret as a friend. It was an unusual combination: she was my friend and she was also my role model."

She sat down as people clapped and there was a long pause while we waited to see if someone else would speak. Pat Capponi came slowly to the lectern. She cleared her throat.

"Since Margaret was an English teacher, a surplus of poems is probably not a bad thing," she said simply, and then read her poem.

there is no shame in losing such a terrible battle
Margaret
we all died before you
cashed in your chips, agreed to leave quietly
cringed under the weight of your skeletal frame
made bargains with God
in unconditional surrender
while you wondered what the fuss was about
and prepared to climb the stairs again

there is no shame in running home
Margaret
for comfort more healing than held hands
we all cursed and cried
and damned injustice
and sought for reason

while you sipped Almond Delight
with shaking hands
choreographing the household
and consoling the consolers

there is no shame in this rainbowed day
Margaret
in the birds and fallen petals that mark your passage
to a new beginning, a new and glorious musical dance
whose shadowy notes you loved to catch
with wavering breath on the silver flute
the trees themselves sing softly
Margaret
in celebration of all that is good
in celebration of all that is eternally you

We were stunned, and then applauded hard.

Eileen Swinton, looking frail and uneasy in total contrast to the firmness of her character, spoke next. "I hope none of you will feel that what I have to say is inappropriate," she said. "Margaret was a very important part of my life for the last ten years, and I know that what I'm going to say is what she would have wanted. The last, I think, the last act that she initiated on her death bed – I should say, her death couch – was a fund-raising event for Nellie's. This is going to take place on Wednesday evening at the Toronto Free Theatre on Berkeley Street. There are still some tickets available ... "

Laughter and applause stopped her. She grinned, "I would like to say that the day before Margaret died she was very concerned that the tickets had not all been sold, and I think she would be very happy if any of you who have not already bought tickets would do so tonight. Gail Flintoff and possibly Jan Hatch will have tickets at the back after this is over. Thank you very much."

The testimonials ended. Bill Whitla rose and said, "Near Margaret when she died was a book that she had filled over the years with quotations. They were not ordinary quotations. It was her commonplace book, but it was far from common. The first entry from forty-five years ago was from Shaw's *Saint Joan*: 'What! Must Christ be crucified in every age because men lack imagination?' She predated the feminist movement, you see.

"Some are witty, some are prayers. And these are the words that she wrote down about halfway through by Cyril Connolly: 'In my religion there would be no exclusive doctrine. All would be love and poetry and doubt. Life would be sacred because it is all we have, and death, our common denominator, the fountain of consideration.'

"Twice in the book she copied out the sonnet of Edna St. Vincent Millay on hearing a symphony of Beethoven: 'Sweet sounds, Oh, beautiful music, do not cease!/ Reject me not into the world again ... Reject me not, sweet sounds/ Oh, let me live,/ Till Doom espy my towers and scatter them,/ A city spellbound under the aging sun./ Music my rampart, and my only one.'

"Just before that sonnet she wote in French, 'Happy is the one who, like Ulysses, has completed a fine voyage.'

"And complete a fine voyage she did, with music all the way. And one of the hymns that she enjoyed up to the second to last day of her life was our offertory hymn, 'The Lord of the Dance'. While we sing it, we will carry the gifts of bread and wine to the altar and, after the Consecration, those who are distributing Communion will go to four places, the far end, the other side, and on either side of the altar. Those who wish to receive it can come forward then."

We stood for "The Lord of the Dance", many of us swept by grief to hear again the music we had come to associate with Margaret.

Michael Creal spoke next. "In this life," he said, "we are clearly celebrating Margaret's life. I think the thanksgivings of the people have been more than eloquently expressed. All I have to say at this point is that Margaret fought the good fight. She fought many good fights. She finished the course, and she kept the faith, and praise be to God."

"Alleluia," said the congregation.

"I think, considering the things that Margaret cared about and the kinds of things that she devoted her life to, we might pray, as she might pray today, for those who died in that Air India crash and their families. Lord, in your mercy ... "

"Hear our prayer."

"For all peoples throughout the world who are oppressed, places like Latin America, the Middle East, South Africa, Afghanistan, Lord, in your mercy ... "

"Hear our prayer."

"For people in this city oppressed with poverty and unemployment and racism and sexism, Lord, in your mercy ... "

"Hear our prayer."

"For people in places like Nellie's giving refuge and hope and strength to oppressed women, Lord, in your mercy ... "

"Hear our prayer."

"For this parish in its manifold ministry, Lord, in your mercy ... "

"Hear our prayer."

"For those who are ill, especially those facing death, that they may know the love that is stronger than death, Lord, in your mercy ... "

"Hear our prayer."

"To all who administer to the sick and the dying, that like the Friends of Margaret they may be able both to give and to receive, Lord, in your mercy ... "

"Hear our prayer."

"And a moment of silence to give our own individual utterance to all our concerns and thanksgivings."

Sheila Mackenzie stood up after the moment of silence. She said, "Margaret got through her dying totally unviolated by the means of her care. Thank God for Linda Rapson, who protected us all."

"Praise the Lord," said the congregation. Bill Whitla shouted, "Alleluia."

Fran Sowton, without leaving her seat, said clearly, "For the children of Margaret's next-door neighbour who gave her such joy, praise the Lord."

"Alleluia."

Someone else said, "For same-sex or sexual-preference people, i.e., gay people; whom Margaret supported, praise the Lord."

"Alleluia."

The prayer of consecration was given and sung — "Holy, holy God of pow'r and might ... " — with a strong guitar accompaniment. Then lines formed in front of Bill, Ginny Peacock, Sheila File, Heather Sutherland, Jack Adam, and Michael Creal, who distributed Communion wafers and sips of wine. Friends of Margaret's from CAMMAC and the Concord Singers sang Bach chorales with Donald Gillies at the organ. 'Becca Whitla's clear trumpet was heard, there were blessings and prayers, and the service ended with Ralph Vaughan Williams' "For All the Saints".

When it was over, people mingled. Holy Trinity provided food, coffee, tea, and juices. I saw Nellie's staff everywhere, and women from the Nellie's fund-raising committee, women from the Nellie's and Jessie's board, an abundance of Holy Trinity friends, Margaret's neighbours, dozens of people I didn't know. After a while, someone put Mary O'Hara on the tape machine and the team linked arms and sang "Bridge Over Troubled Water". It still made us cry, but the service, like the wake, was a healer.

After

A week and a day after Margaret died, Linda Rapson called me to meet her at 47 Deloraine. The work of sorting through Margaret's possessions had begun. Ian Sowton, who with Fran had been given responsibility for the dispersement of the contents of Margaret's house, was waiting for us. Fran once said that she thinks they got the job because she made such good work of reorganizing Margaret's cluttered back porch, home of broken flower pots, scrub pails, trowels, and apple baskets.

"Margaret must have figured that if I could sort out the back porch, I was just the one to organize her house," Fran grinned.

Wendy Farquhar was also at Margaret's. She had come to look

299

at the empty couch, her first visit to Margaret's since before the death. Once there, she had a weep and then pitched in with the back-breaking chores of helping to clean the house so it could be sold.

Ian poured cold wine in Margaret's tall-stemmed glasses and we four sat in the living-room eyeing the empty green couch.

"I've found out the most extraordinary things about Margaret," Ian said reflectively. "Did you know she wrote pieces for the *Encyclopedia of Music in Canada?*"

We didn't, but Ian had discovered that Margaret was the author of the biographies of Maureen Forrester, Pat Patterson, Lois Marshall, Frederic Lord, Dodi Robb, Joanne Ivey, Gerard Kantarjian, Avrahm Galper, Perry Bauman, Morry Kernerman, Hugh Orr, Bertha Carey Morrow, and maybe more.

He had found occasional diaries Margaret kept in school scribblers or on loose-leaf sheets, most of them undated. One began "I came home from Jean's last night, sad to be alone. I need to live with somebody. I wish it could be a man I could love and look after. That's what I keep wanting to get ready for … I have a basic need to look after someone – a man, people I love. And I'd better look after myself – my classroom, office, study, wardrobe …

"My 13E, a class that bristles with problems. Solve them, student by student."

Another: "Why do I so delight in arguing? Pride myself on it? It's part of intolerance, self-righteousness, wanting to set other people right."

And again: "As a hostess I'm a flop. I talk too much about myself…. Often I ask people for facts, about as poor a social question as you can ask. Thinking about this is painful, my talking often a release for pent-up feelings. I want to be a good hostess. Entertaining people is essential, living alone. It is one way I can give to people, have their company. To live alone I must not only entertain, but visit people who need to be visited."

Margaret wrote of the proposal of marriage from her long-time friend, Canadian historian Arthur Lower, when he was eighty-seven years old. She wrote that the marriage was impossible: "After five hours with him doing everything he could think to please me, I was exhausted – chiefly with shouting at him. Surely his hearing is worse. Near the end his honesty broke through. 'Like going into a convent – taking vows,' he said. 'Each person had to be first to the other.' A vocation. His had been teaching. Then as he was going down the front steps, 'I didn't get hold of you soon enough.' How will I tell him? I said I would think about it. I'll wait a few days, and write."

She seemed always to prefer to communicate by mail when matters were intensely personal. Once, in a long period of inter-mittent diary keeping in 1976-80, she seems to have written a passionate letter to a woman she thought felt the same about her, only to have the woman withdraw from her. "She says she is revolted by lesbianism," Margaret noted in an anguished para-graph. "Yet she does feel physically attracted to me, as I to her. I am shattered and shaken. I have to let the pain, hers especially and mine, stay in me until I've sorted it out."

The pages chronicle a busy woman who was at the centre of events at Holy Trinity (it was Margaret, with one other, who was asked to fire three employees during one financial crisis, and Margaret who met with the Eaton's architect to protect the church's interests) and at Nellie's. In only a few places, such as when she spent a birthday or Christmas alone, she confronts her loneliness in a detached way, as something to endure like a bout of flu. She speaks of her longing for love only rarely; more often her most personal entries are impatient criticisms of herself.

For instance, after a meeting of a Nellie's fund-raising commit-tee to make final plans for a bazaar, she wrote, "I was riding high at the meeting yesterday, like a strict teacher telling Eileen she was off the point, going around the table asking everyone when they could come on Saturday morning, etc. Why was I so obtuse as to disregard their feelings? Why was I being so bossy? The important part of running this fair is the planning at my desk."

Ian told us he had spent hours cancelling Margaret's magazine subscriptions and memberships. He showed me the formidable list: Toronto Field Naturalists; Canadian Abortion Rights Action League (CARAL); Canadian Civil Liberties Association; *Radio Guide*; Toronto Symphony Orchestra; *Herizons*; Canadian UNICEF Committee; CJRT Orchestra; United Way; John Howard Society; Ontario Association for Senior Citizens; Metro Zoo Society; Canadian Opera Company; TVOntario; *Saturday Night*; *Maclean's*; *Greenpeace Examiner*; Easter Seal Fund; Royal Conservatory of Music; Stratford Festival; New Democratic Party; Oxfam; Amnesty International; Federation of Toronto Naturalists; Pollution Probe; *Watch*; Chamber Players of Toronto; *Broadside*; *On Air* magazine; Bruce Trail Association; *This Magazine*; Canadian Arctic Resources Committee; *Books In Canada*; Toronto Memorial Society; National Ballet of Canada; Music at Sharon; Frida Craft Stores; *Canadian Churchman*; Friends of the Spit; Art Gallery of Ontario; Music Centre Stage; Canadian Nature Federation; Project Ploughshares; Foster Parents Plan of Canada; Ontario Social Development Council; Toronto Disarmament Network; Operation Dismantle; Frontier College; Women's Electoral Fund; Federation of Ontario Naturalists; Energy Probe; Ontario Committee on the Status of Women; War Amputees of Canada.

"I'm not sure I got them all," Ian said. "These are just the ones I could find so far."

Wendy talked of how much it had meant to Nigel, her husband, to be on the Margaret team. "It was his first encounter with unconditional love," she said. "Margaret was a revelation to him."

I said I thought he had been struggling to express that feeling in the words he spoke at the memorial service, and she nodded.

Linda said, beaming, "We heretics, me and June, thought the service was nifty."

Wendy smiled but shook her head. "I think there is *something*, you know. When my first husband left me he took everything, even the appliances, and I was left with two children, one two and one four, and not one cent. I could only get a low-paying job where I made $9,000 a year, but out of that I managed to pay the baby sitter, the mortgage, everything. I had to rely on mother's allowance to buy food, and when it didn't come I prayed. It was more like a conversation with someone – something – than a prayer. But help always came, *always*. We never went hungry."

I went upstairs to Margaret's den and collected her journals and telephone books. "Take whatever you like," Ian said. "Everything has to go." I wanted something of hers that wrapped around me, so I took the pink sweatshirt I had bought her, the one she had worn most often with her jogging outfits. From the kitchen cupboard I took a tiny vase that Margaret had used for the short-stemmed flowers Gwen Hiseler brought her. What I wanted most, and carried out to my car with care, was Margaret's much-used *Shorter Oxford English Dictionary*.

Ian pointed out that the most valuable articles in Margaret's house were on the walls. Her rugs were cheap and worn, her furniture for the most part unremarkable, but her paintings were by Albert Franck, Florence Vale, and Harold Town, and her pieces of sculpture included one by Frances Loring.

"She had her priorities," he commented approvingly.

As I was leaving we stood in the hall and talked about the team, already with nostalgia, and about the people who had not joined us: Margaret's music friends and some others. I recognized one of the names Linda mentioned. "That person is pretty narcissistic," I observed. "I don't think she would have been able to be on the team."

Wendy smilingly reproved me. "There were several narcissistic people on Margaret's team," she said. "It worked because Margaret taught them. They didn't discover how much Margaret taught them until she died."

Sheila Mackenzie calls Ian Sowton "one of the gardeners of the universe".

She explains, "You know those lines? No? They go, 'Those who are asleep, let them sleep/ Those that are waking, nourish them/ Those who are awake, they are the gardeners of the universe.' That's Ian. He's awake."

At the wake I had announced that I planned to write a book about Margaret and the team, with the team's permission. I would be donating half the royalties to a fund in Margaret's name, and we would agree later on the purpose of such a fund. I asked if anyone on the team felt uneasy about this, but none voiced any objections.

Over the next six months I interviewed team members and I asked each of them what they had learned while caring for Margaret.

Jay MacGillivray: "I learned a lot about dignity. I learned that it really is possible to have control over one's dying. I learned how graciously Margaret received what we had for her. I learned not to be ashamed of the impact music has on me. I learned to revel in it and not be ashamed. I'm sorry I didn't find that out sooner."

Linda Rapson: "Working with the team reaffirmed my faith in people. That's what my faith is, people. I learned so much I don't know what to say. I learned about the dignity of the patient. I learned that the emotional support that came at the end got everyone through. I hardly knew anyone on the team, but at the end I felt close to them all. I'm lucky; I've got a concrete skill that helps. Like Morris, who handled the estate of a relative whose husband had died, it's a concrete thing you can do. But everyone has a concrete skill. The team showed that. Gardening, shopping, cleaning – those are concrete skills."

Nigel Turner: "It wasn't remarkable that the team worked. The remarkable thing is that it doesn't happen very often. Margaret would touch my heart. Toward the end we played some Mozart that had a little waltz in it, something light like a dance. When I was leaving she said, 'I'd like to have a dance with you sometime.' That got to me."

Fran Sowton: "I wouldn't have missed this experience for anything – the energy and dynamic of all that care."

Janice Hatch: "Two days after Margaret died, I saw Marilou McPhedran's newborn baby. I compared that baby, with the stranglehold that his body had on human life, with what Margaret demonstrated. We're not like a TV set, which, when it blows one part, it's finished. Margaret had almost everything blow, but she kept on, she continued to struggle. I lost my fear of my body. I know now that it will struggle to keep me alive. I have a much stronger sense of myself as being safe in the universe."

Vivian Harrower: "She was so vulnerable. It gave me a new insight into vulnerability. I always thought of it as being weak, but she was very strong and able to be open."

Diane Savard: "Margaret taught a lot of people about death. That's one subject people avoid all the time."

Buffy Carruthers: "Jan Hatch called me on the day Margaret died and we cried on the telephone for twenty minutes. The horror of Margaret's death was still very much with her, and she wanted to tell the story. It was fascinating to be part of the team. I could hardly wait to meet the people who signed the notes in the log-book. Wendy, especially, Fran, and Ian. Those Holy Trinity people were full of beans, a vital and interesting group of people."

Hilda Powicke: "I got a lot of reassurance that people could care that much. The friendships at Holy Trinity were there before, but there has been a deepening, an enrichment. We have an experience now that we can draw on. The business with Margaret had some negative things too. It made me feel my own mortality more.... Maybe that's not negative."

Helen Gough: "People pick a time and a way to die. There is an element of dignity in being able to make that decision. We gathered around and went with Margaret through the process to the end. When everything was tidied up, she left. We had to be willing to let her do that. It's like being an usher. It's not very grand or glorious, but it has to be done for each of us. It doesn't happen for many people."

Anne von Egmond: "Because I have retired this year, I think about the fact that Margaret's life seemed to soar after she retired. That's been a real inspiration to me. It is so marvellous that her second career really made more of an impact than her first one. It proves that one can change at any time of life.... Margaret's real immortality is what she has done for us."

Fran and Ian had been cleaning Margaret's house for two months assisted by a few of the team, notably the Whitlas and Wendy Farquhar. The basement had been neglected for years, with so much gluck accumulated on the floor around the furnace it had to be scraped out with a hoe. After a hard scrubbing, they painted the floor a glistening pale grey.

"Margaret kept everything," Fran said. "She seems to have kept every letter and post card, every Christmas card even, that she ever received. Also every glass jar that had a lid and all the flower pots in the world."

The house had been offered for sale, but the first offer was disappointingly low. Ian and Fran did some more cleaning, disposed of more junk, and the price rose astoundingly. On the first day it was offered for the second time, it was snapped up for $170,000. The closing date was August 16. Fran and Ian wanted everything moved out before then in order to allow the new owners time to redecorate if they wished.

Margaret had instructed her executors that her friends were to take whatever they wished. Fran telephoned the team to come. Most were reluctant. "Don't make me coax you," Fran said. "Margaret wanted you to have something of hers. Please come and get it."

Many people had to be telephoned more than once. They protested that they had no need for a souvenir of Margaret. They would never forget her. "I had to strong-arm them," Fran groaned.

Buffy Carruthers bought Margaret's car, paying the market value of it into the estate. She also took the bell that Margaret had used to summon her on those turbulent overnights and a pair of candlesticks – "the bell to remind me of the dying, the candlesticks for living".

Linda Rapson took the wine glasses we had used when she and I ate dinner together while Margaret lay dying on the couch. Grace Ross took linen napkins. Kathy Johns selected some pictures, plants, and ornaments for the Margaret Frazer House. Bill and Nancy Whitla took piano music and some Swedish crystal glasses that matched their wedding gifts. Elizabeth Greaves took a piece of jade that Margaret had bought in China, because Margaret often asked her to rearrange it so she could enjoy how the light fell on it. Vivian Harrower took a soup set: tureen and bowls. Diane Savard wanted personal things, such as the clothes hamper and harmonica – "trivia that she had touched a lot".

Kathy Johns took books for herself, and an African violet. "Margaret told me how to look after her African violets. I never had any luck with my own, but the one I have from Margaret's is blooming."

Pat Capponi, at Linda's suggestion, got the green mohair blanket that Margaret loved.

"Take a cook book," Fran begged everyone. "There are loads and loads and *loads* of cook books."

I talked to Hope Hoey in St. Sauveur. She had been travelling in Europe when Margaret died and didn't know about it until she returned home. She was devastated. When I told her about the disposal Margaret wanted of her possessions, she asked for a picture that meant a good deal to her, an abstract that hung in the dining-room. The Sowtons were travelling to Montreal later that month and delivered it personally.

Margaret's flute was valued at $2,000. Fran observed, "Margaret had a 25-watt light bulb in her kitchen, but she spent her money where she felt it mattered." Margaret, in fact, had purchased the Sankyo flute for $1,712, almost all she had in the bank, more than a year before her death. She marvelled at her extravagance because she was saving at that time for her trip to China. "Is it a crazy thing to do?" she wrote in her journal. "No, now is the time to do both."

The flute was donated to the University of Toronto music department, and Margaret's fine piano was sold to Holy Trinity church, which is what she wished. Christopher Ross took some records, and so did Jay MacGillivray. Someone bought the glass-walled china cabinet and wrote out a cheque for the Margaret Frazer House.

Sheila Mackenzie took Margaret's old stove; it was an improvement on her own. And she took Margaret's coal scuttle.

The Hiseler children were puzzled by the activity in Margaret's house and tried to sort out the names.

"Which one is Fran?" asked Gwen. "Is she the lady who's so nice to us? The one who gardens a lot?"

"Yes," said Jenny. "Margaret was nice to us too."

Gwen agreed. "Of course," Jenny said, "we don't know either of them very well."

Said Gwen, with the lisp of a four-year-old, "But Margaret was *excellent.*"

On August 1, a very hot day, Elizabeth Greaves, Fran Sowton, Heljo Liitoja, a Nellie's staff person, and I spent the afternoon packing Margaret's clothes, dishes, pots and pans, and furniture. Almost everything would be moved to a new house that Nellie's was opening in Toronto's west end, a five-bedroom residence where women and children could stay for a year or more to tide them over a disaster. The decision had just been made to call it Trerise House, after Vicki Trerise, one of the founders of Nellie's.

Because two of Margaret's rocking chairs are fragile and Fran feared they would not survive hard use in Trerise House, Fran insisted that Liz and I take them. Liz chose the one downstairs where most of us sat during the long vigil over the woman on the couch. She made a donation to Jessie's for its value. I gratefully took the chair in Margaret's den; it's a comforting piece of furniture.

When the lamps and ornaments were boxed and Heljo was proceeding rapidly to wrap dishes in newspaper, I went upstairs to begin putting Margaret's clothes in plastic garbage bags. Some would go to Nellie's and some to Trerise House. Margaret had dozens and dozens of blouses, almost all of them blue; one drawer was entirely filled with socks; another drawer contained flannel pyjamas, and another gloves. I folded her trousers and her sturdy tweed skirts, remembering that she had written in her diary about buying such a skirt from a pricey shop. She said she couldn't resist it: "I like the way I look in it," she wrote.

She owned almost no dresses but, in a dusty garment bag, I found some dreadful evening gowns, one of them a dark brown velvet trimmed with orange satin that was difficult to imagine on her. All her dress shoes were sensible ones, with stubby heels and a high vamp. Her clothes for camping and canoeing included weathered sou'wester hats and burly sweaters. Liz helped me, both of us feeling weepy to see favourites of Margaret – an embroidered vest, a blue sweater, a Mexican shirt – that we'd seen her wear a hundred times.

It was the third time I have emptied another woman's closets. The first was my mother's the day after she died; the second, my stepmother's. The process hurts. Clothes, especially old ones, carry not only memories but the shape of the woman's body. We were putting Margaret in green garbage bags. We worked as quickly as we could to get the task behind us.

I was back at Margaret's a few days later, on a Sunday, to finish the packing. Ian was waiting at the house, where everything was gone from the walls, the rugs rolled up, the ornaments packed in cardboard boxes. Fran, he said, would be along in a minute. She had decided to reupholster one of Margaret's chairs and was at home finishing the job.

Joyce Brown arrived in her battered car with Jay MacGillivray and another Nellie's staffer, Carmen Bourbonnais. Joyce and I packed clothes again. We found that Margaret had stored her winter things in the guest-room closet. On the shelf above the garment bags were boxes and boxes of Christmas ornaments.

Ian washed out a garbage pail, into which I put a tall lamp packed securely in newspaper. Carmen was emptying the linen closet when Fran arrived with a prettily covered chair. We six worked companionably for two hours and it was done. The movers were coming the next morning. Margaret's house was ready.

Linda Rapson made up her bills for the Ontario Health Insurance Plan, which has scant provisions for palliative care. She claimed as much time for the thirty house calls she made as she thought the system would allow, but she didn't expect that it would believe, much less pay, for the amount of time she had logged. She decided to claim no visit longer than three hours, though few were that short.

Her anxiety to obtain as much recompense as she could was based on two reasons, neither of them self-interested. The first was a matter of principle. She believes that health-insurance systems should acknowledge the importance of quality home palliative care. Her other reason for wanting as much money as OHIP would allow was that she was donating her entire fee to the Margaret Frazer fund.

"God, how I like that woman!" Sheila Mackenzie exclaimed about Linda. "I always wind up liking most the people I start out disliking."

CAMMAC Southern Ontario presented a concert in Holy Trinity church on November 10,1985, a few days before what would have been Margaret's sixty-ninth birthday. Bev Stainton, a CAMMAC teacher and conductor of the Whiteoaks Choral Society, performed and acted as master of ceremonies. Among the musicians who donated their services was Mimi Gillies, who ended the program movingly with, "You'll Never Walk Alone". Proceeds of the event went to establish a Margaret Frazer Scholarship at CAMMAC's Lake Rosseau Centre.

Sheila File emerged from the experience on Margaret's team determined that Holy Trinity should involve itself in palliative care in the community. She set up a luncheon for three of us — her, me, and Dr. Dorothy Ley, executive director of the Palliative Care Foundation, a nation-wide group. Dorothy is a beautifully groomed, crisp, articulate, poised, straightforward woman who used to specialize in hematology and oncology. She has seen some two thousand people die, from which experience she has developed a passion for palliative care. She believes that death should be allowed more dignity and humanity than hospital procedures usually permit.

"Palliative care is only ten years old in this country," she told us. "We still can't get government recognition for its place in the health-care system. There's only one residential hospice in the country and that's a small one in Quebec. We have a long way to go. One of of the basic problems of palliative care in Canada is the lack of medical involvement. If we don't develop a group of physicians who will do pain and symptom management, as Linda Rapson did for Margaret Frazer, we can't put together a comprehensive plan for palliative care."

Digging into her salad, she added, "You realize we're talking about a middle-class phenomenon. Palliative care goes to people who have relatives and friends who care about them, but bag ladies die, too. All the dispossessed and lonely need palliative care, and where are they going to get it?"

"And people with AIDS need it," I said. "Many of them die completely alone."

"Exactly," she said. "They're this century's lepers. No one wants to touch them."

Sheila said, "Margaret Frazer would have cared about them."

"That's maybe what we should be doing with this money Linda and I are putting into the Margaret fund," I said. "Start a hospice in Toronto for AIDS' victims."

The team met at the end of August for a pot-luck dinner at the home of Bill and Nancy Whitla. I raised the possibility of working to establish a hospice for people dying of AIDS, and the group was enthusiastic. Sheila File spoke of Holy Trinity people forming teams to do palliative care in the community, and everyone liked that approach as well. Someone else said there should be a "how-to" brochure about palliative care based on the team's experience. In the end, the decision was to do it all.

Sheila File took responsibility for developing a palliative-team program at Holy Trinity. She and Linda went to Winnipeg in

October 1985 to attend a conference – Canada's first – on palliative care. Palliative Care: Toward a Quality Future was sponsored
by the Palliative Care Foundation and the St. Boniface Hospital
Palliative Care Service. Linda and Sheila returned full of zest and
ideas.

It was agreed that I would pursue the goal of a residential
hospice for people dying of AIDS, to which fund I would direct
half the royalties of this book and Linda Rapson would give her
medical fees for Margaret's home care. We had a preliminary
meeting of a steering committee in September 1985 at Nellie's
with representatives of the AIDS Committee of Toronto (ACT),
Joyce Brown for Nellie's and Elaine Hall for Holy Trinity. Later
Linda Rapson joined what grew to be a yeasty and determined
group of some twenty people. For a while, two of our most helpful
members were young men with AIDS, but both died. The tragedy
seared us all.

By the summer of 1986 we had a name for the proposed hospice
– Casey House – and a prospective site near Toronto's downtown
core where the great teaching hospitals are located. Margaret
would have rejoiced in the hard work we are doing. Because we
are breaking new ground, the task of creating a hospice takes all
the patience, ingenuity, and nerve we can command; she was
good at all of that, very very good.

We missed her most as spring came around again a year after
her death. Linda and I thought we'd return to the house on
Deloraine and ask permission to look in at the garden for the
giant jack-in-the-pulpit. We didn't find the time. That's odd,
considering that a year before it took no effort at all to find time
for Margaret – all the time in the world.

On June 20, the first anniversary of Margaret Frazer's death,
most of the team had a reunion at Linda's. We came together
with an effortless ease that told us something about ourselves. In
the process of caring for Margaret, we strangers had bonded. We
have a unique knowledge of one another. It is founded on rock.
All our lives, we'll trust each other.

Here's to Margaret....